RAIN CHECK

Baseball in the Pacific Northwest

Edited by Mark Armour
Photos from the David Eskenazi Collection

Published by the
Society for American Baseball Research
for the SABR National Convention
June 28-July 2, 2006, Seattle

Distributed by University of Nebraska Press

In the event that 4½ innings of this game are not played, this coupon will be good for any subsequent regular championship game this season, and may be exchanged at box office for this priced ticket

NO MONEY REFUN

is Ticket No

Front cover:
Tony Conigliaro
waits in the on-
deck circle as
Carl Yastrzemski
swings at a Gene
Brabender pitch
during an
afternoon Seattle
Pilots/Boston
Red Sox game on
July 14, 1969, at
Sick's Stadium.

Back cover:
Posing in 1913 at
Athletic Park in
Vancouver, B.C.,
are All Stars for
the Northwestern
League such as
(back row, first,
second, third,
sixth and eighth
from left) William
"Wheezer" Dell,
future Pacific
Coast League
mainstay J.H.
"Truck" Hannah,
four-time minor
league batting
champ Harry
Jack Meek,
Tacoma Tigers
star hurler Izzy
Hoffman, future
Chicago White
Sox infielder
(and Black
Soxer) Fred
McMullin, and
(front row, third
from left) Tacoma
Tigers slugger Cy
Neighbors.

Title page: For
this ultra-rare
Obak cigarette-
card premium
("ticket" inset),
"Tub" Spencer,
Northwestern
League Seattle
Giants catcher,
poses in 1911. He
also played for
the PCL Seattle
Indians in 1921-
22.

'The great things that took place on all those green fields, through all those long-ago summers'

Imagine spending a summer's day in brand-new Sick's Stadium in 1938 watching Fred Hutchinson pitch for the Rainiers, or seeing Stan Coveleski throw spitballs at Vaughn Street Park in 1915, or sitting in Cheney Stadium in 1960 while the young Juan Marichal kicked his leg to the heavens.

In this book, you will revisit all of the classic ballparks, see the great heroes return to the field and meet the men who organized and ran these teams — John Barnes, W.H. Lucas, Dan Dugdale, W.W. and W.H. McCredie, Bob Brown and Emil Sick. And you will meet veterans such as Eddie Basinski and Edo Vanni, still telling stories 60 years after they lived them.

The major leagues arrived in Seattle briefly in 1969, and more permanently in 1977, but organized baseball has been played in the area for more than a century. If you lived in Seattle in 1969, you watched your city cash in 80 thrilling years for a major-league team, and then saw it disappear in an instant, replaced by ... no baseball at all. The story of the Pilots, depicted on our cover, is best remembered today because of Jim Bouton's remarkable *Ball Four*. Both the Pilots and his book are given their due here, as are the 2001 Mariners, but much of this book's story will be new to almost all of you. I hope it provides you with an appreciation for the great things that took place on all those green fields, through all those long-ago summers.

When asked to edit this book, I was wise enough to understand that my greatest qualification was my friendships with Dave Eskenazi and Eric Sallee. While I grew up in New England and have lived in the idyllic Pacific Northwest for a mere dozen years, Dave and Eric have been immersed in this story their entire lives. They have devoted much of that time to researching and learning about the men, the leagues, and the ballparks featured in these pages. The three of us outlined the contents of the book, identified the writers we wanted to tell the individual stories, and quickly attained their enthusiastic support. Herein lies a wonderful and largely untold story, brought to life by Dave's magnificent collection of photography and ephemera. It was our intention from the beginning that the pictures would be an equal partner to the words, and it is due entirely to Dave Eskenazi that we were able to do this.

Clay Eals wrote the fine chapter on Fred Hutchinson, but he also stepped into the project late to design the book and worked with Dave on the placement of every image. Clay's own love and knowledge of the subject matter comes through on every page. Jim Price, who helped form SABR's Northwest chapter 25 years ago, might be the region's premier historian. He provided four chapters here (he could have written several more if we'd asked him) and

During a June 19, 1949, game at Sick's Stadium, Seattle Rainiers infielder Tony York barely misses beating the throw to San Francisco Seals first baseman Mickey Rocco.

wrote many of the photo captions. Ken Eskenazi also lent invaluable design expertise for the cover.

Finally, I thank the writers whose words grace these pages. For many of them, the work on this book did not begin 18 months ago, as it did for me. It began years or decades ago, when these stories first came to life for them. We all can be grateful that they are sharing their knowledge with the rest of us.

You, dear reader, are in for a treat.

Mark Armour
May 2006

Published by
The Society for American Baseball Research, Inc.
812 Huron Rd, Suite 719
Cleveland, OH 44115-1165

Phone: 216-575-0500
Fax: 216-575-0502
E-mail: info@sabr.org
Internet: http://www.sabr.org

ISBN 1-933599-02-2 (second edition)

What's inside

Page 4

Charlie Swain
Page 34

Page 48

Page 63

Page 114

Page 116

A tale of four cities

Pro baseball in the Northwest had its origins in Seattle, Portland, Tacoma, and Spokane

BY JIM PRICE

With the Lewis & Clark bicentennial having just passed, what took place following their historic journey is well-known. Horses by the thousands brought settlers to the Pacific Northwest, pulling wagons, towing stagecoaches, or hauling humans on their backs. They followed the Oregon Trail, the Columbia River, the Mullan Road, and the upper regions mapped by the adventurous David Thompson. They flowed into what we recognize as Washington and Oregon, western Montana, much of Idaho, and in Canada, the southern parts of British Columbia and Alberta, depositing people everywhere they went. That was less than two centuries ago.

With all that space out there, railroad men caught on to the possibility that there was good money to be made by transporting people and freight to the continent's Western shore. They built new lines, formed complicated alliances with developers and eager communities, and came to realize that promotion was nearly as important as locomotives and track. And what could make idle hours in an up-and-coming city seem more appealing than a professional baseball game?

So, as population centers developed on the far side of the United States, baseball spread, too. It flowered in the upper corner of the country with the creation of the Pacific Northwest League (made up of Seattle, Portland, Tacoma, and Spokane). Today, when it comes to the region's baseball history, it remains primarily a tale of four cities.

Nowadays, Seattle is firmly entrenched in the major leagues. Portland, although sometimes unable to keep a Pacific Coast League team in town, longs to join it. Tacoma has emerged as the senior member of the modern PCL. Spokane, a bit larger than Tacoma, has stepped back in time to cluster with the region's smaller cities in the short-season, Class A Northwest League.

How did we get from there to here?

In 1883, the Northwestern League, far from the Pacific Northwest, became one of the first minor leagues with teams in the north-central part of the U.S, the frontier of its time. By its second year, it included the twin cities of Minneapolis and St. Paul, along with Milwaukee. The league struggled to survive the decade, but it made baseball men out of some fellows whose skills were more inclined to business than bats, balls and gloves. Some of them became friends. John Sloane Barnes, an accomplished athlete, was in charge of the St. Paul franchise. William H. Lucas, heir to a Wisconsin lumber business, managed Duluth (Minnesota) to the 1886 championship, before moving on to the Central Interstate League, where he won a pennant at Davenport, Iowa. W.E. (Billy) Rockwell played at Omaha and Davenport, before turning to the newspaper business. George A. Van Derbeck, a contentious man who may have been involved with Lucas at Duluth, was a land development company official in Toledo, Ohio, another well-established baseball town.

By the fall of 1887, the Pacific Northwest's newspapers carried stories about the possibility of a professional league coming to the region. Although nothing came of it, by then a few pro players had joined the migration, and each city had one or more of them playing for pay on the best team in the area's best league.

In its Sunday edition of March 2, 1890, the *Spokane Falls Review* reported that Van Derbeck and bicycle racing notable W.F. (Senator) Morgan were talking up a league in Portland, and bragging on Barnes' promotional prowess, whom they called "one of the best hustlers in America in ball games and athletic sports generally."

Barnes, who later revealed that he had been dispatched by the Northern Pacific Railroad, arrived on the NP seven days later. He chatted up the business community, raised $10,000 in two hours, and headed to the coast accompanied by bank executive Herbert Moore, who doubled as a partner in Spokane's principal transit company.

Within days, the Pacific Northwest League sprang to life at Tacoma. Banker W.H. Thornell, once a standout semipro player, received the Seattle franchise, with Rockwell tabbed as his manager. Robert C. Washburn served as club president. The Tacoma franchise went to railroad executive W.F. Carson; Lucas became his manager. Portland's ownership took weeks to sort itself out before Van Derbeck regained control from Morgan and took in sporting goods dealer Henry Hudson and tobacco merchant C.Y. Gunst as partners. Dick Dwyer, who may have been one of Rockwell's Omaha teammates, served as captain and manager.

For Spokane, then named Spokan Falls, a partnership of 11 men was formed to co-own the franchise, including F. Rockwood Moore and John Sherwood, the principal stockholders in Washington Water Power Company and investors in the transit company. The partners elected insurance man Tom Jefferson as their president. Another of the partners, Herbert (Sandy) Bolster, a George Babbitt prototype who dealt in real estate and insurance, became the league's president. Barnes retained management of the Spokane franchise with a deal that included a new house for himself, in which he settled with his wife, their

(Opposite page) John Barnes, an early promoter of professional baseball in the Midwest, operated the St. Paul franchise in the late 1880s. In 1890, he organized the Pacific Northwest League, managed Spokane's championship team and, after decades as a globetrotting advocate of physical fitness, died in Seattle in 1929.

Jim Price, a longtime copy editor and sports historian at *The Spokesman-Review* in Spokane, has been a Pacific Coast League play-by-play broadcaster and publicist, Northwest League and California League official scorer and public address announcer and a baseball beat writer. He spent 14 years as announcer and publicist for horse-racing tracks in six Western states and almost a decade as sports information director at Eastern Washington University.

The dapper-hatted John Barnes (center) poses with his 1890 Pacific Northwest League champion Spokane team, whose players are wearing new Navy-blue striped uniforms that Barnes bought after they clinched the title. Barnes' St. Bernard, Prince, anchors the portrait.

PHOTO COURTESY
NORTHWEST MUSEUM OF
ARTS & CULTURE,
SPOKANE, WASHINGTON

Promoter and fitness fan John Barnes became the father of pro baseball in the Northwest

BY JIM PRICE

A very confident man, he chewed gum vigorously and preached physical fitness.

To hear John Barnes tell it, when it came to promoting professional baseball, and himself, he could just about do it all. More surprising still, he did. A native of County Tyrone, Ireland, John Sloane Barnes came to the United States as a boy and became a professional athlete of some renown, at least by his own accounts. He said he was a champion sprinter, broad jumper and snowshoe racer. Purportedly, he won the 100-yard dash at Philadelphia's 1876 Centennial Exposition. In 1905, he claimed the world record in the 50-yard dash for a 50-year-old man.

Barnes boxed for money, sparred with heavyweight champions John L. Sullivan, Bob Fitzsimmons, and Jim Jeffries, wrestled with the legendary Strangler Lewis, and learned to speak several languages. A very confident man, he chewed gum vigorously and preached physical fitness.

Along the way, he became the father of professional baseball in the Pacific Northwest. Barnes cut his teeth as a promoter and businessman during the early years of the Northwestern League, the country's first important minor league. After a spell of operating that league's St. Paul, Minnesota, franchise, he came west in early 1890 at the behest of the Northern Pacific Railroad, which believed a professional league would attract settlers from the Midwest. With a hand from several other men who had ties to baseball in the Midwest, Barnes put together the Pacific Northwest League, reserving the manager's spot in Spokane for himself. Spokane won the championship and nearly won it again in 1891. In 1892, Barnes moved on to Portland.

Returning to the Midwest in the mid-1890s, he claimed to have assisted Charles Comiskey in elevating sportswriter Ban Johnson to the presidency of the reorganized Western League, which, in time, became the American League. Then Barnes spent nearly a decade promoting fitness in China.

Upon returning to the U.S., he directed Butte of the Intermountain League in 1909 and, in 1915, the Aberdeen franchise of the Northwestern League, at that time the latest successor to the original Pacific Northwest League. In 1925, he wrote a series of articles about early Northwest baseball for the sports section of the *Seattle Post-Intelligencer*.

Eventually, Barnes, his wife, Sarah, and daughter Rosie settled in Seattle, where he died Sept. 15, 1929, at age 74. His great grandchildren remain in the area. ⚾

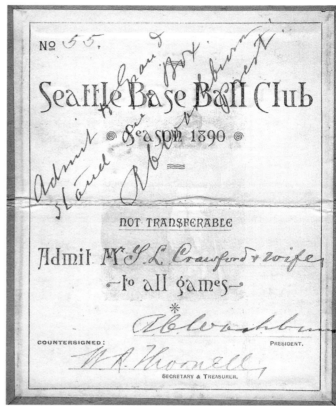

This two-sided, leather-bound pass, signed by Robert C. Washburn, Seattle baseball club president, admitted G.L. Crawford and his wife for a season's worth of games in 1890. The Seattle franchise, playing in the Pacific Northwest League, was backed by banker W.H. Thornell, who named W.E. (Billy) Rockwell as manager. A March 1890 Seattle Post-Intelligencer article indicated the pass cost $15.

daughter, and his purebred mastiff, Prince.

The league's owners agreed to post $1,000 forfeits and limit player salaries to $1,000 per month, with violators obliged to pay a $1,000 fine. However, the forfeits weren't paid, the limit wasn't observed, fines weren't imposed, and it was weeks before the newspapers decided whether the circuit should be known as the Pacific Northwest, North Pacific, Northern Pacific, or Pacific Northwestern League. Opening Day was set for Saturday, May 3.

Seattle arranged to play before an impressive new grandstand at 41st and East Blaine, near the Lake Washington (or eastern) end of the Madison Street Cable Car Company line. Portland made its home at Columbia Park. Tacoma utilized Tacoma Baseball Park, an 1885 field at South 11th and L streets in an area known as the Hilltop. Spokane's directors, who had their own cable system running from downtown along Boone Avenue toward the northwest corner of the city, took down a one-year-old grandstand at the far end of the line and reassembled it closer to town. Near the corner of Boone and A Streets, it became known as the Twickenham Grounds, named after a fledgling amusement park located just a few blocks west on the banks of the Spokane River.

The population of the Pacific Northwest League cities was, of course, far less than today's, barely 160,000 combined. The 1890 census showed Seattle with 42,837 people. In Oregon, where settlement and growth had

preceded that of Washington, Portland had 62,046. Tacoma could claim about 36,000, while Spokane, youngest city of the four, had only 20,142.

Baseball had not yet reached its modern convenience and comfort, and playing conditions reflected the times. Owners catered to their hard-core male fans, permitting rough play, rough talk, and attacks on the umpires. Many players were drunkards, and more than a few were illiterate. Fields were

The "Seattles" warm up in 1890 at Madison Park grounds at the foot of Madison Street. It was the city's Pacific Northwest League debut.

Until Pete Rose, there weren't many players like Frank "Piggy" Ward. A switch-hitting infielder and onetime teammate of Dan Dugdale, Ward hit, stole bushels of bases, dirtied his uniform and whistled while he worked. But he had hands of stone. Although he won two PNL batting titles, his stint (right) with Washington in 1894 was his only full season in the major leagues.

In 1896, after three years of inactivity, teams of the Pacific Northwest League replaced Spokane, adding Victoria. With an optimistic schedule (right), the circuit was renamed the New Pacific League, but it was victimized by torrential rains and failed in mid-June.

Besides his own athletic feats and ventures, John Barnes was keenly interested in promoting his fine dogs, as this 1890 missive on the letterhead of his Spokane team indicates. His Saint Bernard, Prince, was so important to Barnes that he appeared in one version of Spokane's championship team picture (see page 6).

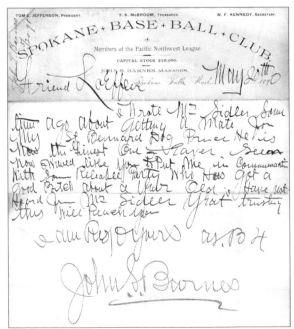

poor, gloves barely covered a player's hand, and the home team could elect to bat first. Flat-sided bats weren't outlawed until 1893. Many pitchers still threw underhand, and they worked from a rectangle that reached to within 50 feet of home plate. Four balls and three strikes did not become the norm until 1889. Men identified as managers usually were the club's business managers, field managers were called captains, and some men did both jobs.

When the Pacific Northwest League season began, Portland played at Spokane and Seattle at Tacoma.

Spokane's players were clad in white with black accessories and the word "Spokane" printed in a shield on the left breast. Portland's men wore buff shirts and breeches accented by maroon caps, stockings, and belts. The visitors hadn't even assembled until they met Dwyer in the Eastern Washington city, but they nevertheless claimed an 8-7 victory in 11 innings. The announced crowd of 1,662 amounted to eight percent of the total population of Spokan Falls. In the other opener, Seattle scored in the last of the ninth to win 7-6. Seattle's uniforms were black with white stockings and lettering, while Tacoma turned out in gray and red.

Portland had an abjectly bad team, leaving the other three bunched atop the standings by mid-June. The Oregonians had long since dispatched Dwyer in favor of Henry Harris, San Francisco's top baseball man. Harris brought along with him a hard-drinking, hell-raising young righthander, George "Chief" Borchers, who was destined to play a major role in the league's first few years.

Courtesy of distant events in other leagues, the Pacific Northwest League pennant race suddenly changed overnight. Apparently tipped by "Honest John" McCloskey (soon to be recognized as the nation's top minor league organizer), Barnes learned that the Texas League had folded because the Galveston club was too strong. Barnes threw the salary limit out the window, and signed five of Galveston's players. Thus reinforced, Spokane quickly took command of the race and finished in first by 6-1/2 games. Borchers, cut by Portland for drunkenness and now with Spokane, pitched the pennant-clinching victory. One former Texas Leaguer, second baseman Frank "Piggy" Ward, won the batting title, while another, pitcher "Happy" Jack

The 1901 Portland Webfooters, Pacific Northwest League champs, included (far left) future Hall-of-Famer Joe Tinker. Manager-first baseman Jack Grim (center) had future club owner Bob Brown at his left. Pitchers George Engel and Bill Salisbury won 49 games between them as Portland dominated the PNL's 1901 season.

Huston, led the league with a dazzling 28-8 record.

In Portland, Harris and the city's best homegrown ballplayer, Tacky Tom Parrott, hadn't gotten along. Late in the season, Harris suspended Parrott for insubordination. When the club's owners overturned the suspension, Harris quit, but the Northwest had not heard the last of him. The same could be said of Lucas, who was bounced by Tacoma at the end of the season and blacklisted for, as the owners put it, "sowing dissension."

Although there were rumors that Barnes would quit Spokane for Portland, he remained in place. The same can't be said of his Texas League stars. McCloskey ignored the reserve agreement to reunite four of them at Sacramento in the California League, although Huston returned to Spokane later in the summer.

There were further changes. Before the 1891 season, Van Derbeck sold his Portland shares to regional Union Ice czar W.B. Bushnell, but he resurfaced a year later as the head of the California League's first Los Angeles entry. Aided by Barnes, he went on in 1894 to found the Detroit club that, in time, became a charter member of the American League.

Despite these shakeups, the new season provided plenty of entertainment. On May 16, 1891, Tacoma edged Seattle 6-5 in a 22-inning game at Tacoma that was hailed as the longest in professional baseball history. Portland, much improved, blew by Spokane in the final week to win the championship.

By the time winter rolled around, there was talk of consolidating the PNL and the California League into a six-

Pacific Northwest League Schedule for 1901

CLUBS	AT PORTLAND	AT SEATTLE	AT SPOKANE	AT TACOMA
Portland	SMOKE LA	May 8, 9, 11, 12 June 12, 13, 15, 16 July 24, 25, 27, 28 Sept. 4, 5, 7, 8	May 1, 2, 4, 5 July 4, a.m., p.m., 6, 7 July 31, Aug. 1, 3, 4 Sept. 11, 12, 14, 15	May 15, 16, 18, 19 June 26, 27, 29, 30 August 7, 8, 10, 11 Sept. 18, 19, 21, 22
Seattle	May 29, 30, June 1, 2 July 10, 11, 13, 14 August 14, 15, 17, 18 Sept. 25, 26, 28, 29	FLOR DE	May 15, 16, 18, 19 June 26, 27, 29, 30 August 7, 8, 10, 11 Sept. 18, 19, 21, 22	May 1, 2, 4, 5 June 20, 22, 23 July 4 a. m. August 21, 22, 24, 25 October 2, 3, 5, 6
Spokane	May 22, 23, 25, 26 June 19, 20, 22, 23 August 21, 22, 24, 25 October 2, 3, 5, 6	June 5, 6, 8, 9 July 17, 18, 20, 21 Aug. 29, 31, Sept. 1, 2 October 9, 10, 12, 13	SEWARD	June 12, 13, 15, 16 July 10, 11, 13, 14 August 14, 15, 17, 18 Sept. 25, 26, 28, 29
Tacoma	June 5, 6, 8, 9 July 17, 18, 20, 21 Aug. 29, 31, Sept. 1, 2 October 9, 10, 12, 13	May 22, 23, 25, 26 July 3, 4, p. m., 6, 7 July 31, Aug. 1, 3, 4 Sept. 11, 12, 14, 15	May 8, 9, 11, 12 May 29, 30, June 1, 2 July 24, 25, 27, 28 Sept. 4, 5, 7, 8	CIGAR

TOM WILLIAMS, 608 SECOND AVENUE

team league that would exclude Spokane. Although Barnes objected fiercely to this proposal, he left Spokane for Portland, taking Huston and a brilliant prospect named Jake Stenzel with him. Over the winter, the National League had absorbed the American Association, reducing the number of major league teams and players by a quarter. Tacoma benefited, adding future Hall of Fame player, manager, and club owner Clark Griffith to its pitching staff.

There were ominous economic clouds on the nation's horizon, clouds that would be realized as the Panic of 1893. The downturn hit the Northwest prematurely. As a result, the 1892 baseball season was cut short. Portland won the first half of a split schedule. Seattle was leading Tacoma by a game on August 14, when the directors called it quits. Despite steady population growth, the region did not

This 1901 schedule for the Pacific Northwest League remains one of the best artifacts from the early days of the region's professional baseball history.

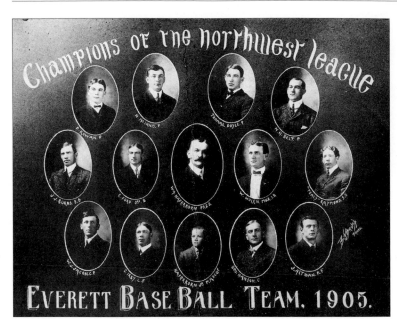

The Everett (Wash.) Smokestackers won the Northwestern League's first pennant in 1905. Skipper Billy Hulen became a successful minor-league manager. Regulars Tealy (actually Tealey) Raymond, the shortstop, and outfielder Charlie Irby became managers, too. The league lasted through 1917.

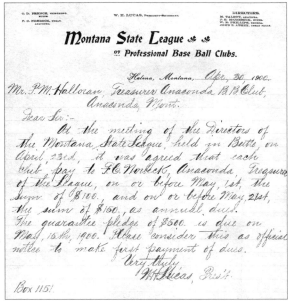

William H. Lucas, signator of this dues notice, became the most important league executive in the Northwest and the intermountain region after launching the Montana State League in 1900. He parlayed that success the next year by reviving, with Dan Dugdale, the Pacific Northwest League and headed four other leagues before his death in 1912.

In typically dignified attire, Dan Dugdale sits with his Seattle Clamdiggers in 1902. Holdovers Jesse Stovall and Jack Hickey won 50 games between them as Seattle made a strong pennant run. Stovall's 29 victories earned him a shot at the big leagues, where he pitched two seasons with Cleveland.

complete another professional season for the rest of the decade. Many of its most prominent citizens lost their fortunes in the economic downturn.

Baseball didn't just go away, however. By 1896, outside money backed a revival with Victoria, B.C., replacing Spokane in what some called the North Pacific League. Wet weather doomed it to an early end on June 14. Spokane and

several southeastern British Columbia mining towns enjoying their heyday, put together a league in 1897. Unfortunately, it was reduced to three teams by opening day, and failed to complete even half of its 44-game schedule. Borchers resurfaced as the player-manager at Kaslo, B.C.

In 1898, the original Pacific Northwest League teams tried again. An old friend of W.H. Lucas, former catcher Dan Dugdale, had moved to Seattle, where he organized a new franchise that played on the YMCA field at 12th and James. Portland arranged to use the new Multnomah Athletic Club field, essentially the site of today's PGE Park. Spokane and Tacoma returned to their original locations.

The season offered events both inspired and frightening. On May 26, Spokane's George Darby, who had managed Victoria in 1896, threw a perfect game at Tacoma in a 15-0 win. The Spokane grandstand burned down on July 4. Perhaps because of the declaration of the Spanish-American War, the PNL barely made it to August. There were no further tries until the next century.

In the meantime, Henry Harris was consolidating his power in the Bay Area, and William H. Lucas, having teamed up with McCloskey to engineer a bang-up season for the Montana State League in 1900, was primed for bigger challenges. Is it a surprise that their paths were about to collide?

Emboldened by their success, Lucas and McCloskey recreated the Pacific Northwest League in 1901, with a hand from Dugdale. It took extra effort from McCloskey, who brought in John M. Maloney of Duluth to organize a

Spokane franchise. McCloskey himself managed Tacoma. Lucas had a hand in organizing the Portland franchise. An ambitious and no-nonsense man, he also established himself as an advocate of a consistent, observed rule book and support for umpires. Decorum also ranked among Lucas' priorities, although it was hard to curb the alcoholic consumption of the players, or the appetite of some club owners for rowdy play.

Dugdale built new stands at Seattle's YMCA grounds, while Spokane moved into a new field in the expanded Twickenham Park, now known as Natatorium Park. Tacoma played again at 11th and L. In May, Portland moved into a new facility at 24th and Vaughn streets, a long streetcar ride from downtown in the northwest part of the city. The Oregon team came to be known as the Webfooters, and with future Hall of Fame member Joe Tinker in its infield and Bob Brown, who spent almost 60 years as a regional ballplayer, manager, and club owner, in its outfield, they led from Opening Day in 1901 and won by 16 games.

The league was on better footing in 1902, when it welcomed two Montana cities, Helena and Butte, into its ranks. McCloskey put together the Butte franchise and led it to the title. His lineup included Piggy Ward, who won a second batting championship, 12 years after his first. Less happily, future big-league southpaw Jack Pfiester and former star Tony Mullane, now 43, couldn't keep Spokane from finishing last. California League champion San Jose defeated Butte ten games to nine in a post-season playoff series.

Although most teams had prominent businessmen as club-owners, Spokane's principal stockholder was Henry G. (Doc) Brown, whose Owl Café was among the city's best-known gambling establishments. Brown started selling his stock during the season, touching off an astonishing three-year flurry of sales and re-sales, all of which apparently became profitable.

W.H. Lucas was active in Northwest baseball for many years, as evidenced by his position in the center of the photo adorning this 1909 scorecard for the Butte team.

The future looked bright for the Pacific Northwest League. Seattle had drawn big crowds. Cities in Montana, British Columbia and Utah were clamoring to join. But a new outlaw circuit to the south, the California League, was about to invade the Northwest, and this successful venture would prove to be the most significant event in the history of baseball in the region.

John Barnes (center), who managed the Spokane team when the Pacific Northwest League was formed, is shown 25 years later as manager of the Northwestern League's 1915 Aberdeen Black Cats.

Sources

Wolff and Johnson, *The Encyclopedia of Minor League Baseball*

Reach Baseball Guide, 1890-1905 editions

The Spokesman-Review, Spokane

The Spokane Daily Chronicle, Spokane

Author's unpublished history of Spokane baseball

Perhaps the irony wasn't intended, but the title of Dan Dugdale's 1902 souvenir booklet for his Seattle entry in the Pacific Northwest League foretold the PNL's 1903 battle with "invaders" from the newly crafted Pacific Coast League.

In bitter 1903 'war,' the Coast was always clear

Population, railway distance, money played key roles in demise of PCL's rival league

The quickest way of ending a war is to lose it.

— George Orwell

By ROB NEYER

On December 10, 1902, Henry Harris, operator of the San Francisco franchise in the four-team, independent California League, made an announcement that sent shivers throughout professional baseball in the eastern third of the United States. In a telegram released to the press, Harris declared, "Arrangements have been completed for Portland and Seattle to join our league," which would, two weeks later, officially be renamed the "Pacific Coast League."

That wasn't precisely accurate. While the directors of the Portland franchise in the two-year-old Pacific Northwest League had agreed to join Harris's league, the existing Seattle franchise remained a question mark. As Harris explained, "Portland has already jumped, and Seattle will either join us or there will be two clubs in Seattle next year."

D.E. Dugdale, who owned the Pacific Northwest League's Seattle franchise, was offered a spot in the new league, but in a meeting he told Harris, "This is too sudden. Give me time." He was given until the next morning and in the meantime showed little enthusiasm for the new venture, telling the *San Francisco Chronicle*:

"The Pacific Northwest League will not give up one of its towns. If Portland has jumped, we will put in another team there. If this combination wants to put another team in Seattle, all right. It means a baseball war, fought to a finish. We will either win fighting or go down fighting.

"I know men with money who stand ready to put up money for a franchise in Portland. The Pacific Northwest League is a member of an aggregation comprising fifteen minor leagues, and we will put up a solid front against this invasion of our territory. The war will prove a bad thing for the game. We will all lose money, but if the war is forced we will not dodge the issue."

In 1902, the four-year-old California League — not a

> **The war will prove a bad thing for the game.**
>
> **Dan Dugdale**

Rob Neyer lives in Oregon and writes about baseball. He thanks Mike Curto, Calvin Bohn, Mike Kopf, and Bob Timmermann for their research help.

Populations of PCL cities exceeded those of Pacific National cities

In the order of their 1900 populations, here are the 10 cities with franchises in the Pacific Coast and Pacific National leagues:

Coast	City	National
342,782	San Francisco	342,782
102,479	Los Angeles	102,749
90,426	Portland	90,426
80,671	Seattle	80,671
66,960	Oakland	
	Butte	48,000
	Spokane	36,848
29,282	Sacramento	
	Tacoma	37,714
	Helena	10,770
120,000	**Average**	**94,000**

part of Organized Baseball and thus considered an "outlaw" league — consisted of only four teams: San Francisco, Los Angeles, Oakland, and Sacramento. The Pacific Northwest League, in just its second season, featured teams in Seattle, Portland, Tacoma, and Spokane, along with Montana entries Butte and Helena. According to an editorial in the *San Francisco Chronicle* published shortly after Harris's announcement, "The strongest reason for seceding was the financial results. Seattle and Portland supported baseball in the other four towns of the league and lost money when away from home."

Dugdale's reluctance might seem foolhardy in retrospect, but apparently he was offered only a piece of a new franchise, rather than an invitation to bring his own franchise in. Also, he was used to being the owner of the biggest team in his league; as an owner in the (soon-to-be-renamed) California League, he would become a lesser figure than he'd been. On December 11, Dugdale announced his decision: "I will not enter the California League. I made $23,000 out of baseball last summer and will spend it all if necessary in fighting these invaders. We have organized baseball back of us, while this California League is an outlaw of the worst type. I will not be wiped off the map."

Initially, there was some talk of the Pacific Northwest League expanding into California, but that talk wasn't taken too seriously, particularly after one promoter of a new club in Los Angeles admitted that he wouldn't field a team in 1903. As the *Chronicle* noted in early February, "This fairly disposes of one end of the promised baseball fight, albeit one that was not given much credence here." A few weeks later, representatives of the National Association of Professional Baseball Leagues traveled to Los Angeles with hopes of making peace on the coast, but nothing came of that either. And in March, with the backing of the National Association — spiritually, if not materially — the PNL revealed its plans to place franchises in San Francisco and Los Angeles.

At 10 in the evening on April 2, 1903, the owners of all Pacific Northwest League teams — including Dr. Emmett Drake, director of a new Portland club — gathered at the Hotel Tacoma (which was, believe it or not, in Tacoma). They didn't get much done that night, but the next day's (Tacoma) *Daily Ledger* reported, "Financial reports from all of the eight clubs show them all very strong and well-equipped to carry on the baseball war, which, the magnates say, will be to a finish. The league has gathered all its financial resources with the determination to either drive the outlaws off the baseball map or be themselves driven off."

The next afternoon, the league took its new name: the Pacific National League.

Initially, the idea was that each club would play 168 games, evenly split between home and road. But considering the population in San Francisco — more on that in a moment — the decision was made to occasionally play league games in that city even when the San Francisco

W. H. LUCAS, President P. N. W. L:

Has the proud distinction of being the head of one of the best minor leagues in the country, comprising six leading cities of the Pacific Northwest. Mr. Lucas was elected president of the league in 1901 and re-elected this year. He is a native of Cleveland, Ohio, and has been connected with base ball for twenty years. He was president of the Montana League in 1900.

A page from Dan Dugdale's 1902 souvenir booklet (previous page). William H. Lucas led his Pacific National League owners astray when he urged them to fight the PCL's invasion of Portland and Seattle by putting teams of their own in San Francisco and Los Angeles and reforming as the Pacific National League.

club was on the road. As first published in the *Oregonian*, the schedule would include 114 games in San Francisco (including three series pitting Butte against Helena), 102 in Los Angeles, 96 in Seattle, 84 in both Portland and Tacoma, 78 in Spokane, and only 57 each in Butte and Helena. As Helena owner W.E. Persell noted in the *Daily Ledger*, "Every club stood willing to concede anything for the good of the league, and this made matters easier than would otherwise have been the case. We think the schedule the best that could be devised under existing war conditions, which, we felt, made it necessary for us to give the two California cities all the National League ball possible. With this object in view, we all conceded something. Montana is satisfied and so are all the other cities."

At that time (see chart), San Francisco easily ranked as the most populous city west of St. Louis. According to the 1900 census, San Francisco's 342,782 citizens ranked ninth in the United States, (slightly) behind Buffalo but ahead of major league cities Cincinnati, Pittsburgh, Detroit, and Washington, D.C. (To be precise, in 1900, Detroit and Washington were not technically "major league" cities, but both would join the ramped-up American League in 1901.) Los Angeles, with slightly more than 100,000, ranked a distant second among the coastal cities.

Obviously, the Pacific National League figured to benefit from its presence in the two largest California cities. But Helena didn't have any business in a league that included the big coastal cities. Today, the trip from Helena to Los Angeles is nearly 1,200 miles by road and was probably of similar length a century ago by train. How far is that? The

> **The league has gathered all its financial resources with the determination to either drive the outlaws off the baseball map or be themselves driven off.**
>
> **Tacoma *Daily Ledger***

A page from Dan Dugdale's 1902 souvenir booklet (see first page of chapter). Dugdale made a big profit with his Pacific Northwest League team in 1902 but lost it all in a vain bid to hold his territory in the face of competition from the faster Pacific Coast League.

D. E. DUGDALE,
President and Manager Seattle Base Ball Team

Mr. Dugdale is one of the best known characters in the base ball world. He began his professional career in 1884 with Peoria in the Northwestern League. Since then he has played in every league in the United States. He retired from active playing two years ago when he accepted the management of the local team. He has worked hard to give the local fans base ball, and the daily attendance proves how successful he has been. He is popular with his men, and this year has brought out the best team in the Pacific Northwest League. He is 37 years old.

distance between Helena and Los Angeles is greater than the distance between Helena and Minneapolis. More obviously, there simply weren't enough people in Helena to support a team in a top minor league. And Helena was merely the weakest link. Butte, Spokane and Tacoma were all less populous than five of the Coast League's six cities.

Nevertheless, on April 6, President W.H. Lucas told an *Oregon Journal* reporter, "We have completed all our arrangements for the season, rented our grounds, signed players, and equipped the teams fully. Our schedule will be arranged to suit the climatic conditions as much as possible. The Pacific National League is financially sound, having the most reputable backing. I think that we will surely win out in the end, as we have the standing with the public that means so much to the success of a game."

On April 14, Opening Day for the Nationals, the war was joined, particularly in Los Angeles, where both leagues were featured. And those two games in Los Angeles perhaps foretold the entire story of this ill-matched war. The Coast League game matched the Los Angeles Angels — or "Looloos," as they were often called — against the San Francisco Seals. The Pacific National League game matched that loop's Los Angeles club (which had no official nickname) against the Helena Senators. If you'd been a baseball fan in Los Angeles, which game would you have chosen to watch? (Making the choice even easier, on the morning of the Pacific National League's first games, the Coast League's Angels entered the day with a perfect record: 14 wins, zero losses.)

> **The Pacific National League is financially sound, having the most reputable backing. I think that we will surely win out in the end, as we have the standing with the public that means so much to the success of a game.**
>
> **W.H. Lucas, Pacific National League president**

According to the *Los Angeles Times*, attendance at the PCL game at Chutes Field was "more than 2,800," but in the PNL opener at Prager Park, attendance was "between 1,300 and 1,500 people." It shouldn't have been a surprise to anyone when, just more than a month later, Portland's *Oregonian* published the following report:

HELENA, May 17 (Special) — Despite all rumors to the contrary Helena is in the Pacific National League to stay. A canvass among the men interested in baseball in this city is authority for this statement. Flannery's men will come home with a large deficit, but anticipating this fact the fans have, during the past week, succeeded in raising sufficient money to insure the team making the second trip to California. People here admit that a mistake was made when the California towns were admitted to the league. As to joining the Salt Lake League, Helena would not for a moment consider it. Unlike larger towns, the business men and mainstays of the town, with a great deal of local pride, feel that whatever mistakes may have been made in the past, Helena is in the league to stay and will remain throughout the season under the present arrangement.

Within a few days, the Pacific National League sent Tacoma and Portland, both scheduled for games in California, northward before they could play those games. Various reasons were given for the schedule change, but Portland's *Journal* probably had it right, noting, "There is reason to believe, however, that the poor attendance in San Francisco is the real reason for the sudden change in plans. The two tail-end teams, Tacoma and Portland, were not drawing well in the California metropolis and the league leaders were forced to shift them. They forgot to agree upon a satisfactory reason to assign for the move."

It wasn't just the Tacoma and Portland clubs that struggled in California. According to a one report, "Butte's share of the proceeds from the series of games at Los Angeles is said to have been less than $48. For five games it is claimed the Miners received less than $8, and one game yielded only 95 cents." Helena did better, but not by much: the Senators made $169 in their Los Angeles series, and drew poorly in San Francisco. And those dollars refer only to gate receipts. When travel costs are factored into the equation, the Montana clubs' expenses far outweighed their income.

With the schedule suddenly in tatters, the eventual outcome of the "war" was obvious. All that remained were the gory details. On July 1, Portland's *Daily Journal* reported, "After a short 11-weeks' struggle with the Pacific Coast League in its own territory, the directors of the Pacific National League last night decided to make a practical surrender. They backed out of a tight hole as gracefully as they could, and having saved themselves by a hair's breadth from total collapse, launched out on a new plan which they hope will succeed better than that which was inaugurated with a blaze of trumpets and many promises last April."

Among the changes? "Having found it impossible to succeed in Portland in opposition to the Coast Leaguers,

President Lucas and his board of directors last night voted unanimously to transfer the Portland franchise to Salt Lake City and today the Portland Nationals were officially wiped from the map."

Wiped from the standings, too. With Portland's "Greengages" in last place — just behind Helena — the new owners in Salt Lake City agreed to join the league only if they could start with a clean slate. And the new club, like both Montana clubs and Tacoma, would not be asked to travel to California. What's more, Los Angeles and San Francisco wouldn't head home until late August. Essentially, the Pacific National League had abandoned California, and thus the war was all but over. Six weeks later — on August 15 — saw this *Daily Ledger* report from Helena: "Forced to the conclusion that the people of the Pacific Northwest do not want league ball sufficiently to patronize the game, and brought face to face with a financial problem that becomes more serious as the daily deficit piles up, the Helena association has been compelled to give up the unequal struggle."

With that domino felled — and various reports of new homes for the franchise unfounded — others fell in quick succession. One day after the dissolution of Helena, the Tacoma franchise also dissolved. Supposedly the Tigers had money in the bank, but were scheduled to play in Helena in two of the next three weeks. As the president of the franchise told the *Daily Ledger*, "It is such a mixed up mess all around that we decided we did not want anything more to do with it. . . Now the plan seems to be to send us on a wild goose chase around the country looking for a team to play with us. We are heartily tired of it." A few days later, two more dominoes fell, and these, reported the *San Francisco Chronicle*, were the biggest:

"The so-called baseball war is at an end, so far as California is concerned. Harry J. Hart, backer and principal owner of the San Francisco and Los Angeles teams of the Pacific National League, threw up the sponge yesterday and ordered the teams disbanded. With that announcement passed what was probably the most expensive venture ever known in a minor baseball league. The loss to Hart and his partners is estimated at between $40,000 and $50,000, all of which was spent without a murmur, and for which there is no hope of return. Even now Hart declines to grumble. 'It was my money and it is gone. The incident is closed,' was all Hart had to say."

On August 27, the directors of the National League's four remaining teams — Seattle, Butte, Spokane, and Salt Lake City — met in Butte to make a new schedule. Somehow, Salt Lake got assigned only six games and Butte with a dozen, while Seattle and Spokane got 18 and 24, respectively. As the *Journal* opined, "Portland fans should congratulate themselves upon getting rid of the Lucas dynasty. Poor old Salt Lake."

Those four clubs did play out the schedule, finishing up on October 4 with Butte's Miners in first place, six games (or four-and-a-half, depending on which source you believe) ahead of the second-place Spokane Indians.

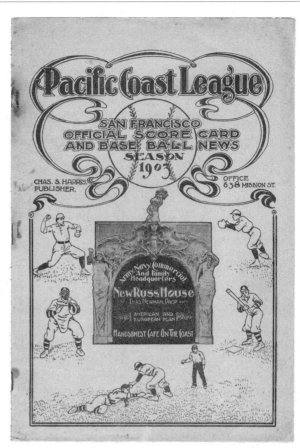

This Pacific Coast League program is from the league's first week of play in 1903. The San Francisco Seals represented the expanded California League, and Portland was the opposing team.

Meanwhile, the Coast League kept playing, and playing, and playing. They had opened their season on March 26, and they closed on... [wait for it] ... November 29. The Los Angeles club, which got off to that wonderful start, wound up with 133 wins and 78 losses, the only Coast League team to finish above .500 (second-place Sacramento won 105 and lost 105).

The War Between the Pacific Leagues just wasn't a fair fight. Fans in the big California cities should have been expected to patronize the old California League teams, and they did. The Montana teams in the Pacific National League — with all the travel and so few home games — should have been expected to lose a lot of money, and they did. Generally, the Coast League teams paid higher salaries, which meant better players, which meant a higher quality of play, which meant more fans. Realistically, the Pacific National League's only hope was to get significant financial help from the National Commission, the governing body of organized baseball (of which the Pacific Coast League was not a member). But aside from theoretically suspending players who signed with Coast League teams — a threat few players took seriously — the Pacific National League's sister leagues did little or nothing to help. And so the Nationals' fate was sealed.

D.E. Dugdale, apparently the most quotable baseball man in the entire western half of North America, provided perhaps the best denouement of the short-lived Pacific National League. After the loop's lone season, Dugdale

Please turn to 'War' on page 47

It is such a mixed up mess all around that we decided we did not want anything more to do with it. …

Now the plan seems to be to send us on a wild goose chase around the country looking for a team to play with us.

We are heartily tired of it.

Tacoma franchise president

"An A-1 catcher" is how the New York Clipper described Dan Dugdale of the Washington Senators in 1894, shown in a cabinet photo from that year. He headed west four years later and began building Seattle minor-league ball.

'He was a nobleman among his fellows'

Ex-catcher Dan Dugdale built teams and stadiums, brought pro baseball to Seattle to stay

BY JEFF OBERMEYER

It was early in the evening on March 9, 1934, as the City Light truck made its way down Fourth Avenue South in downtown Seattle. The driver saw a rotund older man step from the curb to cross the street a short distance ahead.

The truck slowed to allow him to cross, but when he took a step back the driver resumed his normal speed. He was surprised when the man stepped off the curb again and began to make his way to a car on the other side of the street.

There wasn't enough time to react, and the truck struck the pedestrian. He was rushed to Providence Hospital, but his injuries were too severe and he passed away three hours later. Daniel Edward Dugdale, the "Father of Seattle Baseball," was dead at the age of 69.

Dugdale (or Dug, as he was affectionately known) was born in Peoria, Illinois on October 28, 1864, the son of Edward Ryan Dugdale, an Irish immigrant, and Mary Rebecca Lyons. Little is known of his life before he signed as a catcher with the Peoria Reds of the Northwestern League in 1884. He bounced around the Midwest for two years playing with Peoria, Hannibal, Leavenworth, Keokuk, and Denver before coming to the attention of the majors, signing with the Kansas City Cowboys of the National League for the 1886 season. He made his major league debut on May 20, 1886, appearing behind the plate against the New York Giants. Dug picked up two hits (and allowed three passed balls) on the afternoon as the Cowboys defeated the Giants 5-4.

Though he swung the bat well that day, he was hitting only .175 after 12 games when he was forced from the lineup with a sprained knee. Dug still had to work on his game if he wanted to make it in the bigs and not just in the batter's box: his 14 passed balls and eight errors were too many, even for the era. Despite being a work in progress, he caught on with Denver in August, finishing out the season in the Western League.

The next six seasons saw Dugdale move from team to team throughout the minors. After spending 1887 in the International League splitting time between Rochester and Buffalo, he jumped to the Western Association in 1888 and joined the Chicago Maroons. A successful three-year run with the Minneapolis Millers followed before he moved on to the St. Paul/Ft. Wayne club in 1892.

Dug headed south and joined the Chattanooga Warriors of the Southern League in 1893. Gus Schmelz managed the Warriors and liked what he saw in the veteran catcher, so when Schmelz was given the manager job with the Washington Senators of the National League for 1894, he brought the backstop east with him.

Not everyone was enamored with the choice: "What do you think of it?," reported the Oct. 15, 1893, *Washington Post*. Fatty Dugdale has already been signed by Washington for next season [1894]. The Capital is making an early bid for the last hole again." It was around this time that Dugdale's weight became a more and more frequent topic for derision. Much to his dismay, his size was referred to in the papers for the rest of his life.

Despite the unflattering review in the *Post*, the July 21, 1894, *New York Clipper* painted a much more rosy picture of his talents after the season got underway: "Dugdale uses more headwork in a game than three fourths of the catchers and is always on the alert to take advantage of any misplays on the part of the opposing team. He is a fair batsman and base runner, but an A1 catcher."

His performance that season was an improvement over his previous stint in the majors, but still sub-par. He appeared in 38 games and batted .236 (the league average was an amazing .309) with 16 RBIs. Defensively, Dug improved, reducing his passed balls to nine in 33 games behind the plate, though he still had 18 errors charged to him on the season.

Despite the lackluster performance, Schmelz still had faith in the catcher and planned to bring him back in 1895: "[Schmelz] says that the only trouble with Dugdale last year was that he was not given enough work to thoroughly keep his hand in and therefore became too fat and heavy to be of much service when he was needed late in the season," reported the Jan. 10, 1895, *Washington Post*. "In his opinion Dugdale, with enough work to keep him in good playing form, is superior to any of the talent available."

However, Dugdale was not interested in spending another season on the bench backing up Deacon McGuire and sought a release. Schmelz complied, and Dug returned to his hometown of Peoria, where he bought a stake in the city's Western Association franchise, the Distillers. He proved to be an excellent manager, keeping the club in the hunt for most of the season until breaking a finger (he was also the starting catcher) with just under two weeks to go. Without Dug behind the plate, the club faltered and eventually finished in second with a 74-55 record.

In the fall, Dug left for Minneapolis, returning to his off-season job as a molder with the Minneapolis Stove Works. There was talk of him taking over the reins of the Western League club there for the following season, but that never came to fruition. He returned to Peoria in the spring, leading the Distillers to a third-place finish in 1896.

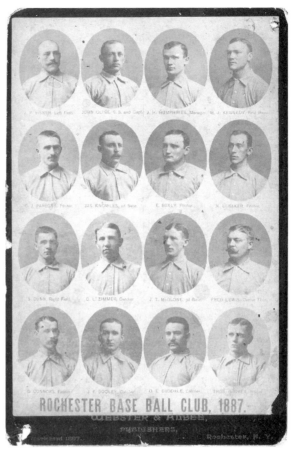

Rochester in 1887 was but one of many minor-league stops for Dan Dugdale (bottom row, third from left).

After watching the Distillers drop to fifth in 1897, Dugdale decided that it was time to move on, heading west in 1898 to seek his fortune in the Klondike Gold Rush. He only made it as far as Seattle, where he took a job as a brakeman on a cable car and immediately set about trying to establish a professional baseball team.

There had been attempts to bring the pro game to Seattle as far back as 1890 with the formation of the Pacific Northwest League ,but these met with only limited success. The PNL was reborn in 1898 with clubs in Seattle, Portland, Spokane and Tacoma. The Seattle entry, owned by Dugdale, was known as the Klondikers and was based at YMCA Park, located on James Street between 12th and 14th avenues.

The Klondikers opened their season against Tacoma on May 18, and Dug made certain it was a big event. Festivities included a parade through downtown Seattle featuring players from both clubs in their uniforms led by a marching band. The parade wound through the city for an hour before ending at the ballpark, after which the teams were given 30 minutes each to warm up. A crowd of 425 fans turned out to watch the Klondikers take an early 1-0 lead before giving way to Tacoma, eventually losing by a score of 14-6.

The league didn't complete the 1898 season and Dugdale had to busy himself with semi-pro ball as well as his expanding real estate portfolio. He got back into the pro game in 1901 with the re-establishment of the Pacific

Dugdale uses more headwork in a game than three-fourths of the catchers and is always on the alert to take advantage of any misplays on the part of the opposing team.

New York Clipper

Jeff Obermeyer is the operations manager at a regional subrogation office for Farmers Insurance. During the off season he does hockey research and his book *Hockey in Seattle* was published by Arcadia in the fall of 2004.

(Above) In the re-established Pacific Northwest League, Dan Dugdale (top center) piloted his Seattle Clamdiggers to third place in 1901, starting a 69-year run of pro baseball in the city.

Northwest League, which included the same four cities as the previous incarnation. Unlike its predecessor, the new PNL was successful financially and Dug piloted his Seattle Clamdiggers to a third-place finish. The league expanded into Montana in 1902 with the addition of clubs in Butte and Helena, increasing in size to six teams. The Clamdiggers improved, finishing second behind Butte. After two successful seasons the Seattle franchise was poised to make a run for the pennant, but a war was on the horizon that would change the complexion of the baseball landscape on the West Coast.

In December 1902 the owners of the independent California League announced an expansion of their operation northward to include franchises in Portland and Seattle. The new league was named the Pacific Coast League and was to consist of six West Coast teams.

The invaders made overtures to PNL representatives, including Dugdale, hoping to lure the Clamdiggers and Portland Webfooters to their league. When Dug refused the offer, the PCL found other backers for its Seattle franchise. The owner in Portland, however, was more receptive and jumped to the new league, a breach of the territorial rights of the PNL (which now stood for Pacific National League).

A protest was filed with the National Association, which sided with the PNL and branded the PCL an outlaw league. All players under contract to PCL clubs were now blacklisted by the Association, preventing any member team from signing them until they were reinstated. The Association also promoted the PNL to a Class A league, the highest minor league designation at the time (other Class A leagues in 1903 included the American Association, the Eastern League, and the Western League).

Dugdale and PNL President William H. Lucas fired back at their rivals by announcing their intention to put franchises in Los Angeles and San Francisco, the two largest PCL cities. The move was a disaster for the PNL. Not only were they still trying to replace the team in Portland, but they also were attempting to establish two new teams more than 800 miles away.

The PCL was already ahead of the game, with five solid clubs and only one new start-up. Allegations also surfaced in the Los Angeles press that Dugdale and Lucas had tried to use Charles Dooley, former owner and manager of the Montreal Royals of the Eastern League, to buy controlling interest in the Seattle PCL club and fold the franchise as soon as he (and therefore they) took ownership. Dirty tricks and shady deals were quickly becoming the norm as the battle between the leagues escalated.

Players began jumping back and forth between the leagues almost immediately, though most of the movement was out of the PNL. Ed Hurlburt left Seattle for the PCL early in the season, and Dugdale didn't take kindly to contract jumpers. While the club was in Portland in June, pitcher Willie Hogg approached his manager outside the team hotel and requested his release to join Hurlburt. When Dug refused the request, the June 13, 1903, *Seattle Daily Times* reported that Hogg "at once assumed a threatening attitude and became abusive. Dugdale, knowing his reputation, concluded that it was proper for him to act in his own defense, which he did, with the result that Hogg was put out of commission with a straight poke to the jaw that would have done credit to any knight of the ring."

That was the last time a player asked the Seattle owner to be released, but it wasn't Dugdale's last fight. Later that summer, he got into a scuffle with captain Gus Klopf of Spokane when the two crossed paths in a Seattle cigar store. There was a history of bad blood between them, and Klopf was knocked down twice by the much larger (265-pound) Dugdale, suffering a number of facial cuts and bruises.

As the summer wore on things got worse for the PNL. The new Portland franchise relocated to Salt Lake City on July 12, Tacoma and Helena disbanded on August 16, and the two California entries followed suit on August 21. The league staggered to the finish line with only four of its eight clubs intact, and the war was effectively over. The PCL had come out on top, and Dugdale sold his team and territorial rights to the victors. The PNL lasted one more year as a four-team circuit, but following the 1904 season it folded for good.

Over the next three years, Dug remained involved in a number of baseball-related projects. He sponsored the Dugdale Pennant of the Puget Sound League, a 20-team semi-pro league that operated in western Washington. He also briefly managed the Portland Browns of the PCL in 1904 and was instrumental in establishing the Class B Northwestern League in 1905. He was slated to manage the Bellingham (WA) club in that circuit during its inaugural season, but backed out before the opener.

This program from the Seattle Giants of 1916 highlights Dan Dugdale's key role in the team's development.

The PCL was forced to abandon Seattle prior to the start of the 1907 season. While most sources indicate this was due to poor attendance and the uncertain future of the league in the wake of the 1906 San Francisco earthquake, PCL President Cal Ewing had another explanation. He told the *Los Angeles Times* that Seattle owner Russ Hall was in collusion with Dugdale in an effort to keep the team off the field.

When Hall was "unable" to field a team and the league failed to find a new ownership group, the territory was automatically relinquished according to the rules of the National Association. This paved the way for Dugdale to establish a new Northwestern League team in the city, the

Dugdale with his 1908 Northwestern League Seattle Siwashes. Northwest baseball mainstays George Engel and Matt Stanley (bottom row, third and fifth from left, flanking Dugdale), and Emil Frisk (middle row, fourth from left), anchored the team.

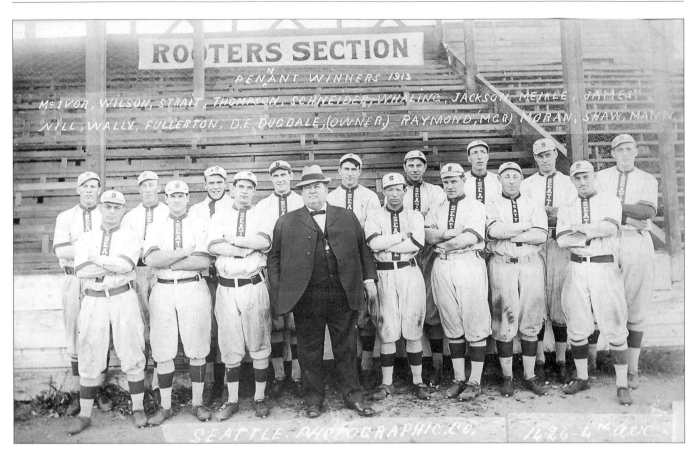

At Yesler Way Park, Dan Dugdale poses with his pennant-winning Seattle Giants in 1912. His franchise also topped the Northwestern League in 1909 and 1915.

Siwashcs (known as the Turks in 1909 and the Giants in 1910-18). Ewing's allegations of underhanded conduct were supported by the fact that Hall was named the manager of the Butte Miners of the NWL following the demise of his PCL club.

Dugdale funded the construction of Yesler Way Park in 1907 to house his new team. The upgraded Northwestern League consisted of six teams, though changes in member cities were still fairly common from season to season. The four cities that made up the backbone of the circuit were Seattle, Spokane, Tacoma and Vancouver, B.C. Other members at various times included Aberdeen (WA), Butte (MT), Great Falls (MT), Victoria (BC) and Portland (OR). The Seattle franchise was successful both at the gate and in the standings, capturing pennants in 1909, 1912, and 1915.

The success of his clubs increased the popularity of the gregarious owner. Always approachable, Dugdale was a fan favorite who usually had a kind word for the local bleacherites and took the time to talk baseball with them. His fellow owners and officials from other leagues respected him for a totally different reason — his commitment to the bottom line. Dug understood that baseball was a business, and he was in business to make money.

While many of his players felt that he was loyal to them, others had a different perspective. Jack Barry resigned as manager of the Giants early in the 1912 season, citing interference by the owner in the handling of players as well as personnel decisions being made for purely economic

reasons. In a tell-all interview in the June 13, 1912, *Sporting News* Barry said of his former boss, "Cut down expenses is his hit-and-run sign."

In 1912 Dugdale began designing a new ballpark that he hoped would be the finest on the West Coast. He got some help in the layout from none other than Connie Mack of the Athletics, who was traveling through Seattle that winter on tour with his world champions. The park (eventually known as Dugdale Park) was completed just prior to the end of the 1913 season. The all-wood structure was located at the intersection of Rainier Avenue and McLellan Street in the Rainier Valley (South Seattle) and was the first stadium on the West Coast with double-decked stands. It was a significant investment, with the stands alone costing $35,000 to construct, and it remained the home of Seattle baseball for the next 18 years.

The first problems within the Northwestern League began in 1915, when Spokane, Vancouver, and Tacoma conspired to alter the schedule late in the season without notifying the other owners or the league president. Dugdale was furious, but powerless to prevent the collusion. He began to drop hints in the press that he would be open to overtures from the PCL if this kind of thing continued.

Teams were struggling financially in the NWL as they were throughout baseball in the wake of America's entry into World War I, and the league was granted approval from the National Association to end the 1917 season on July 15. The approval was necessary as the league did not want to disband and sought to maintain territorial rights to its member cities. The *Los Angeles Times* reported that the Seattle club had lost money over the previous three seasons and that Dugdale was again looking to jump to the PCL.

He gave it one more shot with the NWL, newly reformed as the Pacific Coast International League for the 1918 season. Unfortunately, the new circuit fared no better, struggling at the gate as U.S. involvement in World War I intensified. Two teams disbanded by the end of May, and the league folded on July 7. Dug saw the handwriting on the wall and sold his majority interest in the club to an ownership group headed by cigar store magnate James Brewster for $60,000 in January 1919.

Brewster renamed the team the Rainiers (later changed to Indians early in the 1920 season before changing back to Rainiers in 1938) and transferred it to the PCL, where it remained a mainstay until the American League Pilots came to Seattle in 1969. The sale to Brewster was the close of the Dugdale Era of professional baseball in Seattle and ended his 21-year reign as a local owner.

Dugdale maintained ownership of Dugdale Park, however, and continued leasing it to the club until selling it to the new owner of the Indians, Bill Klepper, in 1928. It remained the home of the Indians until a July 4, 1932 fire left the stands and clubhouse a smoldering ruin.

The fire was discovered by night watchman George Felton, who raced to the clubhouse and called the fire department shortly after midnight. Unfortunately, by the time the first of the three responding fire companies arrived the wood grandstands were already fully engulfed in flames, and it was all they could do to prevent the conflagration from spreading to neighboring businesses and homes. Three houses on the other side of Rainier Avenue also caught fire, but these were quickly contained with only minor damage.

Investigator Frank Harshfield reported that the inferno started in the main runway of the grandstand, and that an oil drum was found nearby in the stands. The investigation didn't turn up much else. It wasn't until serial arsonist Robert Driscoll confessed to setting the blaze three years later that the mystery was finally solved. The damage to the structure was estimated at $100,000, only $24,000 of which was covered by insurance.

It was an inglorious end to a great ballpark that had not only been the home of five championship teams, but had also hosted some of baseball's greatest stars such as Babe Ruth, Ty Cobb, and Bob Meusel, all of whom played exhibition games on its diamond. The Indians relocated to Civic Stadium (near the present-day home of the Space Needle) and remained there until the construction of Sick's Stadium in 1938.

Dugdale stayed involved in the Seattle baseball scene throughout the 1920s and into the 1930s, lending his support to various semi-pro organizations such as the Puget Sound Baseball League, which he led as president in 1931. He was also actively involved in politics as a member of the Democratic Party and was appointed to the legislature

as a representative of the 34th District to replace the incumbent, William Allen. Following the death of his wife Mary in October 1933, Dug moved in with his sister Elizabeth, living with her for the last six months of his life.

At the time of his passing, Dug was president of the Northwest Semi-Pro League and was busy preparing for the upcoming season. He was also looking forward to the fifth annual "Busher's Banquet," the yearly get-together for former baseball players and fans held at the Washington Athletic Club. The event was scheduled for March 10 — the day after the fatal accident. Instead of a celebration, it became a wake for the popular magnate. *Seattle Times* Sports Editor George Varnell wrote a fitting eulogy for his friend:

"The name of Daniel E. Dugdale has on this Pacific Coast been synonymous with all the better things that go with professional baseball. His word in a baseball deal was as good as his bond, as is (sic) was in every other transaction.

"He was a nobleman among his fellows. He was 'Dug' to the multitude of his friends and acquaintances. Baseball was his life and in recent years. ... He devoted his valuable experience and ability to the upbuilding of the lesser light of baseball, the semi-pros.

"But whether it was league ball, semi-pro, amateur or sandlot baseball for the kids, Dugdale always stood ready to put his shoulder to the wheel. And always it was there. Baseball was his first love and his sudden and untimely death robs the Northwest of its greatest individual figure in the national game."

Dug was laid to rest at Calvary Cemetery near the University of Washington. Local fans paid homage to their fallen friend at "Dugdale Night" on June 7, 1934, with the largest night-game crowd of the season (4,500) on hand to watch the Indians knock off the Portland Beavers by a score of 6-1, a fitting tribute to one of Seattle baseball's great larger-than-life figures. ⚾

In the catcher's position of his youth, Dan Dugdale (left) takes part in a 1931 old-timers game at the ballpark named for him. Offering advice was future Hall-of-Famer Amos Rusie ("The Hoosier Thunderbolt"), and listening in was Bill Hurley, who played for Dugdale's 1901 Seattle team.

Sources: *Seattle Daily Times, Seattle Post-Intelligencer, The Sporting News, Washington Post*

The man who won big for Portland

A Beaver to the end, innovative Walter McCredie scorned color line, trumpeted hard work in seeking victory

By BRIAN CAMPF

Walter McCredie, shown in 1911, "one of the most popular ballplayers that ever wore a Portland uniform."

It all started to unravel when they returned from Honolulu. A team of baseball all-stars from the Pacific Coast League had sailed across the blue Pacific for a post-season barnstorming escapade to Hawaii. It was 1914, and the ballplayers were surely enjoying what young men do in the tropics. It's a wonder they ever came home.

Walter McCredie, a 38-year old law school dropout, one-year major leaguer, and manager of the Coast League's Portland Beavers, had good reason to celebrate the island junket. He had signed up a new pitching prospect in Honolulu. McCredie was a superior developer of big league talent. A McCredie acquisition meant something.

The recruit was not a typical busher. He was fluent in Hawaiian, Chinese, and English. Christy Mathewson had personally shown him how to throw his famous fade-away. Ed Walsh gave him tips on pitching the spitball. He had attended a World Series. "A real ball player," said Johnny Kane, a Coast Leaguer who had played against him.

The guy was a catch. But so was his color. He was half Chinese and half Hawaiian. Put differently, he wasn't white. His name was Lang Akana.

Players revolted at the news of Akana's signing. They threatened a walkout. McCredie reluctantly said that he would cut Akana loose. "The Coast Leaguers who played at Honolulu on that recent barnstorming trip came back vowing boycott," McCredie said. "I have received a couple of letters from players telling me Akana is as dark as Jack Johnson [the African-American boxer], so I guess I will have to give him a release."

McCredie refused to back down in the end. He vowed to give Akana a chance to earn a spot on the club. "Akana is going to have a hard time breaking in with this prejudice against him," one reporter observed. And indeed, Akana never became a Beaver.

The Akana episode moved McCredie to openly declare his opposition to baseball's unwritten but very real color line. "I don't think the color of the skin ought to be a barrier in baseball. They have Jim Thorpe, an Indian, in the big leagues; there are Cubans on the rosters of the various clubs. Here in the Pacific Coast League we have a Mexican and a Hawaiian, and yet the laws of baseball bar negroes from organized diamonds. If I had my way, the negro would be welcome inside the fold. I would like to have two such ball players as [Bruce] Petway and [John "Pop"] Lloyd of the Chicago Colored Giants, who play out here every Spring. I think Lloyd is another Hans Wagner around shortstop and Petway is one of the greatest catchers in the world."

McCredie pushed the social boundaries of the day by acquiring Akana, though he could not remove them. His call for baseball's integration was as out of step with the times as someone today urging its segregation. These events reflect McCredie's unwavering commitment to his players, the fans, and himself to field the best team possible. This was not about color. This was about winning. This was about baseball. McCredie knew how to win big.

He led his Portland team to PCL pennants in 1906, 1910, 1911, 1913, and 1914. The number of superb players he graduated to the major leagues would be the envy of any manager. This is his story.

Walter Henry McCredie was born in Manchester, Iowa on November 29, 1876. He played town-lot ball as a youngster and was recognized for his pitching. "Loyal McCredie may not be a good enough boy to go to the Olive street school, but he proved yesterday that he was a good enough pitcher to shut out the Bunker Hills to the tune of 8 to 0. His team was the Ida Street Juniors," one early account reported.

He also pitched for the High School baseball nine. A game summary notes that the opposing team, the Athletics, "could do nothing with McCredie" and that "McCredie once more pitched one of his masterful games, allowing the Athletics only two scattered hits and letting only one man walk." Score: High School 2, Athletics 1.

Pitching took a back seat to playing the infield and the outfield as his baseball career progressed. There are historical discrepancies regarding the teams McCredie played for, and when, prior to his joining Portland in 1904. The following likely chronology is based largely on a *Sporting News* article published at the time of his death.

He started with the Des Moines ball club in 1896-97. There, he was nearly shot in a shoe store shooting that killed the proprietor. "I've been mixed up in several shootings, and I'm mighty leery of 'em now," McCredie said later. "I feel it stands me in hand to get out of the way when there are any bullets flying around loose in the air."

He next played for Quincy and Minneapolis (1898). While with Youngstown in 1899 McCredie broke his right leg sliding into a base, but he recovered and joined Newcastle and Sioux City (1900) and Minneapolis (1901). He then headed west and led the Oakland Clamdiggers to the pennant in 1902, topping the California League with a .319 batting average.

Bill Lange signed McCredie for Ned Hanlon's Brooklyn Dodgers in 1903. His father John was proud of Walter's good fortune. "He got $300 spot cash for signing the contract," the elder McCredie boasted, "and his salary for the season is to be $1,000 for three months' work." He batted .324 in 56 games before Brooklyn traded him to Baltimore of the Eastern League on July 3, 1903. McCredie played 74 games in the outfield for Baltimore, averaging .318 with 18 stolen bases.

Recognizing that baseball careers tend to be short, McCredie enrolled in Drake University's law program with a plan to quit the game once he had his degree. "I find ball playing is a sort of lottery after all," explained McCredie. "You are always getting hurt at it and there is so much uncertainty that I am tired of it. I want to study law and settle down some place and practice. I believe it will be a lot more certain, and there is not the danger attached to it, either." The *Washington Post* noted in 1903 that McCredie had been "reading law, and will graduate next year."

However, McCredie's legal education was teaching him a valuable lesson that many lawyers secretly know but only admit to themselves while reading the morning's box scores: baseball is a lot more fun than law. With nothing but an uncertain future before him, and probably an unhappy mother behind him, he abandoned his budding legal career to continue playing baseball full time.

McCredie landed a right field job in Portland in 1904 after visiting friends there. Baseball in Portland was in a very bad way when he arrived. The *Sporting News* declared that the Portland club, "owing to the way it has been run in the past, had become decidedly unpopular."

In 1903, the Portland Browns (as the team was then called) lost 15 of their first 20 games on their way to a last-place 95-108 season. Twenty-five players and two managers came and went that year. One bright spot was pitcher Jake Thielman's league-leading 2.12 earned run average. Less impressive was Isaac Butler leading the league in losses with 31.

Things got worse in 1904, a year that could have inspired Abbott and Costello to ask, "Who's on first? And second? And third?" The Browns used 37 players, wearing out three managers and two owners along the way. Isaac Butler had another league-leading 31-loss season, and the team finished dead last with a 79-136 record. Worse yet, the team was hemorrhaging money.

Through this darkness McCredie emerged as the lone star of his new team. He was big and handsome, 6-foot-2 and 195 pounds. He batted left, threw right, and was a .300 hitter in 1904. Still, given the precarious state of Portland baseball that year, it could not have come as a complete surprise that in 1904 the team president ordered him to accept a pay cut. McCredie refused and was fined $100.00.

Rather than being branded an upstart, the plucky outfielder captured the public's eye. In 1904, the Sporting News lauded Big Mac's playing abilities, his "gentlemanly manner," and called him "one of the most popular ball players that ever wore a Portland uniform."

McCredie's leadership skills were evident from the beginning. His teammate Jack Holland remarked after the 1904 season that Portland's owners "made a big mistake ... in not turning the management over to Walter McCredie, by far the most capable man on the club, and [who] was popular with players and patrons."

So there he was, a smash hit with the players and the fans, stuck on a team that was losing money and losing games. Most people would have run, not walked, to greener outfields. Yet McCredie saw opportunity in this chaos. He and his uncle bought the Portland club at the end of 1904 for $9,000 (about $185,000 in today's dollars).

Having a successful uncle did not hurt. William Wallace McCredie was born in Montrose, Pennsylvania in 1862. His father, a Union army officer, was killed at Gettysburg. In 1890, he moved to Portland, Oregon, began practicing law in nearby Vancouver, Washington, and went on to serve one term as a prosecuting attorney in Clark County,

> I find ball playing is a sort of lottery, after all.
>
> You are always getting hurt at it, and there is so much uncertainty that I am tired of it.
>
> I want to study law and settle down someplace and practice.
>
> I believe it will be a lot more certain, and there is not the danger attached to it, either.
>
> **Walter McCredie**

Walter McCredie (bottom row, fourth from left) paced the 1905 Portland Giants. A highlight of the season came June 21 when second baseman Larry Schlafly (bottom row, far right) executed an unassisted triple play.

Mac runs the club as though he owned it.

The players realize that there is no appeal from his decision in any matter affecting the conduct of the club, and as a result he is able to enforce a high degree of discipline.

Hap Hogan, Vernon Tigers manager

Washington, hold one term and part of another as a superior court judge in Vancouver, and become a representative for Washington state in the U.S. Congress.

Uncle William also adored baseball. In 1909, the *Washington Post* described him as a "former professional player" who in his early days "was considered one of the best curve pitchers in the West and was regarded as of major league timber."

The McCredies made Portland baseball a family affair. Bill Rodgers, Portland's second baseman from 1911-14 and 1916-17, explained, "[t]he judge was president; Walter was manager; Hugh McCredie, Walter's first cousin, was business manager; and Alice, the judge's wife, sold the tickets and handled the cash money at the gate. The judge and Walter were absolute owners of the club. It was a 50-50 partnership, one of the best and soundest baseball organizations ever operated."

The judge's first orders of business were to name his nephew Walter as the team's manager and right fielder, and to change the team's name from the dreary "Browns" to the imposing "Giants." They renamed the team again in 1906, switching over from "Giants" to "Beavers."

Fixing the broken-down team was made easier with Judge McCredie sticking to running things off the field while giving Walter carte blanche over what happened on the diamond. Hap Hogan, the Vernon Tigers manager who led teams that challenged McCredie in the standings, called this division of labor a secret of their success.

"Mac runs the club as though he owned it," Hogan said. With Judge McCredie vesting in his nephew the absolute power to hire and fire at his discretion, "[t]he players realize that there is no appeal from his decision in any matter affecting the conduct of the club, and as a result he is able to enforce a high degree of discipline."

Only one player with 200 or more at-bats on Portland's 1904 team returned in 1905: McCredie. He found his new players the old fashioned way. "Spaulding's [sic] guide and

Reach's guide have been carefully scanned until the new manager has selected his men," it was reported. "Once he had 'doped' out the players he wanted, he got busy with the mails and telegraph and was soon in communication with them."

Additions in 1905 included future major leaguer Jake Atz at shortstop. Big Larry McLean was behind the plate, all 6-foot-5 and 228 pounds of him (though his girth could not stop the bullet that killed him in a 1921 bar fight). Mike "Swat Kid" Mitchell, another future big leaguer, was in the outfield.

A 1905 season highlight was an unassisted triple play by Portland second baseman Larry Schlafly in a June 21 game against Seattle. Possibly the year's worst point came July 8 when Seattle's Charlie Shields struck out 19 Portland players in a 4-1 win. But the season low might instead have been on November 8, when only one person came to see Portland play the home team Oakland Commuters. Portland finished 94-110, in fifth place out of six teams, in 1905. Pitcher and future New York Yankees scout Bill Essick lost 30 games, more than anyone else in the PCL.

Not even Walter McCredie could float that sinking ship in just one year. He needed two. In 1906, the team captured McCredie's first pennant with a 115-60 record. The season almost stalled following the 1906 San Francisco earthquake and fire, but his uncle personally came to the financial aid of the league to guarantee transportation costs for PCL ball clubs for the full season. The judge even reached into his own bank account to help one failing club. Portland outfielder Mike Mitchell topped the league in batting average, home runs, and total bases. McCredie hit .300 for the second time in his three seasons with Portland. Even the out-of-town press praised Walter. "Mac is a fine fielder, a good batter, knows a ball player when he sees him coming and is a cracking good fellow whose many friends are glad that his ability in handling a team showed itself in the pennant winners of this year," the *Los Angeles Times* gushed.

The team sagged to a 72-114 last place finish in 1907 with a mostly new roster. McCredie was the only Beaver who hit .300, and he also led the league in triples. The most notable moment of Portland's season came when pitcher Bob Groom no-hit the Los Angeles team in a 1-0 victory.

From there, reaching second place with a 95-90 record in 1908 was a marked improvement. Portland players led the league in batting average (Babe Danzig) and wins (Bob Groom). The Beavers made another strong showing in 1909 with a 112-87 record, good enough again for second place. Third baseman Otis Johnson was the league's home run champion, and Alex Carson threw a no hitter.

An informal relationship with the Cleveland Naps that lasted from 1909 through 1915 strengthened the Beavers during this period. Portland received young players from junior clubs with ties to Cleveland, and sent them East ready for prime time. Also starting in 1909, McCredie had the benefit of his own junior team. Judge McCredie backed not only the Class A Beavers, but Portland entries in the Class B Northwestern League (1909, 1911-14). The Class B team was called the "Colts" except in 1911, when it was named the "Pippins." In addition to giving Portlanders local baseball every day at Vaughn Street, the farm club provided the Beavers with a stream of talent that included future Hall of Famer Dave Bancroft.

These affiliations with Cleveland and with Portland's Class B junior teams helped push the Beavers to the next level. McCredie led Portland to pennants in 1910 (114-87), 1911 (113-79), 1913 (109-86), and 1914 (113-84). The 1912 season was a disappointing aberration: the team finished 85-100 and in fourth place, the most notable event being an unassisted triple play turned in by first baseman "Roaring" Bill Rapps in a game against Oakland.

Portland's championship teams during this stretch boasted terrific talent. In 1910, McCredie's pitchers tossed 88 consecutive scoreless innings from October 6-16. Pitcher Vean Gregg led the league with 376 strikeouts and 14 shutouts on his way to a 32-18 record. He also threw a no-hitter during which he struck out eight Los Angeles batters in a row. Behind Gregg in 1910 were other outstanding hurlers who eventually matriculated to the majors: the unfortunately named Gene Krapp (29-16), Bill Steen (23-17), and Tom Seaton (17-17). Pitching was the key ingredient for the 1910 Beavers, but so it was for all of the PCL teams that year: San Francisco's team batting average of .226 led the league, with Portland's .218 average placing it third amongst the six Coast League clubs.

The Beavers' offense exploded in 1911 thanks to both a new cork-centered ball and to outfielder Buddy Ryan, who led the PCL in batting average, hits, and home runs. On the mound, Bill Steen was the league leader in wins and its co-leader in winning percentage, and Ferdinand Henkle tossed a sparkling 1-0 no hitter against Sacramento.

Portland players continued to steamroll the league after they recovered from the 1912 debacle. Individual Beavers led the PCL in hits (Bill Rodgers) and strikeouts (Bill James) in 1913, and took home top honors in 1914 in home

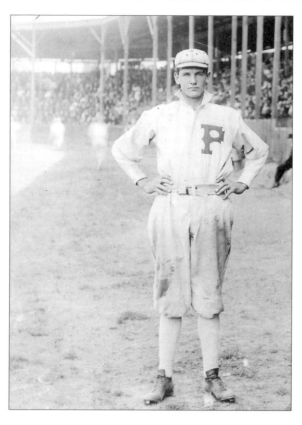

Portland Beavers pitcher Vean Gregg led the Pacific Coast League in 1910 with 376 strikeouts and 14 shutouts on his way to a 32-18 record.

runs (Ty Lober), doubles and triples (Art Kores), and wins (Irv Higginbotham). Pitchers Johnny Lush and Rube Evans pitched no hitters within four weeks of one another in 1914.

As a tribute to their achievements, the Beavers welcomed the 1912 season with a refurbished stadium. Called Vaughn Street Park, it was originally built in 1901. The facelift that the McCredies gave it reportedly made Vaughn Street the finest ballpark in the minor leagues, notably featuring individual theater seats in the grandstand instead of benches. The McCredie business plan was a winner: make money through ticket sales, give each fan a comfortable seat with leg room, and sell concessions as cheaply as possible, even if the team makes no money from it.

On the diamond, Walter McCredie played right field regularly for Portland until the 1910 season. He was a high-strung player, pacing back and forth during close games like a sentry nervously awaiting the delayed sound of a far off crack. He wore a visible 20-foot pathway that paralleled the fence. The *Los Angeles Times* joked in 1909 that some fans "think he must have been in jail once and learned how to walk back and forth in a cell."

Hard work was the McCredie way. When a bush league pitcher cautioned him during 1913 spring training, "don't work me too hard at first," McCredie retorted "no danger, I won't have time even to notice you." The busher went home. Even once he had stopped playing regularly after 1909, McCredie would suit up and work out with his team during spring training for two hours in the morning and two hours in the afternoon.

> Mac is a fine fielder, a good batter, knows a ball player when he sees him coming and is a cracking good fellow whose many friends are glad that his ability in handling a team showed itself in the pennant winners of this year.
>
> *Los Angeles Times*

Future Hall-of-Famers Dave Bancroft (left) and Harry Heilmann were among many top ballplayers whom Walter McCredie groomed.

Like many players of his day, McCredie was superstitious. Fearing bad luck from torn bits of paper, he would drop to his hands and knees to pick up tiny scraps that a player had dropped in the dugout. He hated the sight of blood so much that he avoided going onto the field to check on a bleeding, spiked player. He also had a terrible fear of snakes, something pitcher Irv Higginbotham loved to exploit by sneaking up on him and, with a shriek, throwing a harmless snake at McCredie's feet.

McCredie had a tremendous ability to turn raw recruits into major leaguers. "Unquestionably the greatest developer of talent in the minor leagues," is how the *Los Angeles Times* described him in 1915. "His record in this respect is unparalleled. In the past nine years he has contributed something like thirty ball players to the majors who have made good, an average of slightly better than three a year."

A list of some of them reads like a baseball university's roll call of successful alumni. They include Hall of Famers Dave Bancroft, Harry Heilmann, and Stan Coveleski, and also Roger Peckinpaugh, Carl Mays, Ken Williams, Babe Pinelli, Allen Sothoron, Jack Graney, Vean Gregg, Ivan Olson, and Mike Mitchell. This Beavers fraternity led to some reunion match-ups. In a 1912 game between Cleveland and Washington, ex-Beavers Vean Gregg, Buddy Ryan, Roger Peckinpaugh, and Ivy Olson helped Cleveland defeat ex-Portland pitcher Bob Groom.

With the McCredies' successes came other opportunities. Hall of Famer Joe Tinker, who had led the Portland Webfooters to a 1901 Pacific Northwest League pennant, authorized an offer to buy the Beavers in 1912, but it went nowhere. Judge McCredie turned down a chance in 1914 to obtain a controlling interest in the St. Louis Browns. Walter even rejected an offer to manage the Cleveland Naps in 1915, though that same year the *Los Angeles Times* called him "a major league manager in every sense of the word."

The arc of Walter's career in the game peaked in 1914. He would never have another winning season as a manager. Two events coincided with this downturn. One was the demise of the Class B Portland Colts in 1914, when it became too expensive for Judge McCredie to support both teams. The other was the end of the player arrangement with Cleveland after 1915, when financial difficulties forced out Cleveland owner Charlie Somers, a personal friend of Walter's. Portland finished 78-116 and in last place in 1915.

The Beavers ended the 1916 season second to last in the PCL with a 93-98 mark. A bright spot was Allen Sothoron's league-leading 30 wins, but the rest of Portland's pitching staff struggled that year. Just three weeks into the 1916 season, beneath the blunt headline "Beaver Fans Getting Mad," one writer accurately described the team's hurlers as being "divided between the uncertain and the certainly ineffective."

The losses that followed only hardened McCredie's resolve. During one 1916 match, he watched his 24-year old pitcher, Herb "Moke" Kelly, whom the *Los Angeles*

He always thought about how to give his team an edge. McCredie was so innovative that in 1905 he considered hiring a Japanese jiu-jitsu expert to teach his players how to slide into bases without getting hurt. Having broken a leg six years earlier while sliding, he knew firsthand that an injury could jeopardize a promising career. Portland's trainers assisted Big Mac in readying his men for action. The squad was expected to obey the trainer just as they would the manager. Today's players would recognize some of one Beaver trainer's methods ("[n]ever stay in the game if you feel your arm getting sore") and would welcome others ("[i]f you feel soggy and lazy at times through the long season, drink a little ale or good beer at meals").

McCredie kept clubhouse distractions to a minimum. He barred poker playing in 1914 because the bets got big and so did the losses, and with that came hard feelings. "The team that plays poker is not the ball machine which it should be," he said. (What gaming he allowed at a billiard parlor he owned in Portland has been lost to history.)

He treated all of his players alike. Gruff and blunt, McCredie knew just the right balance between criticism and encouragement. One of his pitchers observed in 1914, "McCredie nearly chews my head off sometimes, but I guess I have it coming when he does. The old man [he was 37 then] knows what he is talking about. On the other hand, he is just as quick to speak a word of praise."

McCredie had little praise for umpires, though, and he was not afraid to let them know it. Accounts of his encounters with them read like a rap sheet: McCredie tossed from a 1909 game, telling Umpire McGreevy that he will "get him" and "you will be sorry for this" (fine: $20); McCredie shoving Umpire Finney in 1911 and unleashing "language that would have scared a pirate" (fine: $10); McCredie shoving Umpire Hildebrand in 1911 and being kicked off the grounds by the police (and suspended).

> **(Walter McCredie's) record in this respect is unparalleled.**
>
> **In the past nine years, he has contributed something like 30 ballplayers to the majors who have made good — an average of slightly better than three a year.**
>
> *Los Angeles Times*

Times described as having "nothing but a roundhouse curve and an ambition to eat supper," let a 3-0 lead over the home team Vernon Tigers evaporate into a 10-3 deficit. With five runs across the plate for Vernon in the eighth inning, two outs, and no end in sight, McCredie stomped out to the pitching rubber to put pitcher Kelly out of his misery, and to give his Portland team a lesson in leadership by example. Just six weeks shy of his fortieth birthday, McCredie pitched the last out of the inning himself, getting the Vernon batter to pop up for the final out of the inning. Even the Vernon crowd applauded.

In 1917, Portland finished a disappointing 98-102 and in fourth place. Outfielder Ken Williams, just around the corner from his outstanding major league career, led the PCL in home runs. World War I travel problems led to a shortened Pacific Coast League season and no PCL baseball in Portland in 1918, though the Portland Buckaroos of the Pacific Coast International League temporarily filled the void. McCredie managed Salt Lake that year. Still, "his heart is with Portland," Judge McCredie said.

Walter and his Beavers returned to Portland the next season, but he never regained his magic touch. The club's record dropped to 78-96 in 1919 (second to last), 81-103 in 1920 (last), and 51-134 in 1921 (last, and 55-1/2 games out of first place). When Portland outfielder Hazen Paton came to after knocking himself out sliding into second base in 1921, he looked up at McCredie and said, "All I can see is stars." McCredie replied, "Not on this ball club."

Through it all, Judge McCredie stuck loyally by his nephew. However, Portland fans grew tired of losing. The McCredies had spoiled them with pennants in earlier years, but the Beavers had not finished over .500 since 1914. On the investment side, it is a safe bet that the McCredies were no longer enjoying the profits of their winning seasons. In 1912, for example, when Portland did not win the pennant, the season's profits were nearly half of what they had been in their 1911 championship year.

The inevitable finally came in July 1921, when Judge McCredie announced, "new blood, not only in the club, but in management would be gratifying to many Portland fans." The McCredies sold the Beavers. Big Mac stepped aside after the season ended. Even so, Portland would not win another Coast League pennant until 1932.

Walter McCredie still had his own road ahead of him. He briefly managed the Seattle Indians in 1922 to a 34-48 record. There, he was reunited with ex-Beaver Vean Gregg, who had come back down to the minors. McCredie then became a scout for the Detroit Tigers. He declined an offer to take the reins of the Coast League's Vernon Tigers in 1925. The Mission Bears lured him back to the PCL for a short time in 1926, and McCredie led them to a 16-19 mark. In spring 1927, he coached the Hollywood Stars before returning to his scouting job with the Tigers. McCredie eventually left his post with the Tigers, retired from baseball in 1931, and moved back to Portland.

In fall 1933, as if the clock were turned back to 1904,

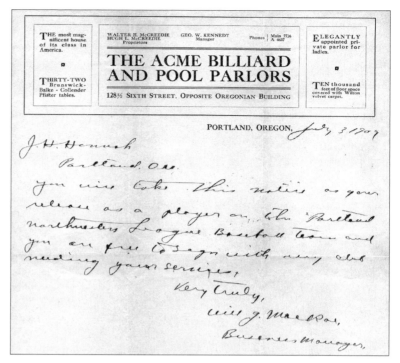

Signing and releasing ballplayers was a frequent task for Walter McCredie — even on his billiard-parlor stationery.

McCredie was offered, and accepted, the job of managing the 1934 Portland squad. "The Portland Beavers have always been my favorite team," he said upon accepting the position. His tenure was to be a short one. Although he was just 57 years old, his health was bad and getting worse. Rheumatism hobbled him and kept him from the ballpark. The team's poor showing had made the once invincible McCredie unpopular with a new generation of Portland fans. By late April 1934, he had to be replaced as Portland's manager.

McCredie would only live for another three months. Seeing his final days approaching, the Portland club arranged for former Beavers Irv Higginbotham, Gus Fisher, Vean Gregg, Carl Mays, and Lyle Bigbee to take the home field with members of the current Beavers team in a benefit game in McCredie's honor against Sacramento. Sadly, the benefit turned into a memorial. Walter McCredie died on July 29, 1934, on the eve of the game that was to be played in his honor. He picked his pallbearers (players from the 1934 Portland team) and honorary pallbearers (players from his earlier Beavers clubs) while on his deathbed.

Baseball was on his mind to the last. "Toward the end his mind wandered and he imagined that he was playing again. " 'Hit it out!' they heard him say once, and 'Slide!' " the Portland *Oregonian* reported. "And at the very last, his final words, just a few minutes before he ceased to breath[e], 'Let the game go on.' "

So it did, with Portland winning 10-7 before only 3,200 fans. As McCredie had requested, all the proceeds went to his widow Etta. The final chapter on the McCredie era closed when Judge McCredie died the following year on May 11, 1935, at age 73. Speaking at a baseball banquet a year before he died, Walter McCredie wrote his own epitaph. He simply stated, "Baseball is my life." ⚾

The Portland Beavers have always been my favorite team.

Walter McCredie

Sources: contemporary newspaper accounts about Walter McCredie and the Portland team

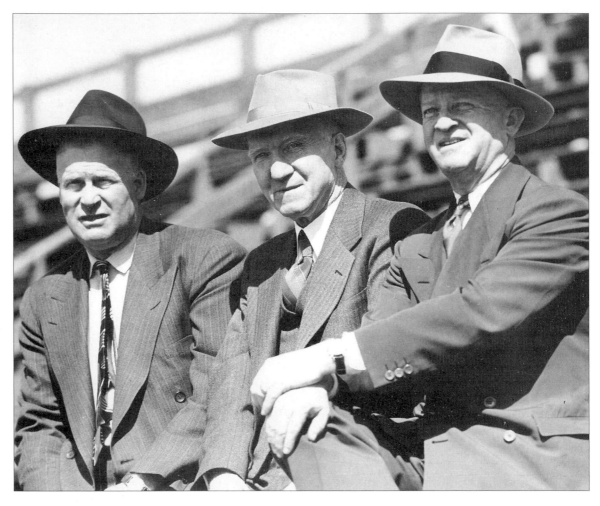

In a circa 1950 photo representing more than a century of West Coast minor-league experience, Bob Brown, the "Mr. Baseball" of Vancouver, B.C., is flanked by (left) Earl Sheely, star player and manager who became Seattle Rainiers' general manager, and Torchy Torrance, Seattle sports booster who spent many years as Rainiers vice-president.

'I was never accused of lack of life'

'Vancouver's Connie Mack' Bob Brown figured B.C. port city 'had a real future,' by jingo

By TOM HAWTHORN

Tom Hawthorn is a magazine and newspaper writer in Victoria, B.C., Canada. His nickname is E5.

Bob Brown was a sickly old man by the time he died at St. Paul's Hospital in Vancouver, British Columbia. He had spent 61 of his 85 years in Organized Baseball as a player, manager, owner, scout, and league president. Unhappy in his retirement, he complained that "this loafing is hard work."

His final public appearance had come a few weeks earlier, when he left a sickbed to catch the Vancouver Mounties play their home opener for the 1962 Pacific Coast League season. He walked slowly, leaning on a cane, and needed an escort to his box seat, No. 42, right behind home plate at Capilano Stadium. He had built the park — his second — only 11 years earlier.

His weakened state offered no hint of the scrappy fireplug he had once been. Brown had a big potato-nose in the middle of a face that seemed untouched by a smile or sense of whimsy. Some called him a sanctimonious old Puritan, for his courteous Old World manners seemed out of place in the rough-and-tumble world of baseball. He wore high-collared shirts, a vest, and a pocket watch with fob. The writers called him Ruby Robert in the early days, and the Old Redhead as time passed. Until he got sick, he seemed as eternal as the game itself.

His harshest oath was said to be a hearty, "By jingo!" Yet, as a player, he eagerly engaged in diamond dust-ups, and as a manager, he was known to drop a bat on an umpire's toes. As an owner, he was as unyielding a bargainer as the most steadfast umpire.

The *Vancouver Sun* greeted his death with the headline: "City loses Mr. Baseball. The *Province* replied: "Local baseball will not forget Bob Brown."

As early as 1917, *The Sporting News* was hailing Brown in a headline as "Vancouver's Connie Mack." He kept baseball alive in the city for decades, through the

Depression and both world wars. He brought the great Babe Ruth to town, introduced night ball to Canada, carved a ballpark out of forest with his bare hands (and the occasional stick of dynamite), and later helped construct a gem of a diamond in which teenaged professionals still play ball and dream of the major leagues.

But today, he is forgotten, and no street bears his name. His ballpark still stands, but carries the name of a man he hired to sell peanuts. The anniversaries of his death pass without notice. Only die-hard fans have ever even heard of him. "People have forgotten lots of things from that era," said Clancy Loranger, a *Province* sportswriter who covered baseball for decades. "They've forgotten lots of old boxers and wrestlers and soccer players. They just fade away, I guess."

Robert Paul Brown was born in Scranton, Pennsylvania, on July 5, 1876, missing by a day the country's wild centennial celebrations. It was also the year in which the National League began play. He was the son of Anthony Brown, a foundry worker and coal miner who had immigrated to the United States from Ireland. The growing Brown family, which would eventually total four boys and three girls, later settled on farmland near Blencoe, Iowa. At a young age, Robert was in the saddle to tend cattle, but at 17, his father dispatched him to St. Joseph's College at Dubuque, where he spent two years before entering Notre Dame University in South Bend, Indiana, in 1895. There, he won letters in baseball and football.

Brown earned a reputation as a pugnacious and relentless halfback despite his smallish 150-pound frame. His playing coach, H.G. Hadden, stood 6-foot-5 and weighed 240 pounds. "In those days we had three downs to make 5 yards, and if we'd find ourselves just a couple of feet short, the other backs used to pick me up and toss me right over the line," Brown reminisced many years later. He scored a touchdown in a 32-0 whipping of the College of Physicians and Surgeons and scored two majors in an 18-0 defeat of the Chicago Cycling Club.

Fifty players turned out to attend the start of baseball training camp on February 1, 1895. The varsity team was beginning its third season. By mid-March, half had been cut, but Brown survived to win a spot in right field.

In 1898, a bout of dizziness, including fainting spells, led Brown to seek recovery in the fresh air of Miles City, Montana. A decision to forego tobacco seemed to repair his health. As a result, he never again smoked or chewed a wad.

After recuperating, Brown volunteered as a cavalryman to fight in the Spanish-American War. Upon enlisting, he gave his occupation as "cowpuncher." Though he would later recall his eagerness to fight in Cuba, he spent most of the war as a private at a dusty camp in Georgia. The *Vancouver Sun*'s archives include a biographical form Brown filled in by hand in the spring of 1955. Under the entry for honors under military service, Brown wrote: "was returned on furlough to enlisted base Miles City Montana account typhoid malaria."

BROWN, VANCOUVER, N. W. L.

Despite his small stature, Bob Brown, shown in this 1911 Obak cigarette card, cast a big shadow in Pacific Northwest minor-league circles. He played at least a decade and managed four teams in three leagues before becoming part-owner and manager of Vancouver's Northwestern League franchise in 1910. He remained active into his 80s, playing a key role in bringing the Pacific Coast League to the British Columbia city in 1956.

He survived malaria, returning to Indiana to finish his schooling at Notre Dame. Football teammate Albert J. "Wild Bill" Galen, who had been born on a Montana ranch and would be a future state attorney general and Supreme Court justice, found Brown a $125-a-month job with baseball's Helena Senators, whose Montana State League rivals included the Anaconda Serpents, Butte Smoke Eaters, and Great Falls Indians. The Senators only had 12 players: one for each fielding position and four pitchers. One of his teammates was Joe Tinker, an infielder of great promise. Brown was an outfielder and backup catcher, breaking every finger on both hands in the days when pitchers could legally throw spitballs and mudballs and shineballs (daubed with polish from baseball shoes). The breaks were set with splints jury-rigged from a cigar box.

Baseball offered men an escape from lives of toil down on the farm, or down in the mine, or on the factory floor. These rough-hewn men did not easily give up a day job in the sunshine. "Salaries? Well, I won't say we just played for the principle of the thing, but none of us fussed much about the money, there not being much to fuss with anyway," Brown said in 1956. "A couple of hundred dollars per month was a pretty good average in those days, and

> **I won't say we just played for the principle of the thing, but none of us fussed much about the money, there not being much to fuss with anyway.**
>
> **Bob Brown**

Bob Brown (bottom row, far right) managed the Aberdeen, Washington, team in the Southwest Washington League in 1904-05 at the same time that he was a partner in an Aberdeen shoe store.

Bob Brown not only declined this 1901 opportunity to manage Portland, but he left the Pacific Northwest League team to make his managerial debut with Pendleton of the newly formed Inland Empire League.

Had the reputation of being pretty rough out on the field.

Bob Brown

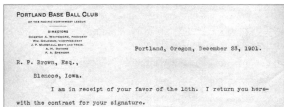

$1.50 per day looked pretty good for eating money on the road."

Nor was the diamond a place for milquetoasts. Fights were not unknown, on or off the field. "I had a pretty reckless mouth," Brown admitted, "and a hot temper."

The Helena club folded with the rest of the league after the season. When ex-league president W.M. Lucas started up a Pacific Northwest League on the coast, Brown and Tinker joined a Portland club known as the Webfooters. "Joe Tinker hit .322 that year, which was real good hitting then," Brown said. "I managed .245, but I was never a hitter. Couldn't hit much, but I guess I was never accused of lack of life. Had the reputation of being pretty rough out on the field."

Brown knew that if he were to stay in baseball, he'd be better off trying to do so as a manager. He lost a competition to become the playing manager at Portland to teammate Sam Vigneaux, so instead Brown helped form a team in Pendleton, Oregon, in an unaffiliated league. (His friend Tinker signed after the 1901 season with the Chicago Cubs.) Brown quit the Class D Pendleton team at midseason to play for a new club at Helena, but the club would not complete its second full season.

In 1904, he moved to Aberdeen, Washington, where he became a partner in the Brown-Elmore Shoe Company. His name would be associated with the store for more than a half-century, long after he sold his interest. In 1904, he played and managed the Aberdeen Pippins of the Southwest Washington League, piloted the team in 1905, then became manager of the local Grays Harbor Lumbermen in the Northwestern League in 1906.

As a playing-manager, Brown led the Aberdeen Black Cats to a pennant in 1907, a season during which he had his share of playing time. "Manager 'Red' Brown, who is something of an all-round ball player, came in from the outfield to cover shortstop and when both his catchers were injured went behind the bat regularly and the team continued to win games," *The Sporting News* reported.

In the fall of 1908, the same newspaper covered Brown's negotiations for an interest in the Spokane team. The headline read: "Aspires to be magnate." He signed a two-year contract to manage the Indians, and was sold, for one dollar, a quarter interest in the club.

He realized the Vancouver franchise was in trouble when the league had to cover the cost of the club's return home from a series in Spokane. Brown set up a secret off-season meeting with two of the club's directors, renting a lavish suite at the old Hotel Vancouver, stocking it with fine whiskey and a box of first-class cigars. He walked away with an option to buy after handing over a check for just $500.

Spokane majority partner Joseph Cohn, who had rebuffed all Brown's requests for a sale, wound up paying his manager $3,000 for the stock he had acquired for a dollar. Brown had made another $3,000 in salary, as well as a $2,500 dividend.

The British Columbia port city, which had a population of 100,000, a four-fold increase over the past decade, held great promise as a sports Mecca. The Patrick brothers — Lester and Frank — were soon to open a 10,000-seat hockey rink. "I liked this town first time I saw it," Brown wrote in 1957. "Figured it had a real future, industrially, and in baseball, too."

When the 1910 season opened, Bob Brown was owner, manager and starting shortstop of the Vancouver Beavers. The club finished second, and the report on the Northwestern League for Spalding's *Official Base Ball Guide* saw in Brown a budding tycoon. "Vancouver probably cleaned up the biggest roll on the season through the sales of pitcher Harry Gardner to Pittsburg, third baseman (Dick) Breen to Cincinnati, (Charles) Swain to Washington and the drafting of another outfielder, (Bill) Brinker, by the Chicago White Sox," Roscoe Fawcett reported. "Vancouver's profits were close to $3,500, Spokane's $1,500, Seattle's $1,000 and Tacoma's minus several hundred."

After winning the league pennant in 1911 with Brown no longer managing, and a season named the Vancouver "Champions," Brown turned down a $35,000 offer for the

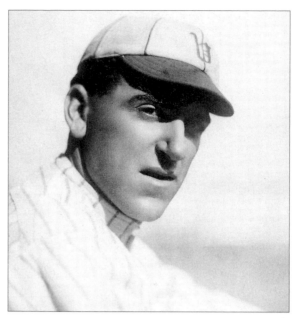

Charlie Schmutz, one of several future pro ballplayers on Seattle's brilliant 1907 Seattle (later Broadway) High School nine, won 16 games for Bob Brown's Vancouver team that took the Northwestern League title in 1913. Schmutz spent parts of the next two seasons pitching for Brooklyn.

Though Vancouver lacked pro ball in 1923-36, Bob Brown managed Athletic Park as the city's top semipro facility, reflected by this 1934 scorebook.

One traveling troupe that played in a downpour in 1934 included Babe Ruth, Lou Gehrig and six other future Hall-of-Famers. Gehrig played first base in galoshes while holding an umbrella in his throwing hand.

club from a San Francisco syndicate. He had greater ambitions.

The Beavers played out of Recreation Park, a small stadium at Homer and Smythe on the downtown peninsula owned by the Canadian Pacific Railway and leased by city businessmen to whom he paid rent. When he found out the park was to be closed for more profitable use as warehousing, Brown bought the bleachers for $500. He covered the cost by forcing the local lacrosse team to share the proceeds of bleacher-ticket sales from their big series against the Eastern champions. Then, he began felling trees and blasting stumps in the forest at a leased site on the south shore of False Creek.

Brown's Athletic Park, which opened in 1913 at the corner of Fifth and Hemlock, would be the home of Vancouver baseball for the next 38 years. Several major leaguers began their career in the wooden bandbox, among them spitballer Charlie Schmutz (whose name sounded like what he did to the ball) and Dutch Ruether, who later starred for the Cincinnati Reds in the infamous 1919 World Series. Even 47-year-old righthander "Iron Man" Joe McGinnity took to the mound at the park on his way to closing out a Hall of Fame career.

Athletic Park helped put Vancouver on baseball's map. Barnstorming teams of major league All-Stars would play games in the city, stopping on their way to exhibition series in Japan. One traveling troupe that played in a downpour in 1934 included Babe Ruth, Lou Gehrig, and six other future Hall of Famers. Gehrig played first base in galoshes while holding an umbrella in his throwing hand.

The park lured such itinerant entertainers as the Bloomer Girls, all-black all-stars, and the House of David, a team sponsored by a religious sect whose members wore unshorn hair. Players took the field with beards down to their

bellies. On July 3, 1931, a game billed as the first to be played at night in Canada and west of the Mississippi was played at the park. The light fixtures cost $8,000.

The professional minor leagues faltered after the Great War, not to be revived until the late 1930s. Brown launched the semipro Senior City League at his park with teams sponsored by a local clothier, a distiller, and a transport company. Arrows, Home Gas, Arnold & Quigley and others had their devoted fans, as did the Asahi, a team of Japanese-Canadians that won respect for their clever style of baseball.

Norm "Bananas" Trasolini, Billy Adshead, Johnny Nestman, and Coleman "Coley" Hall became Vancouver household names, as did pitcher Ernie Kershaw, a teacher known as "The Professor," "The Master Mathematician," and "The Slinging Schoolmaster." Kershaw later pitched for the Vancouver Capilanos, who made their home at the park, renamed Capilano Stadium, from 1939 until 1951, at which point they moved to a new stadium of the same name in the lee of Little Mountain.

The old ballpark was knocked down to make way for an on-ramp for the Granville Street Bridge, a rich history literally overshadowed by concrete and blacktop. Brown had to twice rebuild his old wooden stadium. "His ball parks kept burning down on him," Loranger said. That he kept baseball alive through the Spanish Flu pandemic of 1919 and the Depression and the sacrifices of two wars was proof both of his tenacity and his penny-pinching. "He could squeeze a nickel as well as anybody," recalled sports reporter Jim Kearney, "and he had to."

To put it simply, Bob Brown was cheap. He sort of obeyed a league dictate that the umpire be given a dozen balls at the start of each game. Brown's daily supply included six fresh balls — and six scuffed balls. He

Bob Brown (center row, far right) poses proudly with his 1942 Vancouver Capilanos. Manager Don Osborn (center row, fourth from left) pitched the team to the 1942 Western International League title, with 22 wins and a 1.63 ERA. Osborn later managed Spokane to a Northwest League title and spent many seasons as pitching coach for the Pittsburgh Pirates.

Season's Greetings

Capilano Stadium

Join us Opening Day, May First at the New Home of your Capilanos

SICKS' CAPILANO BASEBALL CLUB
VANCOUVER, B.C.

N. C. K. (Chuck) WILLS
PRESIDENT

R. P. (Bob) BROWN
VICE-PRES. GEN. MGR.

Bob Brown was still on the job as general manager when Vancouver used its Christmas card and calendar to announce that it would begin play in new Capilano Stadium during the 1951 season.

encouraged street urchins to retrieve fouls that flew out of the park. The reward for their shagging? Free admission for what remained of the game.

Still, Brown could be a soft touch. In 1928, he bought a train ticket to Eastern Canada for a frail-looking schoolboy who wished to compete at the Olympic trials. It proved money well spent when Percy Williams later returned from Amsterdam with two Olympic gold medals.

Brown was 77 when he became president of the Western International League in 1953. His single year as boss is notable for his hiring of an up-and-coming umpire by the name of Emmett Ashford, who went on to become the first African American to officiate in the major leagues in 1966.

Brown went into retirement at the end of the season, having spent more than a half-century in baseball. He returned to action to lobby for Vancouver as a new home for the Oakland Oaks. A Pacific Coast League franchise had long been his dream. During World War II, he had gone to Sacramento with satchels of cash to try and purchase the team. Instead, local interests managed to raise enough money to keep the club in California. Brown subsequently always referred to his failure as the great disappointment of his life.

The Oakland Oaks moved to Vancouver and became the Mounties for the 1956 season. Brown was made public relations director for the inaugural season. He was also put in charge of a youth program. He insisted plenty of youngsters in British Columbia could make careers in professional baseball, even though the province had only ever graduated a handful of talents in the past. It would take many years before his prediction came true, and

homegrown talents like Larry Walker, Jason Bay, and Rich Harden put the province on baseball's map.

Brown died on June 21, 1962, once again cared for by his wife, the former Jean Campion, a nurse whom he had met in a hospital. He passed five days short of their 29th wedding anniversary. They had no children. He was buried at Ocean View Cemetery in Burnaby.

The Mounties folded after the 1962 season, and pro baseball disappeared from Vancouver for two years, as though in mourning for the man they called Mr. Baseball.

Brown's was the first name included in a Vancouver Baseball Hall of Fame, which was no more than a plaque inside the stadium. He has also been posthumously inducted in the British Columbia Sports Hall of Fame and the Canadian Baseball Hall of Fame in St. Marys, Ontario.

Nat Bailey Stadium, as the second Capilano Stadium was dubbed in 1977, deservedly carries the name of the man who owned the Mounties for several years. What is often forgotten is that Nat Bailey, who launched the White Spot restaurant chain, got his start as a restaurateur and baseball entrepreneur by flogging peanuts and hot dogs at Bob Brown's old park. They called him Caruso Nat for his sing-along vendor's sales pitch: "A loaf of bread, a pound of meat, and all the mustard you can eat!"

The street to the park is Clancy Loranger Way, a worthy tribute to the indefatigable baseball writer who chronicled the sport for decades. Loranger thinks a proper tribute to Brown would be a plaque in center field, just like at Yankee Stadium. That's a swell idea, by jingo. ⚾

Sources

The Sporting News

Spalding's *Official Base Ball Guide,* 1911

Vancouver Sun

Vancouver Daily Province

Chicago Daily Tribune

Filichia, Peter. *Professional Baseball Franchises: From the Abbeville Athletics to the Zanesville Indians.* New York: Facts on File, Inc., 1993

The 1913 Spokane Indians had many minor league veterans, but pitchers Stan Coveleski (ninth from left) and Shufflin' Phil Douglas (not pictured) proved to be the only good big league players. Other notables: longtime Northwestern League third baseman-catcher Dutch Altman (fifth from left), Manager Harry Ostdiek (11th from left) and a future member of the infamous Black Sox of 1919, "Swede" Risberg (far right).

Spitballing to the Hall of Fame

Colorful contemporaries paved Stan Coveleski's way to majors

"The brand of stuff which Coveleskie was putting on the ball today beats anything seen here since [Big] Bill James used to fan 'em out two years ago. The Portland twirler simply had the locals eating out of his hand, and he looked like he could keep on doing it all day."

— **Seattle sportswriter Royal Brougham,** quoted in *The Oregonian*, **Sept. 21, 1915**

By STEVE STEINBERG

Steve Steinberg spends most of his time in the early 20th century, where he focuses on spitball pitchers, St. Louis teams, and the New York Yankees. This is his first foray into Northwest baseball. He lives in Seattle with his wife and three children.

He came from the mining town of Shamokin, Pennsylvania, the youngest of five brothers who worked in the mines and played baseball. On his way to a Hall-of-Fame career, he spent three formative years in the Pacific Northwest: 1913-14 with the Spokane Indians of the Northwestern League (NWL) and 1915 with the Portland

Beavers of the Pacific Coast League (PCL). Little did Stan Coveleski know that his journey so far from the eastern epicenter of baseball would put him very much in the middle of larger baseball trends, conflicts, and competition. Following his western trail helped make him an emerging star in the heart of baseball's Deadball Era.

It was a hard life for the youngster at the start of the 20th century. He was born Stanislaus Kowalewski in 1889, but he went by Coveleskie as a pro, and dropped the "e" at the end of his name after his baseball career had ended. "There was nothing strange in those days about a twelve-year old Polish kid in the mines for 72 hours a week at a nickel an hour," he told baseball historian Larry Ritter. "What was strange was that I ever got out of there."

In four seasons in the Tri-State League, playing with Lancaster and Atlantic City from 1909 to 1912, Coveleski won 73 games and caught the eye of one of Connie Mack's scouts. Coveleski made his major league debut in September 1912 for the Athletics and hurled a shutout in his first start. With a surplus of talented pitchers, Mack chose not to offer Coveleski a contract for 1913. Mack felt he was set with young hurlers Joe Bush and Byron "Duke" Houck, who would combine to win 29 games between them for the 1913 Athletics.

In this era, major league teams often had informal relationships with the owners of minor league clubs. Mack had such an understanding with Joe Cohn, president and part owner of the Spokane Indians. Cohn had sent pitcher Houck to Mack a year earlier, and the pitcher had won eight

Coveleski's contemporaries: Ill-fated Charlie Swain was the Northwestern League's premier power-hitter, starring for five teams during the Deadball Era from 1905-1914. The stocky slugger, a fine defensive outfielder, reached his peak by hitting 34 home runs in 1913. After another bang-up season in 1914, he lost his right leg following a traffic accident and died less than four years later in the worldwide flu epidemic.

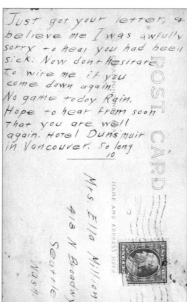

games for the 1912 A's. Since Houck had performed better than the player Spokane got in return, Tiny Leonard, Mack "was persuaded to let Cohn have the youngster for a season," wrote the *Spokane Chronicle* on March 20, 1913.

The Northwestern League was a "fast" Class B league of six teams: Spokane, Seattle, Tacoma, Portland, Vancouver, B. C., and Victoria, B. C. However, the National Association allowed the league to have a higher payroll than other Class B leagues. In its eight years as a circuit, the NWL had a reputation for developing many prospects. Fielder Jones, the former manager and outfielder of the 1906 world champion Chicago White Sox, had been the league's president since 1912. Tacoma's new owner and manager, "Iron Man" Joe McGinnity, had left the majors with 246 wins, and now pitched for his own ball club at the age of 42 in 1913, tossing 436 innings in 68 games, and winning 22 games while giving up only 66 walks.

Stan Coveleski's Northwest League debut was

impressive: a 2-0 shutout of Portland. "POLISH PITCHER IS GAME," read the next day's *Chronicle* headline, and the article talked about the pitcher who was "cool as cracked ice." Next, after 16 consecutive shutout innings, he turned a tie game over to 18-year-old pitcher "Swede" Risberg, who had appeared in only one pro game. This was the same Risberg who would become the starting shortstop of the 1917 world champion Chicago White Sox and one of the eight 1919 Black Sox banned from baseball. Risberg came to Spokane as a pitcher, but the *Chronicle* noted that he "has been anxious to get away from pitching all season." In early June, Joe Cohn sent Risberg to Ogden of the Class D Union Association for seasoning.

Coveleski soon gained a reputation as "steady and dependable" and, perhaps more important, "invincible in pinches." He finished May with two shutouts, over McGinnity and Vancouver's Charlie Schmutz (the future Brooklyn Dodger). In the summer of 1907, Schmutz and other members of his Seattle High School team — including future New York Yankee Charlie Mullen and Coveleski's Spokane teammate Ten Million — barnstormed across the country. Million was the son of Seattle judge Charles Million.

The Spokane club was not doing nearly so well. The 1913 Indians quickly sunk to last place and had an early July record of 25-50. With attendance dwindling to a few hundred fans a game, the Spokane and Inland Empire Railway Company bought out Joe Cohn. The railroad owned the streetcar line to Recreation Park, as well as the land and the ballpark, and had stepped in to protect its investments. New team president F.C. Farr was the superintendent of the streetcar line, known as the Spokane Traction Company. Just under a year later, Farr would put together a syndicate to buy the Indians from the railway for $15,000.

The new owners moved decisively that summer of 1913. First, they signed Mike Lynch to be the club's player-

Coveleski's contemporaries: Ten Million, the son of a Seattle judge, bore one of baseball's most intriguing names. A member of the famed 1907 Seattle (later Broadway) High School team, Million played at Moose Jaw, Tacoma, Spokane and Victoria before becoming a top Puget Sound sports official. He is shown in a pose on a penny postcard that he mailed to his mother. Note his numerical signature.

Coveleski's contemporaries: George Kelly began his professional career with Spokane in 1914, but the Indians sent him to Victoria within a few weeks as part of a league arrangement to shore up that faltering franchise. Sold to the New York Giants late the next season, Kelly went on to join several Giants teammates in the Hall of Fame.

George L. Kelly

On Sept. 9, 1913, Spokane came to Seattle to open the new Dugdale Park in the Rainier Valley.

alcohol. He had worn out his welcome in the Bay Area, just as he later would in the majors. When Brooklyn signed him in 1915, manager Wilbert Robinson declared, "If I can get this fellow sober, I've got the best pitcher in the league." As it turned out, "Uncle Robbie" could not, and Douglas shuffled to the Cubs before the season's end. Douglas, like pitcher Risberg, who had left Spokane earlier in the season, would one day be banished from organized baseball.

In this summer of 1913, however, Douglas's star was on the rise. He won ten games in a little over two months, and Coveleski had an opportunity to see this skilled spitballer up close. Another rising star was pitching for the league's Portland Colts, a pitcher named Carl Mays. Before the season ended, Douglas and Mays faced off twice, each winning a game by one run. Mays was a terror at the plate — he hit .364 this year (in 118 at bats) and would hit .268 in his major league career. Eight years later, in the 1921 World Series, Douglas of the Giants and Mays of the Yankees would face off in three classic games, with Douglas winning two of them and the Giants winning the Series.

On September 9, Spokane came to Seattle to open brand-new Dugdale Park in the Rainier Valley. In front of almost 10,000 fans, Seattle's ace Wheezer Dell beat Phil Douglas, 1-0, in ten innings. Though Dell won only 19 games in the majors, he would accumulate 231 minor league victories. After winning 41 games for Seattle in 1913-1914, he was a Dodger in 1915 and 1916, pitching briefly in the 1916 World Series. Dell returned to the minors and won 103 games for Vernon in the Coast League in just four seasons, 1919 to 1922.

Coveleski's final start of 1913 was "the greatest game on the home grounds this season," in the words of the *Chronicle*, a 1-0 win over Portland in 11 innings. Coveleski finished the year 17-20 with a 2.82 earned run average for a team that ended 70-97. A last-place finish was a disappointment, but the team had stabilized by winning about half its games after Mike Lynch took over, and could also take pride in providing local fans with the sterling performances of Coveleski and Douglas.

A couple of aging sluggers garnered the biggest league headlines in 1913. Victoria's Harry Jack Meek, in the minors since 1896, led the league with a .358 batting average, following up on his NWL-best .344 in 1912. Weighing 300 pounds and sporting a career average well over .300, and a winner of four batting titles, Meek was "perhaps the slowest man on his feet who ever tried to play major league ball," wrote *Sporting Life* (July 17, 1915).

There was also Meek's teammate, Charlie Swain, who'd played for Spokane back in 1905-07. Taking advantage of Victoria's short fences, Swain broke the league home run record with 34; the previous mark was 27, set by Seattle's Art Bues in 1911. (By way of comparison, the PCL record at the time was 30, set by San Francisco's Ping Bodie in 1910.) Swain also finished second in batting with a .329 average. A year later, after a successful 1914 season with Seattle, and on the verge of a big league call-up, tragedy

manager. Lynch had already played in almost 2,000 games, and was the player-manager of two NWL pennant winners, the 1906 Tacoma Tigers and the 1909 Seattle Turks. In 1906 Lynch had led the league in many offensive categories, including batting average (.355) and home runs (7), yet he had also released a young pitcher named Walter Johnson, suggesting that the youngster try playing the outfield instead.

In mid-July "Shuffling" Phil Douglas, a spitball pitcher, joined Spokane from San Francisco of the Coast League, with whom the Indians had a close working relationship. Douglas was a big man (6-foot-3,190 pounds), with enormous natural pitching talent and a prodigious thirst for struck. Swain fell off a truck, which rolled over his leg and crushed it, requiring amputation. Numerous benefit games were held on his behalf in early 1915. *Sporting Life* (May 15, 1915) reported that 7,000 fans turned out for his game in Tacoma in early May.

Judge W.W. McCredie and his nephew, Walter McCredie, owned the Portland Colts of the Northwestern League, as well as the Portland Beavers of the Coast League. Walter also managed the Beavers. While the Colts never drew big crowds (turnout was usually in the hundreds and not the thousands), the McCredies used their NWL club as a farm team for their Class A Beavers. They often sold players to themselves, either to avoid the players being drafted by other teams or to get the higher draft price a Class A club commanded. Dave Bancroft moved from the Beavers to the Colts and back to the Beavers in this way between 1912 and 1914.

As the 1914 season came around, Stan Coveleski was back with Spokane. The Indians had a couple of future big leaguers in their infield: 21-year-old Walter Holke and 18-year-old George Lange Kelly. Kelly was the nephew of Bill Lange, who'd hit .330 in seven seasons with the Cubs in the 1890s. Holke and Kelly would go on to long major league careers, with more than 3,000 hits between them. *The Sporting News* recognized Holke's talent on July 16, calling him "the best first baseman that ever pulled on a glove in the Northwestern."

Kelly, the first-year professional, turned heads as early as spring training. "The wonderful showing of the youthful Kelly," wrote the *Chronicle* on March 20, "is too good to pass over." Yet in early May, before ever playing a regular-season game for Spokane, Kelly was sent to the struggling Victoria club, as part of the league's effort to help the new owner of the last-place team.

Around the same time, Spokane acquired Emil Frisk, "the Wagner of the Minors." A career .300 hitter in the minors, Frisk had starred with Seattle of the Coast League in 1904 with 272 hits in 808 at bats. With the temperate climate out west, the PCL season usually ran more than 200 games, from late March until late October. The Northwestern League, on the other hand, ran a more traditional mid-April until late September schedule.

Another new Spokane player was pitcher Dave Gregg, the brother of Cleveland Indian star Vean Gregg. Dave won three games in April, in which he gave up just eight hits in 27 innings. Unfortunately, he also walked 21 men in those games. "His wildness was fierce," wrote the *Chronicle* on April 20 of his first start. He soon began giving up more hits and losing games. By late spring, Dave Gregg was gone from Spokane, and his professional baseball career was over.

The [Spokane] *Spokesman-Review* reported in a April 21, 1914 story: "Coveleskie had his spitter working just right, and it was impossible for the Colts to hit the ball squarely." The *Chronicle* also noticed Coveleski's spitter that day, writing that it "broke nicely through the game." Coveleski was destined to become one of baseball's great spitball

FRISK, SPOKANE, N. W. L.

Coveleski's contemporaries: Emil Frisk was the winning pitcher when Detroit defeated Milwaukee 14-13 in the first official American League game on April 25, 1901, but he turned to the outfield the next year and played the last eight years of his career in the Northwestern League. Frisk compiled 2,284 minor-league hits and a .302 average.

pitchers in his long major league career. Yet just when and where he picked up and mastered the pitch is not clear.

In interviews late in his life, with both Larry Ritter and Eugene Murdock, Coveleski claimed that he took up the spitter "on the coast" and, more specifically, when he joined the Portland Beavers in 1915. It was then, he told Murdock, "I had to get more stuff. I heard the fellows talking about the spitball, but I didn't even know what it was." He explained that pitchers Joe McGinnity and Harry Krause showed him how to throw it. Similarly, he told Ritter, "That year in Portland — 1915 — was the turning point." After watching a Portland pitcher throw spitballs, "I started working on the spitter, and before long I had that thing down pat. Had never thrown it before in my life."

Yet the evidence is not quite so clear-cut. It is simply not accurate that Coveleski turned around his career in Portland; it was very good in Spokane in 1914. Consider the numbers: 1914: 314 innings, 269 hits, 109 runs, 20-15 record, 2.41 ERA. 1915: 293 innings, 279 hits, 123 runs, 17-17 record, 2.67 ERA.

Then there is the fact that Joe McGinnity pitched in the Coast League only briefly, for Venice at the end of the 1914 season. When Coveleski was in Portland in 1915, the Iron Man was back with his NWL Tacoma team.

> **I saw a few pitchers throwing the spitball during my years in Lancaster and started working on that pitch.**
>
> **I could make it do practically anything I wanted it to.**
>
> **Stan Coveleski**

Stan Coveleski, flanked by outfielders Watt Powell (left) and Jimmy Lewis, showed flashes of his future Hall-of-Fame skills while winning 20 games for Spokane in 1914. This photo is from Athletic Park in Tacoma.

Coveleski's interviews were done decades after he retired from baseball, and recollections grow fuzzy over time. In a 1969 interview quoted in William Kashatus' *Diamonds in the Coalfields*, Coveleski said, "I saw a few pitchers throwing the spitball during my years in Lancaster and started working on that pitch. I could make it do practically anything I wanted it to."

While it is true that some of Coveleski's 1915 Portland teammates threw the spitter (Harry Krause and Johnny Lush were two), one of the masters of the pitch — Phil Douglas — was his teammate in the second half of the 1913 season. The first Northwest newspaper accounts of Coveleski's spitter appeared in 1914, starting with those April quotes (see above). References to his spitball appeared with increasing frequency in Portland, in 1915.

Most likely, Coveleski was aware of the pitch and even dabbled in it as early as his Tri-State League days. In the next few years, he perfected it, probably with some advice from the several spitballers he came into contact with. We can accept his statement, "At Portland, the spitter became one of my best pitches," and after he reached the majors in 1916, he was still refining it.

New pitch or no, Coveleski had some tough early-season 1914 losses. In early May, he lost to Tacoma in a game in which former teammate Ten Million shone in the field: ten putouts, including five catches "that were labeled two-base hits when they left the bat" (*Spokesman-Review*, May 10). Coveleski closed out the month with two extra-inning 2-1 losses.

The second of these defeats was a 12-inning loss to Victoria and a kid named Ruether, who gained his first professional win. Reuther went on to hit .340 in 1914 (32

At Portland, the spitter became one of my best pitches.

Stan Coveleski

for 94) and would be one of the best-hitting pitchers during his major league career, with a .258 average. More than a decade later, Dutch Ruether and Stan Coveleski were teammates on the 1925 pennant-winning Washington Senators. After winning 137 games in the majors, Ruether returned to the West Coast in 1928 — pitching for the San Francisco Seals, he led the Coast League with 29 wins.

June 1914 was a terrific month for Coveleski: six wins, in which he gave up only six earned runs, "pitching big league ball." In a 3-1 win over Tiny Leonard and Portland, he allowed his first run in 29 innings. Coveleski won his eighth straight game in early July, as Spokane completed a seven-game sweep of Portland. When Coveleski's six innings of relief helped edge Wheezer Dell and Seattle on July 13, the Spokane Indians took over first place.

Win Noyes had returned to Spokane after spending 1913 with the Boston Braves. His 25-9 record in 1912 had kept Spokane in the pennant race, and in midsummer 1914 he threw three shutouts and a 14-inning 1-1 tie (the game was called when the teams had trains to catch). On July 19, in the longest game ever played in Seattle, Noyes went 20 innings in a 6-1 Spokane win over the Giants.

On July 22, the Portland Colts — who had been drawing so poorly that they had played the past two months on the road — were formally transferred to Ballard, a suburb of Seattle. They played their home games at Seattle's Dugdale Park, which now had "year-round ball." The move tightened the league's geographic spread and reduced transportation costs. League president Fielder Jones, who lived in Portland to tend to family lumber interests, announced his resignation because, he said, the president should reside in a NWL city. A month later, he left Portland when he received a lucrative offer to manage the Federal League's St. Louis Terriers.

As Jones departed, his conflict with Seattle owner Dugdale boiled to the surface. Dugdale said he opposed Jones over the poor quality of the league's umpires. He was also unhappy that he didn't gain control of the Ballard franchise. Jones responded to the *Chronicle* on August 22, "His [Dugdale's] object was to make it a one-man league, with Dugdale posing as the man in control." Before Jones took over as president, he said, Dugdale insisted on 115 to 130 home games each year. Dugdale defended such scheduling by explaining that the big city of Seattle drew the biggest crowds, and revenue was shared with visiting teams. In an article entitled, "TOO MUCH DUGDALE," the August 27 edition of *The Sporting News* suggested that the Seattle manager helped Jones make his decision to leave. Jones later announced that he would not recruit players for the Federal League from the NWL... except for Seattle players.

In late July and early August, both Coveleski and the Indians faltered. After Seattle beat Spokane for the seventh straight time on August 23, the Indians were settling into third place with a 73-57 record. The *Chronicle* wrote that the pitching staff was demoralized and that even Coveleski couldn't be depended on. But, noted the paper, he's "too

SCANLON. DRISCOLL. WILHOIT. KELLY. SMITH. McKENRY. HOFFMAN. CUNNINHAM. MORAN. CALVO. LAMB. DELMAS. NYE. STEELE. NARVESON.

Coveleski's contemporaries: Up-and-coming minor-league great Joe Wilhoit and future Hall of Fame member George Kelly were key players for Victoria's Northwestern League team in 1914. The young Cuban outfielder Jacinto (Jack) Calvo also contributed to a potent offense.

classy ... to be out of condition for any length of time."

Two very different "wars" had an enormous impact on baseball in these years, and the Northwestern League in particular. First, in the spring of 1914, the upstart Federal League claimed major league status by raiding the existing major leagues of established stars. Attendance in the established leagues plummeted and salaries rose, as players now had an alternative to the team that controlled them. The ripple effect on the minors was twofold. First, players who were released by big league teams, known as "comebacks," were no longer reporting to minor league clubs — because they too now had another option. Second, minor league teams could no longer maximize the sale of their emerging stars to big league clubs because the players were threatening to jump to the "Feds." To salvage some value from these players, the minor league teams were forced to sell them quickly and at fire sale prices.

Thus Seattle lost pitcher Pete Schneider to the Cincinnati Reds, and Spokane lost Walter Holke to the New York Giants at midseason, long before the pennant race was over and at a fraction of the price they would have generated in more peaceful times. In these two cases, the Federal League may have "been foiled," as the *Chronicle* wrote on September 30. Both players stayed with Organized Ball, as the opportunity to play in the majors eliminated their need to jump to the Feds. Yet the loss of these stars had a major impact on the outcome of the 1914 NWL pennant race.

Spokane certainly could have used George Lange Kelly now, but he was firmly settled in Victoria. The following year he too would rebuff the call of the Feds and join the New York Giants. His uncle, Bill Lange, had given him advice before he made his decision: "Be sure and have nothing to do with the Federal League as they are in a very shaky condition, and I am sure [New York Giants' owner and manager John] McGraw will take care of you."

The second war was a much bigger deal, because it reached far beyond baseball. In August, most of Europe entered into the Great War. While the United States would not join the conflict until 1917, Canada, as a member of the British Empire, was a full combatant from the start. Canada would suffer enormous casualties for a country of only eight million — more than 40 percent of its 600,000 enlistees were killed or wounded. The outlook of Canadians changed markedly and suddenly. As early as September 10, 1914, *The Sporting News* described Vancouver as a "veritable armed camp buzzing with the preparations of war." Not surprisingly, attendance at games in Vancouver and Victoria plummeted. After getting the approval of the National Association, the league's owners cut the season short by a couple of weeks. Vancouver held on to win its second straight pennant, edging Seattle by three games. Spokane had no last-month rush, finishing in third place, 12 games back at 84-68.

Coveleski finished strong, with four wins and a 1-0 loss. His final win, against Seattle, was both improbable and dramatic. Seattle's Al Gipe, going for his 19th win, had pitched a no-hitter his last time out. Coveleski came into the game with one out in the first inning and the Indians already down 4-0. When they rallied for an 8-6 win, he had his 20th win (against 15 losses), and earned a $100 bonus for reaching the milestone. Coveleski also led the league in strikeouts with 214. Reviewing his feats on September 24, *The Sporting News* wrote, "Coveleskie is one of the best pitchers out of the big show."

As the season came to a close, the *Spokesman-Review* wrote that the club was "a grievous disappointment ... a gloomy page in Spokane baseball history." The paper elaborated that the team "threw down" owner Farr with "midseason dissipations." A couple of weeks later, Farr addressed the vexing problem: "Am I thinking of quitting?

I don't care if a man can present credentials that he was raised a Quaker and never took a drop in his life. His word won't go. He's got to sign a contract with me that his salary stops with the first glass of beer.

F.C. Farr
Spokane Indians owner

HUNT.REUTHER. HARSTAD. BRINKER. FRISK. M^cCARL. DOTY. HALL. WOTELL. SCHARNWEBER. GRANT. HEISTER. CLARK. SHAW. JONES. GRINDELL. CHEEK. BENNETT.

Coveleski's contemporaries: In 1914, Vancouver won its second straight pennant with Northwest mainstays Harry Scharnweber, Dode Brinker, Emil Frisk, Bert Hall, Jimmy Clark, Hunky Shaw and Pug Bennett, as well as fine young pitchers Dutch Ruether and Oscar Harstad.

No pitcher can expect to get by in the Coast League without a good change of pace.

Walter McCredie Portland Beavers co-owner

Not on your trolley." Looking ahead to 1915, he was quoted September 25, 1914 in the *Spokesman-Review*, "I'm going to have no boozers. I don't care if a man can present credentials that he was raised a Quaker and never took a drop in his life. His word won't go. He's got to sign a contract with me that his salary stops with the first glass of beer."

Spokane had a close working relationship with the San Francisco Seals of the Coast League, from whom they'd received Phil Douglas a year earlier. But as Seals owner Cal Ewing was getting out of baseball, the Indians' informal relationship with the Seals ended. At the same time, the McCredies were looking for a NWL team to hook up with, since the Portland Colts were dissolved. *The Sporting News* reported on December 5 that Walter McCredie "naturally is looking to Spokane as his logical little brother," especially since he thought highly of Indians' owner Farr.

And so the Spokane Indians became an informal farm club of the Portland Beavers. If Stan Coveleski had been sent to Spokane "with strings," as was probably the case, the deal was done between Connie Mack and Joe Cohn. The latter was long gone, and with him went whatever right the Athletics had to recall Coveleski. The [Portland] *Oregonian* reported on December 14 that Farr didn't want to let Covey go but felt that he "may have to do so to protect himself" because "Coveleskie wants to graduate and has several options." While the article doesn't spell out those options, the reference most likely is to the Federal League. The first major deal between the two teams sent Coveleski to Portland, in exchange for five players. Only one, pitcher Suds Sutherland, had modest success on the Coast, and none became regulars in the major leagues.

With two wars raging, the baseball talk the next off-season was on retrenchment. Attendance and revenue

would continue to be down in 1915, so expenses had to drop. In Portland, Judge McCredie promised to cut the salaries of star pitchers Irv Higginbotham and Harry Krause. Should his pitchers decide to jump to the Feds, said McCredie, so be it. In the meantime, players of the NWL pushed back by asking the National Association for the two weeks' pay they lost when the 1914 season was shortened, threatening civil action. Nothing came from their challenge.

The Portland club Coveleski joined was the two-time defending PCL champion. The 1915 team had lost a couple of powerful bats — Dave Bancroft had graduated to the Phillies, and Buddy Ryan joined the new Salt Lake City franchise, where he'd hit .340. The Beavers would depend on a powerful trio of pitchers: Irv Higginbotham (21-14 and 31-20 the past two seasons), Harry Krause (17-11 and 22-18), and Johnny Lush (7-4 in 1914). All three men had already spent a few seasons in the majors, and all three resisted overtures to jump to the Federal League.

Credited by *Sporting Life* on August 29, 1914, with being "the shrewdest judge of baseball horse-flesh west of the Mississippi river," Walter McCredie wanted Coveleski, "a strikeout king of some renown." "Coveleskie is to be the meteor of the 1915 Coast season," McCredie predicted to the *Oregonian* on January 17, 1915. He planned to hook Coveleski up with Johnny Lush, to help his new pitcher develop an effective slow ball. "No pitcher can expect to get by in the Coast League without a good change of pace," said McCredie.

Trick pitches were the rage in baseball during these years, and the Coast League was no exception. Lush had already gained some notoriety out of a suspicion of his throwing the emery ball. In one interview, Coveleski admitted he threw the pitch "every once in a while." Two other probable purveyors of the pitch in the PCL were

"Skeeter" Fanning and Jack Ryan, who were also thought to be masters of the mudball. Fanning won 77 games for the San Francisco Seals from 1913 to 1915. From 1914 to 1916, Ryan won 79 games for the Los Angeles Angels. All these "freak" pitches proved easier to ban than to eradicate.

Before Coveleski came out west for 1915 spring training, he married Mae Shivetts in Shamokin. After they had two children, she died in 1920, and Coveleski married her sister Frances, who had been tending to the kids, in 1922. They were married for more than 60 years.

Ever interested in improving his arsenal, Coveleski proved a quick learner. By the end of spring training, the *Oregonian* noted that he had a good slow ball (March 24). On January 17, the paper captured the personality that Coveleski would be known for throughout his big league career: "He is a most willing learner, never complains over the 'breaks' and never makes trouble with his teammates over support, as was the case with Tom Seaton and some others of a crabbing temperament."

Back in 1913, the Spokane *Chronicle* had noted Coveleski's almost painful shyness. He wouldn't "earn his salt talking" and rarely said more than a few words. Instead, he let his pitching do his talking. Now, near the end of spring training 1915, on March 24 the *Oregonian* reported, "Coveleskie has a world of speed and a good change of pace. In addition to this he uses his head at all points."

Ticket prices in the Coast League would stay the same for 1915: 25 cents for the bleachers and 50 cents for grandstand seats. The new Salt Lake City franchise, transferred from Sacramento, faced high transportation costs, and would charge 50 cents and 75 cents, but still drew very well. The first-year club would be a rare bright spot in 1915, with strong fan support and attendance. In Portland, Judge McCredie installed "pay-as-you-play" turnstiles, the latest technology. As fans entered the ballpark and dropped their quarters into the turnstiles, the judge could sit in his office and watch the totals register on "electronically-connected dials," the *Oregonian* reported on February 6, 1915.

The McCredies announced cutbacks on a number of fronts. They would no longer provide their players with fancy green sweaters, which usually ended up with their lady friends and could be spotted on Guild's Lake during the winter skating season. The players would be provided with only two meals a day and transportation to the ballpark only one way. The players would walk back the three miles the other way. In the Beavers' promotional push at the start of the season, former world featherweight champion and future Black Sox personality Abe Attell — who was appearing at Portland's Orpheum Theater — sold booster buttons for the team.

The McCredies scheduled spring exhibition games in Fresno against Rube Foster's Chicago American Giants. At the end of the series, Foster reviewed the Beavers and told the April 2 *Oregonian*, "Of the youngsters I like Coveleskie best because he has all the natural requirements." The *Spokesman-Review* of December 26, 1914, had noted that these black players were "wizards who could easily make any major league team except for their complexion." Yet even such exhibition games were controversial. *Sporting Life* had reported a year earlier, February 21, 1914, that the McCredies had come under criticism from Coast League president Baum for scheduling such matches.

In the first few weeks of the 1915 season, Coveleski was used both as a starter and in relief. "McCredie kept switching pitchers like Muggsy McGraw in a World's series," wrote the *Oregonian* on April 12, after Coveleski and three other Beavers relieved in an 8-7 win over Lefty Williams and Salt Lake City. Williams, another future Black Sox player, would go on to a spectacular 1915 season, producing a 33-12 record with 294 strikeouts in 419 innings.

By this point, Coveleski's spitter had become a major weapon. In his four-hit win over Salt Lake City in April, the *Oregon Journal* wrote that Coveleski's "sharp-breaking spitball had the locals completely baffled." On June 4, the *Oregonian* noted how he got out of tight spots in a 5-1 win "by a prodigious use of his spitter." On June 10, the *Oregon Journal* wrote, "the expectorating Pole had all sorts of saliva on the ball," as he shut out Salt Lake, 5-0. A few days later, manager McCredie and umpire Red Held fought under the grandstand after a game in which Held had ejected the manager. Such an event was not rare in these rough-and-tumble days. Held said on June 14 in the *Oregonian* that he wouldn't ask for a suspension of McCredie. "These occasional spats are all in the business. We umpires are not perfect, and neither are the managers."

On June 25 Coveleski suffered perhaps the most dramatic loss of his minor league career. League-leading San Francisco rallied for an 8-7 win on Harry Heilmann's eighth-inning homer, knocking in slugger Ping Bodie ahead of him. Bodie hit 19 home runs this year, while Heilmann would hammer Coast League pitching for a .364 batting average.

In July 1915 the spotlight of the Coast League was on Jack Ness of Oakland, as he hit safely in game after game. On July 4 Coveleski gave up a double to Ness, his 32nd straight game with a hit. Portland won in extra innings, as McCredie used seven pitchers, "switched with such rapidity that the fans were bewildered." Ness would go on to break Ty Cobb's "world record" by hitting safely in 49 straight games. [Newspapers made no mention of the longer streaks — pre-1901 — of Willie Keeler (44 games) and Bill Dahlen (42 games). Joe Wilhoit would set a new record of

Booster buttons for the 1915 Portland Beavers sought a 20,000 attendance mark for the 1915 opening series at Vaughan Street Park, which had been expanded three years earlier to a capacity of 12,000. One of the button promoters was former world featherweight champion and future Chicago Black Sox personality Abe Attell.

Coveleski's contemporaries: Pete Schneider started as a good-hitting pitcher with Seattle and Medicine Hat, spent five seasons with Cincinnati, where he won 20 games in 1917, and returned west as a high-average, power-hitting outfielder. On May 11, 1923, playing for Vernon in a Pacific Coast League game at Salt Lake City, he hit five home runs, two of them grand slams, and drove in 14 runs.

hitting in 69 consecutive games in 1919, with Wichita of the Western League.] Ness would hit .339 in 1915, enough to gain him a return call to the big leagues.

In late August, Stan Coveleski had a remarkable stretch doing double duty as both staff workhorse and relief pitcher extraordinaire. In the short space of eight games and nine days, Coveleski pitched in seven games (five in relief) and appeared in the eighth as a pinch runner. In the first game, the winning run scored off Coveleski in the 9th inning on a passed ball. Yet the *Oregonian* almost suggested otherwise: "The young Pole's saliva made the spheroid so slippery that one of his fast ones got away." In the second game, Coveleski struck out Salt Lake City pinch-hitter Dutch Ruether on three pitches in the 9th. Coveleski's heroics were just starting.

Looking back on this string of games, the *Oregon Journal* ran a photo of Covey on September 5, with the headline, "CRACK RELIEF PITCHER OF BEAVERS." The caption read: "The eminent spitballist ... 'saved' two games during last week, striking out Los Angeles players in the ninth." The *Journal* saluted Coveleski: "As a finisher up, this bird is as good as Bill Steen in his palmiest days." Steen had won 57 games over1910 and 1911 for the pennant-winning Beavers.

One of the games was described as "quarrelsome," with Portland complaining about Jack Ryan's mud ball and Los Angeles protesting Johnny Lush's emery ball. Coveleski

ended the quarrel — and the game — with a ninth-inning strikeout. He ended this Herculean stretch of games with a start, beating the Angels' Slim Love, who would lead the Coast League in earned run average in 1915.

After hovering around .500 well into the summer, the Beavers had a rough August. They lost 18 of 23 games until meeting Los Angeles and beating the first-place Angels three straight, when Coveleski got two saves and a win. He went back to winning games as a starter in September, with four victories, culminating in a 9-0 win over Oakland on the 28th. "COVELESKIE INVINCIBLE," shouted the headline of the *Oregon Journal*. "His spitters were breaking all over the place," wrote the *Oregonian*.

Earlier in the month, Coveleski tossed a four-hit shutout over Vernon (the Venice club had relocated to nearby Vernon on July 11) and their pitcher-manager, Doc White. White had won 189 games in the majors and was a star of the 1906 world champion Chicago White Sox (Fielder Jones's "Hitless Wonders"). He had joined the California club in 1914 and won 17 games for them. Early in 1915, when popular manager Happy Hogan died suddenly of pneumonia, White stepped in to manage the club.

A late-season bright spot for the Beavers was Billy Southworth, an outfielder the Cleveland Indians sent to Portland in early September. Southworth had hit only .220 in 60 games with the Indians that season, but his home run on September 5th helped Coveleski edge pitcher Bill Steen and the Seals, and he followed with another homer the next day. Southworth had not hit a home run in 177 at bats with Cleveland, but he would finish with a .320 batting average and would hit .300 in a full season with Portland in 1916 before going on to a long major league career.

Portland went into a free-fall towards the end of the season, including 14 straight losses in October, and finished in last place at 78-116. In doing so, the Beavers lost 60 of their final 82 games. The McCredies spoke about making a total housecleaning and going with younger, less expensive players for 1916. "I've tried until I'm sick, sore and disgusted. It can't be done," moaned Walter to the *Journal* on September 12, 1915, about his efforts to mold the current group into a winner. Little did he realize that — having won four pennants between 1910 and 1914 — he would win no more. He and his uncle would stay with Portland through 1921 (except for one year, 1918, when Portland did not field a team, and Walter managed Salt Lake City), and they would not come close to another Coast League pennant.

Coveleski had been a bright spot in an otherwise disappointing year: he appeared in a league-leading 64 games, posting a 2.67 earned run average and a 17-17 record. The aces of the 1914 staff — Higginbotham, Krause, and Lush — had won only 37 games between them, against 50 losses. All saw their earned run averages rise about a full run over their 1914 numbers.

Coveleski further solidified his position as an emerging star when he excelled in post-season exhibition games between the PCL champions, the San Francisco Seals, and

Stan Coveleski (center), refined his spitball with Portland in 1915, his lone season in the Pacific Coast League, and it helped propel him to stardom with the Cleveland Indians and a berth in the Hall of Fame.

a squad made up of Coast League All-Stars, among them Fred Snodgrass and George Kelly. Coveleski pitched in two of the games in San Francisco. On October 29 he went 11 innings in a 3-3 tie, called because of darkness. Just three days later, he pitched the All-Stars to a 13-3 win.

The *Oregon Journal* reported on August 19 that the Cleveland Indians would request the transfer of Coveleski's contract, to keep him from the upcoming (August 26) minor league draft. Charles Somers was one of the founders and original financial backers of the American League, and his Indians had enjoyed a close relationship with the Portland Beavers for many years. Walter McCredie emphasized the importance of this personal relationship when he noted, "The squareness of Charley Somers made our relationship extremely pleasant and profitable to both of us," in an interview with the *Oregon Journal* on December 18. As 1915 was drawing to a close, Somers was experiencing severe financial difficulties. Were he to sell his team, the working agreement with Portland would end, and Stan Coveleski would not go to the Indians.

The run-up to the Coveleski deal provides insight into "working relationships" between the majors and the minors at this time. As the *Journal* wrote on December 10, "McCredie, in the event of a sale [of the Cleveland ball club], would feel that he was under no obligations to the new owners and would step out and get a better price than even Cleveland had offered." McCredie elaborated in the December 11, 1915, *Oregonian*: "My deal with Cleveland [for Coveleski] was practically closed, but it was a personal matter between Somers and myself. We have always found Charley Somers a prince to do business with, and have never had to have any written contracts or agreements."

McCredie said in the December 18, 1915, *Oregon*

Journal that if Somers did exit baseball, the Beavers would "immediately seek an alliance with the St. Louis club [the Browns]" managed by Fielder Jones. "Jones knows what we need in the Pacific Coast league and above all, he would be square with a fellow. Too many of the major league managers and owners are always trying to jip a minor league club."

The year ended with great news for minor league owners: settlement of the Federal League war. Walter McCredie claimed in the December 17 *Oregonian* that his club was worth $20,000 with the baseball war and $100,000 with peace. Besides the upward pressure on salaries, it was impossible to maintain discipline, with players threatening to jump to the Feds. Now, he recognized that many players would soon be dumped onto a shrinking market. "Baseball players," he told the *Journal* on December 9, "are the cheapest commodity on the market, cheaper even than cheesecloth." The limited free agency that baseball's war had created was at an end.

Coveleski was formally transferred to Cleveland and signed with the Indians at the end of the year. Ironically, Somers did indeed sell his team just a few weeks later. The breaker boy from the mines of Shamokin had come a long way during his years out west. He had traveled far from the East Coast and had progressed far in his nascent baseball career. "THE SPOKANE SPITBALLIST BREAKS BALL WHERE BEES CAN'T SEE IT" was the April 10, 1915 headline of the *Oregon Journal*. A lot more than bees were about to struggle with his spitter. His big league career, highlighted by 215 wins, 38 shutouts and a 2.89 earned run average, was about to begin, but his three years in the Pacific Northwest were the foundation of that future success. ⚾

> **Baseball players are the cheapest commodity on the market, cheaper even than cheesecloth.**
>
> **Walter McCredie**

Sources:

Newspapers, 1912 to early 1916:

Spokane Chronicle

Spokane Press

Spokesman-Review, Spokane

Oregon Journal, Portland

Oregonian, Portland

Sporting Life

The Sporting News

The rocky saga of vagabond 'tribesman' Jimmy Claxton

First African-American depicted on a baseball card first played at 13 in tiny Washington state towns of Roslyn and Chester

BY TOM HAWTHORN

Although Jimmy Claxton spent barely a week on Oakland's roster, he was with the Oaks long enough to be photographed for this prized Zeenut trading card.

On the morning of May 28, 1916, a lean, lefthanded pitcher took the mound in Oakland for the hometown Oaks. Jimmy Claxton's debut in the Pacific Coast League was with a team desperate for pitching. The Oaks had already slipped into the basement, where they would remain for the rest of the season, finishing 72-136.

The 23-year-old was a coal-miner's son born in a coal-mining town. He would spend much of his life as a baseball vagabond, pitching for barnstorming and semiprofessional teams well into his 40s. His wandering ways had brought him to the Bay Area, where he hurled for a local semi-pro team before coming to the attention of the Oaks.

Claxton got through the first inning against Los Angeles without allowing a run to score, but the visiting Angels touched him for a run in the second. He was pulled in the top of the third, having surrendered four hits and three walks. He'd committed an error, and recorded two assists, one of those starting a pitcher-to-second-to-first double play. The Angels had a 3-0 lead before the Oaks pulled ahead by a run. The visitors scored another run in the eighth to tie the score. In the top of the ninth with two outs, left fielder Rube Ellis, the former St. Louis Cardinals outfielder, singled, stole second, and took third on an overthrow. He scored when Harry Wolter beat out a grounder to shortstop. The umpire's verdict on the close call at first was not shared by hometown fans.

"As the Oaks were retired with no scoring," the *Los Angeles Times* reported the next day, "the right field bleacherites moved on the field en masse. A share of the grandstanders backed them up and before he knew what was happening, (umpire) Guthrie was the target for cushions, scantlings and anything that came handy."

Los Angeles manager Frank Chance and Oaks pitcher Dutch Klawitter, who had relieved Claxton, braved a fusillade of pop bottles to escort the beleaguered umpire off the field. Both of them carried a bat.

The umpire returned to the field for the concluding afternoon game of the Sunday doubleheader. The Angels got to Oaks starter Speed Martin early and often. Claxton came on in relief in the ninth, issuing a walk before recording the final Angels out. By then, the score was 10-0 for the visitors, and a five-run outburst in the home half of the inning only made a game that had been a laugher look respectable.

Claxton's work for the day: 2-1/3 innings pitched, four hits, three runs (two earned), four walks, and no strikeouts. The reviews the next day were considerate. Claxton "was obviously nervous and cannot be fairly judged by his showing," the *San Francisco Chronicle* reported. The rival *Call* told readers the rookie hailed from an Indian reservation back east. "The Redskin had a nice windup and a frightened look on his face, but not quite enough stuff to bother L.A.," the newspaper noted. "He lasted two innings. However, he may do better in the future."

He never got get the chance. Claxton was released by manager Rowdy Elliott on June 3 without ever again taking to the mound.

"According to Rowdy, the heaver had nothing on the

> **The Redskin had a nice windup and a frightened look on his face, but not quite enough stuff to bother L.A.**
>
> San Francisco *Call*

Tom Hawthorn is a magazine and newspaper writer in Victoria, B.C., Canada. His nickname is E5.

ball, and he couldn't afford to bother with him," *Chronicle* sports editor Harry B. Smith reported. "Claxton pitched last year, according to reports, with the Oakland Giants [a black team], but Manager Rowdy declared that he had appeared at the Oakland headquarters with an affidavit signed before a notary showing him to be from one of the reservations in North Dakota."

He was indeed from the north, but not the Dakotas. James Edgar Claxton, known all his life as Jimmy, or Jimmie, was born on December 14, 1892, at Wellington, a British Columbia mining town at the northern terminus of the Esquimalt and Nanaimo Railway on Vancouver Island. Though he was born in Canada, both his parents were American. His father, William Edgar Claxton, was a stout miner from Lynchburg, Virginia, where his father had been a farmer, and his older sisters worked as domestic servants. Jimmy Claxton's mother, Emma Richards, was born in Illinois to a farmer, and by age 13 was living on a farm in Kittitas County, Washington.

In Wellington, William E. Claxton, a widower, lived in a boarding house with a dozen other American coal miners, where a Chinese cook, Mah Ping, prepared meals for the men and the house's keeper, a 29-year-old widow and her two daughters. On January 14, 1892, Claxton and Richards, who had turned 18 just 24 days earlier, were wed by Reverend John W. Flinton, an English-born minister with the Church of England. In a section reserved for remarks on their marriage registration, the minister wrote: "The bridegroom is a coloured man; the bride a white woman." Those words would define Jimmy Claxton's working life, as well as limit his possibilities on the baseball diamond.

In a 1964 newspaper interview, the pitcher recounted his career, including how his brief tenure with the Oaks stemmed from his time pitching for the Giants.

"A fellow named Hastings, a part-Indian from Oklahoma, I believe, followed every game we played. He was a baseball nut," Claxton said. "He introduced me to Herb McFarland, secretary of the Oakland Coast League club, and told him I was a fellow tribesman. I was signed to an Organized Baseball contract."

Claxton's memory was somewhat faulty in recounting events from almost 40 years earlier. He told Tacoma *News Tribune* sports editor Dan Walton that he had three starts and two relief appearances with the Oaks, although his name, misspelled Klaxton, only appears in boxscores for the May 28 doubleheader. He was on the roster for about a week, not the month he remembered.

In any case, Claxton felt he had been betrayed by a friend who told management about his racial heritage. "I had been with Oakland about a month when I got notice that I was released," he said. "No reason was given, but I knew." The pitcher also blamed Rowdy Elliott for doing "everything to keep from giving me a fair chance."

Claxton described his ethnic heritage as being Negro, French and Indian on his father's side, and Irish and English on his mother's. The 1891 census in Canada, in

Jimmy Claxton said it was longtime club secretary Herb McFarland (above) who encouraged him to join the Oakland Oaks in May 1916 for what turned out to be a brief attempt at breaking the Pacific Coast League color line.

which his father was recorded living at the boarding house, did not record race. The census takers in America first accounted for Claxton's father as a nine-year-old in Campbell County, Virginia, in 1870. Jimmy's paternal grandfather John Claxton, 48, was recorded as mulatto, while wife Susan, 43, was listed as black. Their six children were mulatto, a designation Jimmy himself would have recorded beside his name in the 1910 census, by which time he was living with his father in the coal-mining town of Ravensdale, Washington. Ten years later, Jimmy Claxton's race would be recorded by the census taker as black. He was working then as a stevedore in Oakland.

"When he bares back his shirt his skin is as white as that of a Nordic," Walton wrote 41 years ago. "Perhaps from his Indian blood his hair is straight and jet black — or was before grey hairs and a high forehead came with the years."

His sister, Emma Elmary Josephin Claxton, was born in Wellington in 1896, and raised by her maternal grandparents in Washington state. She appears in the U.S. census as being white.

Claxton was referred to as a Native American for much

Please turn to 'Claxton' on page 126

> I had been with Oakland about a month when I got notice that I was released. No reason was given, but I knew.
>
> Jimmy Claxton

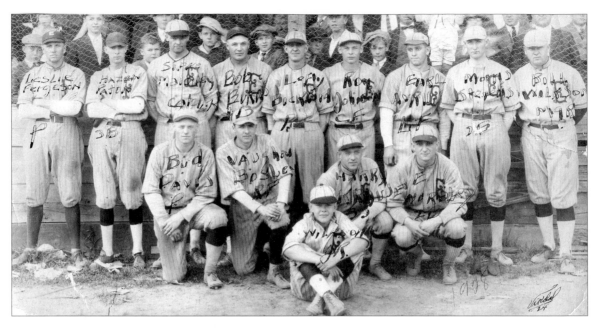

The semipro Everett Seagulls who defeated the barnstorming Brooklyn Dodgers in 1924: (Back row, from left) pitcher Leslie Ferguson, third baseman Hazen Paton, catcher Spike Maloney, first baseman Bob Burns, pitcher Earl Bickford, center fielder Roy Johnson, postseason left fielder (and future Hall of Famer) Earl Averill, utility infielder Morris Stevens, manager Bill Wilkinson, (front row, from left) left fielder Bud Davis, right fielder Vaughn Bosley, the batboy and manager's son, shortstop Harry Krause and second baseman Carl Nordley.

Brooklyn Dodgers were no match for high-flying Gulls

Drunken brawl the day before in Wenatchee led to 15-3 win for semipro Everett team

BY DAVE LARSON

On October 20, 1924, the semi-pro Seagulls of Everett, Washington, surprised the baseball world by walloping the Brooklyn Dodgers 15-3. Pitching for Brooklyn that day was spitballer and future Hall of Famer Burleigh Grimes, whose spitter was not working that day in the Pacific Northwest.

Brooklyn had a formidable 1924 team, finishing second in the National League, 1-1/2 games behind New York. While the Giants battled the Washington Senators in a memorable seven-game World Series, the Dodgers barnstormed the northern states. Brooklyn featured pitcher Dazzy Vance, the NL's MVP with a record of 28-6, 262 strikeouts, and a 2.16 ERA, all major league-leading figures. Backing up Vance with a 22-13 record was Grimes. Brooklyn first baseman Jack Fournier, the NL's home run leader who hailed from Aberdeen, Washington, acted as the team manager for the tour.

Dave Larson is a researcher-author living at Alexander Beach near Anacortes, Washington. He has recently completed a book on early baseball in Northwest Washington, *Wide Awakes, Invincibles, & Smokestackers.*

Meanwhile, the Seagulls were winning the semi-pro Northwest Washington League title by beating the Mount Vernon Milkmaids in the playoffs. Everett fielded good players for the Brooklyn game, including second baseman Roy Grover, who had played for three seasons in the American League. The center fielder was young Roy Johnson, who later teamed with Earl Averill and Smead Jolley for the 1928 San Francisco Seals in one of the hardest hitting outfields in minor league history. Johnson went on to play ten years in the bigs, batting .296 lifetime.

The Everett-Brooklyn game was played on a Monday afternoon. Few, if any, Everett children had ever seen major leaguers in action, so school was dismissed early to let them watch the leviathans. The ballpark had hosted a horse show the previous day, so a crew worked steadily up until game time to sanitize the grounds and level the infield.

The umpire called "Play Ball" at 2:30. Brooklyn drew first blood by scoring an unearned run in the second inning when Everett made its only two errors of the game, but the Seagulls went ahead in the third and boosted the lead from there. Roy Johnson led the attack with two doubles and a single. Roy Grover made the defensive play of the game in the sixth, with a sensational stop of Fournier's hot grounder back of first base that threw the big leaguer out at first.

Grimes lasted through the seventh but ten runs were charged to him. The Dodgers' eight errors, including three by Grimes, didn't help. Everett southpaw Earl Bickford allowed only seven hits in seven innings. After the game Fournier said, "You have the best semi-pro ball club we have played on this trip. This was the first game we lost on the tour. That boy Bickford sure has a wonderful arm."

There were, however, extenuating circumstances for Brooklyn. The day before the game, the Dodgers had played a game in Wenatchee against a pickup team of the best local players. The Wenatchee Commercial Club had come up with a $1,000 guarantee to induce the Dodgers to play at this stop on the rail line. The club knew it would not make money on the game but believed the advertising and pride in being "selected" to meet the Dodgers more than offset the meager pay the locals would receive.

Brooklyn's starting pitcher that afternoon was Rube Ehrhardt, who in seven innings staked the Dodgers to a 7-1 lead. With the result sealed, the crowd clamored for Dazzy Vance, who pitched the last two innings. This was fun time, and Vance called his fielders to line up behind him. They all went into a pitching motion — lefties, righties, all arms flailing away — when a pitched ball came out from somewhere. The catcher was smoking and exhaled puffs of smoke as the ball smacked into his glove. One local player sorted out the confusion enough to blast a triple to left field. The left fielder, of course, had abandoned his post to participate in the clowning behind the pitcher's mound. The crowd laughed and cheered the comic routines.

Afterward, the Dodgers repaired to the Elman Hotel for refreshments and rest before catching the train for Everett. Prohibition reigned, but a Brooklyn delegation came up with corn squeezings of questionable pedigree and soon got rather rowdy. H. D. Miller, hotel manager, made several requests for players to stop disturbing guests, to no avail. Miller resorted to calling the police around 11:20 PM.

William Weaver, 16-year-old bellboy, upstairs on an errand, was knocked down by the players. Miller came to Weaver's defense, and a brouhaha broke out. Police later reported that the players hurled cuspidors and other heavy objects and broke all the glass in the hotel office. One Dodger slugged Weaver, knocking out two teeth, and hospitalizing him with a lacerated and possibly broken jaw.

Police arrested players Bernie Neis, Johnny Mitchell, Eddie Brown, and Milt Stock, who spent the night in jail and missed the train to Everett. They were held on charges of being drunk and disorderly, and assault in the third degree. The next day they were released on bail of $400 each, with trial set for the following Monday.

The players did not return and were represented at the trial by two attorneys, one local and one from Seattle. Judge John Porter awarded Weaver $750 for his injuries and the hotel $200 for damages, and fined each player $200 on criminal charges. The players also had to pay attorneys' fees and the cost of refreshments. A local paper reported, "The moonshine party given by the Brooklyn ball players at the Elman Hotel was one of the most elaborate and expensive social affairs ever held in that city."

Charles Ebbets, owner of the Dodgers, sent a telegram: "Please mail me record of court proceedings in disgraceful brawl involving Brooklyn players. Also itemized statement of damage and cost to replace same, including doctor bill and services for boy, William Weaver. Please present our sympathy to him with a wish for a speedy recovery."

Baseball Commissioner Kenesaw Mountain Landis declined jurisdiction "as the players involved were playing on their own hook after the close of the season."

Even though Brooklyn was short-handed, nothing could dampen the celebration of the Everett semi-pros after beating the Dodgers and Burleigh Grimes, 15-3. ⚾

You have the best semipro ball club we have played on this trip.

Jack Fournier, first baseman and manager for Brooklyn Dodgers brainstorming tour

Sources: *Everett Daily Herald, Everett News, Seattle Post-Intelligencer, Seattle Times, Wenatchee Daily World, Tonasket Times*

War, continued from page 15

talked to the Seattle correspondent for *Sporting Life*:

"Say, do you know I have figured that the sum of $114,000 was lost in base ball on the Pacific Coast this year? Yes, you can say that if they keep up the money I think I would buy a New York block and put a lunch counter in the basement. No, I didn't lose any of it myself, for I broke even — just even. Why, we lost $12,000 in Portland, and Tacoma and Helena both lost.

"But think of it, $114,000! Why, say, when men do such things, they are bordering on the nut factory. Sure. When your children grow up, you can tell them: 'Why, away back in 1903, base ball was killed on the Coast because we paid men anywhere from $200 to $400 a month to play ball.' Yes, you can. And if they keep up the salaries next year — puff — there'll be a bit of smoke, and it will be back to the James street power house with a lot of us. Oh I don't know anything about consolidation. I am open to any good business proposition where the stock isn't watered. But not any of that steel trust business for Dugdale."

Dugdale, who said so many nasty things about the Coast League in 1903, went back to it to manage Portland's PCL franchise in 1904. Lucas's Pacific National League did return, but neither "Pacific" nor "National" belonged in the league's name. With Dugdale's Chinooks vanquished, the new four-team PNL didn't get any closer to the Pacific Ocean than Spokane (joined by Boise and holdovers Butte and Salt Lake City). In 1905, the Pacific National League and all its 1904 cities were out of professional baseball.

The Pacific Coast League, undisputed winner of the 1903 war, joined Organized Baseball in 1904 as one of the top four minor leagues. In another Coast League change, Tacoma replaced Sacramento, and the new Tigers, despite hailing from the league's least-populous city, went 130-94 and won both halves of the split season.

But Tacoma was just too small to support a PCL franchise, and in 1906 the Tigers were replaced by the Fresno Raisin Eaters. That club didn't last, either, and neither did the Seattle franchise. In 1907, the PCL was once again a four-team circuit, identical to the old California League, except that Portland was in the league and Sacramento was not. The PCL did re-expand to six teams in 1909, but it wasn't until 1915 — when Salt Lake City replaced the Mission entry — that a non-California city other than Portland would host a Pacific Coast League franchise. The "war" was probably fought a decade earlier than it should have been. ⚾

Sources: *San Francisco Chronicle,* the *Daily Ledger* (Tacoma), the *Oregonian* and *Oregon Journal* (both Portland), the *Los Angeles Times, Spalding's Official Base Ball Guide* (1904), the second edition of *The Encyclopedia of Minor League Baseball* (Baseball America 1997) and *Reach's Official Base Ball Guide* (1904)

'The thought of losing was just abhorrent'

Grit of Seattle's 'boy wonder' Fred Hutchinson endures long after his untimely cancer death

By CLAY EALS

I n the sizzling summer heat of the 1957 National League pennant race, Fred Hutchinson turned philosophical. "Baseball doesn't have many naturals, a lot less than you might imagine," said the Seattle-born-and-bred skipper of the St. Louis Cardinals. "The ones who work the hardest are the ones who make it, the ones who win. Sometimes that's the only difference. If you don't work hard at this game, you might as well hang them up. Sweat is your only salvation."

It was such a telling utterance that Emmett Watson — his close friend and high-school catcher, who subsequently became Seattle's preeminent newspaper columnist — used it to end a lengthy profile of the stone-faced "Hutch" that ran in the August 26 edition of *Sports Illustrated*.

At no time did Hutch build a better case for his own admonition than in coping with his major-league debut 18 years earlier. Just 19 years old and steeped in a manly Pacific Northwest upbringing, Hutch had become the quintessential local boy made good. After graduating from Franklin High School, where he had racked up four sterling years as a pitcher, outfielder and hitter, and triggered countless "Hutch" headlines in the city's three newspapers a generation before the Pilots and Mariners landed in Seattle, he crafted a storybook season in 1938. Pitching for the just-minted Seattle Rainiers of the Double A Pacific Coast League in his professional debut, Hutch went 25-7 with 29 complete games and a 2.48 ERA, leading his team to second place and prompting *The Sporting News* to name him the country's minor-league player of the year.

But in 1938, even the "American Idol" of baseball needed to attract the contract offers of major league teams from the Mississippi River east to reach the peak of pro success. Near season's end, the New York Yankees' Col. Jacob Ruppert rejected a demand by Rainiers owner Emil Sick for $250,000 and 10 players in exchange for the rookie. The off-season scramble to sign Hutch tempered only a bit, as the Detroit Tigers outbid the Yankees,

Pittsburgh Pirates and Chicago Cubs, securing him for a still whopping $50,000 and four players. As spring training opened in 1939, the hype for Hutch, nicknamed "the Iceman," built to proportions that were literally Ruthian. In the March 11 *Liberty* magazine, Royal Brougham of the *Seattle Post-Intelligencer* said Hutch possessed "the pitching magic of a Christy Mathewson" and christened him "a second Ruth come to judgment."

Judgment, indeed. Under deep pressure, Hutch, strictly a control pitcher in his Rainiers stint, had lost his control. His first action as a Tiger — three innings in an intra-squad game in Lakeland, Florida, and one day after *Liberty* hit the newsstands — was inauspicious. Hutch couldn't find the corners of the plate, giving up five runs and six hits, including two triples and a homer. Though writers predicted otherwise ("Much of the success of the Detroit pitching situation depends upon young Freddy Hutchinson," opined *Wind Up* magazine), Hutch endured a weary wait for his official big-league entrée. A full two weeks after opening day, Hutch finally got into a game — one for the ages.

It was Tuesday, May 2, 1939. Making their first western swing of the season, the Bronx Bombers had boarded a train to Detroit, where star Joe DiMaggio would not be patrolling center field at Briggs Stadium, owing to a strained ankle. But their first contest against the Tigers was to be far more notable for the absence of another Yankee star. After a jaw-dropping record 2,130 consecutive games, first baseman Lou Gehrig finally sat out. Fired up, the New Yorkers devoured Detroit pitching, scoring six runs in the first inning, and led 13-0 by the top of the seventh when, with the bases full and no outs, the call went to Hutch. He lasted just two-thirds of an inning, giving up four hits and five walks. On Hutch's fleeting watch, the Yanks scored their final nine runs, seven of which were tagged to him, resulting in a rout with the football score of 22-2.

The next day, the Tigers banished Hutch to their Double A team 120 miles south, the Toledo Mud Hens. "I've never had trouble like this before," Hutch told the *New York Herald Tribune*. "Control is the one thing which never bothered me." He refused to admit that pressure could crack his code of determination. "I'm not trying too hard to live up to all those headlines," he said. "I just cannot explain it." "He should get plenty of work at Toledo," Tigers' skipper Del Baker told *The Sporting News*. "That's what he needs to regain control."

The strategy eventually worked. Over the next two and a half months, Hutch went 9-9 for the last-place Mud Hens, emerging as the team's lone American Association All Star. He rebounded to Detroit on July 21, posting a 3-6 record for the fifth-place Tigers. Thus began his lengthy major league ascendance.

Never blessed with a blazing fast ball, Hutch used his control and domineering glare to amass a 95-71 record (3.73 ERA) in ten seasons with the Tigers, pitching in a World Series (1940) and an All-Star game (1951). An anchor of the pitching-rich, postwar Tigers, he notched 18- and 17-win totals in 1947 and 1950, respectively, and for

If you don't work hard at this game, you might as well hang them up. Sweat is your only salvation.

Fred Hutchinson

(Opposite page) The sterling 25-7 record carved in 1938 by Fred Hutchinson in his only year pitching for the Seattle Rainiers resulted in hype of Ruthian proportions.

Clay Eals is a Seattle writer and 15-year newspaper journalist who also worked from 1990 to 2003 at the Fred Hutchinson Cancer Research Center.

Clay is finishing a biography of singer/ songwriter Steve Goodman, author of "The Dying Cub Fan's Last Request," and is researching and writing a biography of Fred Hutchinson. He can be reached at ceals@comcast.net.

Fred Hutchinson warms up after being sent down to Toledo on May 3, 1939. He went 9-9 for the last-place Mud Hens, emerging as the team's lone American Association All Star.

every three of his 591 strikeouts, he recorded only two walks (388). He completed nearly half the games he started (81 of 169). He was versatile, his .263 batting average reflecting and justifying Hutch's frequent use as a pinch-hitter. In his last at-bat as a pitcher, in 1953, he homered.

As a manager, Hutch rode a similar arc. Plucked at age 32 in mid-1952 to lead the last-place Tigers, he continued as their skipper through 1954, when he nudged the team to fifth place. After a triumphant return to Seattle, leading the Rainiers to the 1955 PCL pennant, Hutch bounced back to the bigs, piloting the St. Louis Cardinals for nearly three years and becoming NL Manager of the Year in 1957 when his Redbirds finished second.

The zenith of his time as a field general was yet to come. Hutch again helmed the Rainiers in 1959 but was tapped mid-season to lead the parent Cincinnati Reds, elevating the second-division team to the 1961 NL crown. The Reds lost the World Series in five games that year, but the berth earned Hutch esteem even greater than his phenom status of 23 years earlier. He posted three more winning seasons for Cincinnati, coming within one game of the pennant in 1964, his final year, and as a skipper ended up three games over .500 (830-827) lifetime.

The story of Hutch, however, is far more than his stats. His most memorable feats were those of character. Of an athlete driven to win. Of a tempestuous gentleman who embodied every element of that dichotomy. And, in the end, of a mortal who lived the final year of his life with the countenance of an everyday hero.

Hutch's die was cast in the southern section of Seattle, in a part of town bordering Lake Washington called Rainier Beach, where he was raised in a three-story hillside home by his parents, Joseph

and Nona Hutchinson. The boy's father was a respected family physician and surgeon with a neighborhood storefront and who did hospital work downtown. A dignified goatee decorated his no-nonsense, tobacco-chewing persona. The legendary story that defined him had "the old doctor" airing his ire over a streetcar fare hike by stubbornly walking the last half of its route in front of the car on its track, impeding its progress for the afternoon.

In his dad's work-related absences, Fred's older brothers Bill and John became deep influences. They groomed the imposing Fred for physical, if not emotional prowess. Though he was a natural righty, they posted him against a garage door and pelted him with tennis balls while he wielded a broomstick left-handed, hoping to give their slow-footed brother a jump in getting to first base.

To some young peers, he was a bully, "a brutal son of a bitch," says neighbor Roland Watson, who bitterly recalls fierce soccer games. "He kicked hell out of me and everyone else with those big boots." Fred even was expelled from his grade school for punching a shop teacher who chided him for an inability to make square corners on a wooden trivet. To others, however, Fred became a loyal protector. One friend, a news carrier whose daily batch of papers was delivered by streetcar but was continually short because the motorman stole a few copies, gleefully recalls a Saturday morning at the Rainier Beach streetcar switching station when Fred locked the motorman in an outhouse.

Though all sports beckoned, baseball soon became Fred's passion, and his family's admonition was to win and never be satisfied with less. A catcher, he sparked his grade-school teams to city championships, and he did the same at Franklin High as a pitcher. His first official mound work came after his freshman year in 1934 for Palace Fish, an American Legion squad consisting of Franklin players that went undefeated through the summer's city, state and Northwest regional playoffs.

"He could throw it where he wanted," recalls one of Fred's catchers, J.B. Parker. "He couldn't throw fast, he didn't have a great curve ball, but he had good control, and he was such a competitor that he just made himself a pitcher. I was always trying to find the weakness of the batter and work on the guy's weakness. We could find it, and Fred would exploit it."

Fred's fierceness sanded down a batter's confidence. "If a batter started to dig in with his back foot, he immediately got one thrown right at his chin," says Parker, who signaled Fred for a knockdown pitch by flicking his thumb. "The first pitch Fred would throw would be right under the guy's chin, and down he'd go, and the next time he'd get in the batter's box, he wasn't digging around with that back foot. But if it looked like he was going to, he got another one under his chin. Fred would never, never allow anybody to come in and dig in on him."

Such determination lent Fred the reputation of a "Boy Wonder Pitcher," the label used in the *Chelan Valley Mirror* for a visit by Palace Fish. His temper flared as well when the team finally fell in its march to the national Legion championship during the Western U.S. playoff in Topeka, Kansas. There, Fred won the first game (his 14th straight). But the next day, though he batted 4 for 4 with two doubles and pitched creditably in relief after the team fell behind 8-1, he couldn't single-handedly eke out a team victory.

Seattle papers labeled Fred's effort heroic but overlooked what followed. At Topeka's Jayhawker Hotel, Fred, barely 15, led his 16- and 17-year-old teammates in a tantrum. He fed coach Ralph "Pop" Reed's straw skimmer hat into a circulating fan, dropped water balloons on passers-by from his third-floor window, tore framed pictures from the walls and slipped them under rug runners where they were crushed underfoot, and tried to steal the hotel's parrot-shaped water pitchers by hiding them in players' suitcases. "It was nothing really malicious," Parker recalls. "but we were so discouraged and disgusted losing that game that we just took out our frustrations on what was close and what was there, and Fred was the ringleader. It was a frustration that he couldn't control, I guess. The thought of losing was just abhorrent to him."

Posting a 60-2 record at Franklin and dominating the summer Legion contests (his no-hitter for Gibson's Carpet Cleaners included 22 K's and hitting 4-for-6), Fred was a natural for the PCL's Seattle Indians, renamed the Rainiers early in 1938. Signing for $2,500 and 20 percent of any sale to a major league team, Fred — already dubbed "Hutch" by friends and writers alike — was ruggedly handsome, with looks likened to those of actor Spencer Tracy. The rookie was easily the biggest draw at beer baron Emil Sick's sparkling new stadium, built not much farther than a stone's throw from Hutch's alma mater.

Sick's Stadium thus became the site for a legend in the making. In July, the city learned of Hutch's brash act 180 miles south in Portland, where he halted a tense game with the bases loaded, one out, and two capable hitters, Johnny Frederick and Harry Rosenberg, on deck. He walked off the mound and into the Rainiers dugout, leaned over the water fountain, washed his face and took a drink. Returning to the mound, he struck out Frederick and induced Rosenberg to pop out. Why, L.H. Gregory of *The Oregonian* asked him later, had he interrupted the action for a drink of water? His reply was the self-assured stuff of allegory: "I was thirsty."

So at Sick's Stadium on August 12, when Hutch sought his 19th season win on his 19th birthday, a PCL-record crowd showed up. Turnstiles recorded an overflow turnout of 16,354, some fans filling the bullpens and lining the outfield fence as the first batter, San Francisco Seals center fielder Dom DiMaggio, ripped a single off Hutch. But one hour and 55 minutes later, Hutch had thrown a five-hitter, striking out three and walking six on the way to a gutsy 3-2 victory, with DiMaggio flying to left for the final out.

By the next morning, the journalistic mythmakers had Hutch squarely in sight. "The historians WHO DON'T KNOW will probably tell you he was 'cool as the proverbial iceberg.' Don't you believe one word of it," wrote Cliff Harrison of the *Seattle Star*. "The big boy was fired like one of the Queen Mary's Scotch boilers."

(Above) The catcher for Brighton Elementary, the second grade school he attended, was Fred Hutchinson (lower left).

(Left) An astounding 60-2 record as a pitcher for Franklin High School earned Fred Hutchinson a quick signing with Seattle's PCL team.

Ballyhoo over Hutch naturally spilled over into talk that he should demand a hike in his $250 monthly pay. But the response of Hutch's father underscored his son's youth as much as the family's integrity. As Emmett Watson later reported, when the doctor heard of the salary speculation, he roared at his son, "By the Lord, you're a Hutchinson! You made a bargain, and you'll stick to it, or you can pack up and move out right now."

If Hutch's Seattle season was a fairy tale, a coda hinted at the reality of his life to come. On Friday night, Oct. 7, 1938, a barnstorming major league team of mostly Cleveland Indians rolled into Seattle to play the Rainiers. The starters were Hutch and a 19-year-old fireballer who five days earlier had set a new big league record by striking out 18 batters in a game — Bob Feller. Six thousand fans

The nattily dressed Bob Feller (left) and Fred Hutchinson compare notes prior to their Oct. 7, 1938, duel at Sick's Stadium in Seattle.

If I needed one game, upon which my whole season was based, if my career depended on that one victory, I'd pick Hutch to pitch it for me.

Steve O'Neill, Detroit Tigers manager

---

streamed into Sick's for the so-called "schoolboy" duel, but it fizzled midway through. Feller tossed five-plus innings, while Hutch left after six, trailing 6-3. (The visitors eventually won, 9-8, in 10 innings.) The road ahead for Hutch was to be similarly spotty.

As Hutch stumbled in Detroit and proved fallible in Toledo the following year, his woes made for banner news back in Seattle. Royal Brougham quoted anonymous wags: "The kid's lost his nerve." "Maybe his arm has gone dead." "He is just an overrated pitcher who didn't have anything but a prayer and a million dollars worth of luck." Brougham even half-seriously suggested that Emil Sick buy him back. "Maybe all Hutch needs is a few of Ma Hutchinson's home-cooked meals and a friendly pat on the shoulder. If Del Baker is tired of looking at him, we'll take the boy off his hands, won't we, mates?"

Hutch's 1940 performance was not a big improvement: 3-7 with Detroit, and the reverse for the Buffalo Bisons, the Tigers' new Double-A affiliate. Even his one-inning stint in the World Series, while not crucial to the Tigers' 4-0 sixth-game defeat or the overall outcome, was marred by a homer over the left field fence by Cincinnati hurler Bucky Walters. Talk turned to whether Hutch should revert to his childhood positions of outfield or first base, so that he might play daily. But then came a 1941 Bisons season in which he bettered his heady Rainiers record: 26-7, 31 complete games, 171 K's against only 47 walks, and a 2.44 ERA.

Hitting in 72 games, twice the number in which he pitched, Hutch batted .385, with 13 doubles, a triple, two homers and 23 RBI. The International League MVP was a sure bet to join the Tigers full-time in 1942.

But as with Bob Feller, Hank Greenberg, and scores of other big leaguers, that was not to be. After the Pearl Harbor attack, Hutch sidestepped the draft by joining a Navy physical conditioning program led by heavyweight boxing champ Gene Tunney. (Look for Hutch's uncredited enlistment cameo with Feller in newsreel footage in the 1992 film "A League of Their Own.") As one of the Navy's "Tunney fish," Hutch played for four years on teams in Norfolk, Seattle and Honolulu. (He also married a high school girlfriend, Patsy Finley.) Playing outfield as much he pitched, he told *The Sporting News*, "When the war is over, I want a real try for about three or four years just to see whether or not I really can pitch major league ball. If I can't pitch, and if I'm not too old, then I'd like to try it in the outfield. ... I like to hit that ball, you know, but I like to throw it, too. It's a lot of fun to fool a smart batter."

With World War II's end, Hutch plunged into such fun. Joining other servicemen in returning to former teams, Hutch entered the most stable period of his playing career, sticking with pitching and winning 87 games for the Tigers (against 57 losses) from 1946 to 1951. With Hal Newhouser, Dizzy Trout, and Virgil Trucks, Hutch anchored a powerful staff and pitched many crucial games.

Perhaps his biggest was a startling, 8-0 home victory over New York on July 18, 1947, after a one-month hiatus due to shoulder pain — a gem in which Hutch faced 28 batters, gave up two singles, struck out eight, walked none, batted 3 for 4, and denied the Yanks an American League-record 20 consecutive wins. Such performances stirred Steve O'Neill, Hutch's manager at Detroit in 1946-48, to unqualified praise. "If I needed one game upon which my whole season was based, if my career depended on that one victory," O'Neill said, "I'd pick Hutch to pitch it for me."

Tenacity became Hutch's identity and his "angry scowl," as Emmett Watson labeled it, a fearsome calling card. After a bad outing, the dozen light bulbs lining the narrow tunnel to the Briggs Stadium clubhouse fell victim to his fists. He unleashed similar fury at other ballparks. "I always know how Hutch did when we follow Detroit into a town," Yankees catcher Yogi Berra classically observed. "If we got stools in the dressing room, I know he won. If we got kindling, he lost."

Nicknamed "The Bear," Hutch earned the moniker in part from a spring-training incident in Lakeland in which he wrestled the real thing. "They had a little sideshow circus at the ballpark, and they had a bear there," recalls Virgil Trucks. "This bear was staked out by the trainer, but the bear broke the stake and got loose and was coming toward Fred — and Fred just grabbed him by the throat and the neck, had an arm around his neck. He probably didn't weigh any more than Hutch did, but you know bears, they got claws and everything else they can retaliate with. But that didn't bother Fred. The trainer came over and said,

'Hey, man, you let go of my bear. You're gonna kill him.' He probably would have, but Fred said, 'You get him away from me. He might kill me, too.' But he held on to him. That bear couldn't do nothin'. Oh, he was really strong."

Hutch's strength was endorsed in 1947 by his teammates, who elected him their delegate to the fledgling player union, and in 1948 by his foes, who elevated him to AL player rep. In four-plus years in that post, he helped secure from owners a $25-per-week spring-training expense fund, a $5,000 minimum salary, and designation of radio and TV All Star Game and World Series proceeds to the players' pension fund.

His player-rep stint ended only because of a further promotion in July 1952, to management. He had pitched three innings in the previous year's All-Star Game, and the press was enamored of his control, Lyall Smith of the *Detroit Free Press* tagging him "baseball's most amazing modern pitching personage." But Hutch was undergoing the worst arm trouble of his career as the Tigers stagnated in last place. Five weeks shy of his 33rd birthday, Hutch was hired to replace popular skipper Red Rolfe. Though he pitched and pinch-hit in 21 more games through the 1952 and 1953 seasons, Hutch largely devoted himself to managing, inching the cellar dwellers to sixth place in 1953 and fifth in 1954, and nurturing promising rookies, such as 18-year-old future Hall of Famer Al Kaline.

"The one thing he demanded was a 100 percent effort, no alibi-ing at all," recalls Kaline, who never played a game of minor league ball. "He was a guy who didn't like to be embarrassed, and maybe that one word might be what he really stood for. He wanted his teams to be competitive and not embarrass themselves when they play. If they lose, fine. Lose in the right way. But don't embarrass yourself. ... When you played for him, you knew what to expect. There was no behind the back. He let you know, and you knew where you stood all the time, which is really what anybody really likes to know. He was an up-front type guy."

Up front for fans to see was Hutch's fiery temper, vented not at his or opposing teams' players so much as at the men in blue. *The Sporting News* delighted in reporting that Hutch's first managerial beef with an umpire came just 26 minutes into his first game on the job. Hutch lost the appeal but stayed in the game — which was not his fate in countless later beefs in which umps gave him the boot.

When Hutch resigned his Detroit post after the Tigers denied him a two-year contract at the end of 1954, he embraced an offer by Seattle GM Dewey Soriano, a childhood pitching chum, to manage the team on which he earned his first national fame in 1938. Aware of Hutch's famous fury, Soriano installed at Sick's Stadium a heavy punching bag on which was painted the glowering cartoon face of an umpire. "The punishment the bag took was comparatively light," joked *The Sporting News*, because despite 67 player transactions and no 20-game winner or .300 hitter, Hutch pieced together a ragtag Rainiers team that ran away with the 1955 PCL title.

Nevertheless, Hutch ached to return to the bigs. He

After World War II, Hutchinson came into his own as a big-league pitcher, compiling a record of 87-57 for the Detroit Tigers.

switched to the National League when he hired on as St. Louis skipper from 1956 through 1958, witnessing landmark feats of future Hall of Famer Stan Musial, including his NL record-breaking 823rd straight game. Plans for another Musial milestone wound up altered by Hutch's winning resolve. On May 13, 1958, the Cardinals had opted to sit "The Man" from the last game of a series at Chicago's Wrigley Field so that he could record his 3,000th hit back home. But with the Redbirds trailing 3-1 in the sixth, Hutch needed a pinch-hitter. Musial obliged with a double to left field, igniting a rally that turned the game in St. Louis' favor. Stopping play and jogging to second base to congratulate Musial on his feat, Hutch beamed.

He steamed, however, in his relationships with St. Louis GM "Trader" Frank Lane, a loose cannon with the press, and hands-on team owner and beer baron August "Gussie" Busch. As revealed by Emmett Watson, Hutch didn't hesitate to call his bosses onto the carpet.

In July 1957, Lane fumed when Hutch stuck with lefty Vinegar Bend Mizell to pitch to righty Gil Hodges, who homered to trigger a Brooklyn win. In a closed meeting, Hutch lashed out, "I've got to be left alone to do my job. It's hard enough to fight the opposition on the field every day without answering to my own front office in the newspapers. Criticize me all you want. Second-guess me in private. I get paid to take that. But when your criticism hits every newspaper in the country, it can wreck the morale of this ball club. That's one thing we can't stand."

One year earlier, Busch had ordered Hutch to insert awkward first baseman Tom Alston into the Cards lineup, and the manager refused, telling the owner during a meeting with Lane, "Mr. Busch, do you want me to say what I really think or what you want to hear? If I wanted to play a clown, I'd go hire Emmett Kelly." After Hutch left the room, Lane told Busch, "That man is worth a million dollars to you because he always tells the truth."

He was a guy who didn't like to be embarrassed, and maybe that one word might be what he really stood for.

He wanted his teams to be competitive and not embarrass themselves when they play. If they lose, fine. Lose in the right way. But don't embarrass yourself.

Al Kaline, who played for Fred Hutchinson in 1953-54

Opening day for the 1955 Seattle Rainiers carried special excitement, as it marked Fred Hutchinson's return to the team for which he had pitched brilliantly 17 years prior.

On May 13, 1958, after pinch-hitting a double for his 3,000th career hit, Stan Musial (far left) receives congratulations from his manager, Fred Hutchinson, as photographers record the moment and umpires stand by.

All I got to say to that is if somebody bumps your head, the only thing to do is bump back.

Fred Hutchinson

The sad truth, however, was that by the end of 1958, the Cardinal team that had climbed to second place under Hutch the year before had slumped to fifth, and ten games before the season's end Hutch became Busch's sacrificial lamb. Welcomed back to Seattle, he took the helm of the PCL Rainiers in 1959 and was cajoled to serve as GM as well. By this time, though, long-independent Seattle had linked with the Cincinnati Reds, and when the parent team foundered in seventh place in July and the brass wanted to replace Mayo Smith, they called on Hutch.

Hutch's years with Cincinnati were to be both his most challenging and triumphant. He failed to take a team loaded with talent above fifth place in 1959 or sixth in 1960. Relatively inexperienced and indifferent about racial sensitivity, the ties he forged with African American stars Vada Pinson and Frank Robinson were labored and distant. But on the plus side, the Reds were ready for a surprise.

"I like to win," Hutch told players his first day at Crosley Field (as quoted by pitcher and author-on-the-side Jim Brosnan). "That's the only way to play this game. To win. We're all like that. ... Some people say you've been playing a little too conservative, that you don't bump heads enough on the field. All I got to say to that is if somebody bumps your head, the only thing to do is bump back. Now, I'm not going to say to you pitchers that you should knock somebody down just because they're takin' a shot at you. I can't say that, and I won't say that. But I don't care if you brush a hitter back once in a while. Just to let 'em know you're out there. ... I'm glad to be up here with you. We're going to start winning. We might as well start tonight."

When they truly started winning was in 1961. No one had pegged them as contenders, but Hutch achieved "my biggest thrill in baseball, so far" by leading the Reds to a 93-61 season and the NL flag. The night of the clincher, more than 30,000 people mobbed Cincinnati's Fountain Square as an ebullient Hutch stepped off the team bus, hoisted the arm of General Manager Bill DeWitt, and joined a players' party at the nearby Netherland Hilton. Once again, he was named NL Manager of the Year.

The celebration was short-lived, though, as in the World Series the Reds ran into one of the best-ever Yankee teams, sparked by the Maris/Mantle home-run derby that resulted in the asterisked breaking of Babe Ruth's season record. Cincinnati dropped the tilt 4-1, but Hutch nevertheless strode to the Yankee dressing room to congratulate winning skipper Ralph Houk. The AP photo of the encounter, which ran in hundreds of newspapers the next morning, said it all — Houk giddy with laughter, and Hutch in equal parts grin and grimace. Given his mental makeup, Hutch's expression was as brave as humanly possible.

The Reds carved a record equally impressive during the new, 162-game schedule of 1962 yet fell to third place. In 1963, when Hutch guided Pete Rose to Rookie of the Year, the team won ten more games than it lost but slipped two slots to fifth. Attention turned to the singular personality of Hutch — headlined as "Baseball's Angriest Man" in a lengthy *Climax* magazine profile, "explosive" in a *Sport* magazine feature, and "Angry boss of the Reds" in a *Look* magazine photo essay. Writers also enjoyed toying with a quote about Hutch that Emmett Watson first brought to national attention in 1957: "He's really kind of a happy guy inside," observed broadcaster and former catcher Joe Garagiola, "only his face doesn't know it."

The finality of fate marked his face and brought him back to Seattle in 1964. A week before New Year's, Hutch felt soreness and swelling on the right side of his neck. From the home he had made in Florida for 15 years, he flew to his hometown to be examined by his surgeon brother, Bill. The diagnosis was unequivocal: the 44-year-old Hutch, a smoker of three to four packs of cigarettes a day since his Navy stint two decades prior, had inoperable lung cancer. To many, the notion that this relatively young and burly, 6-foot-1, 210-pound "Bear" could be so easily cut down was inconceivable.

His honesty and courage were reflected in a January 3 press conference in the Seattle office of his old friend Dewey Soriano. There he divulged his disease to the world, and — just eight days prior to the first Surgeon General's Report on Smoking and Cancer — it became big national news. As Hutch spoke, his matter-of-fact tone belied his heartbreaking words. "It's like having the rug jerked out from under you," he said. "You're feeling fine, then somebody tells you that you have cancer. You just don't know what to think. ... Naturally, with the thing like this, you're bound to be concerned. But you don't feel you're alone in it, either."

He was anything but alone in 1964. Fitting in radiation

and rest, Hutch surrounded himself with Reds players and staff. To supervise at spring training, he perched in a lifeguard chair and tooled around in a golf cart. In the regular season, Cincinnati became a contender, with Hutch a resolute presence, moving all who saw or came in contact with him to introspection or tears. "I have a hunch that God sends cancer only to those who can handle it," wrote columnist Bill Gleason of the *Chicago American*, "those like Hutch, who, in their handling of it, ennoble us all."

Hutch's relentless weight loss and emaciation were hard to miss. By his 45th birthday on August 12, when the Reds feted him with a 500-pound cake and color TV in a pre-game tribute, his left eye, drooped by a distended tumor, jarringly did not match his right. "What a lucky man I am," he intoned into a microphone that carried his voice to the 18,000 fans. The next day, he officially took a leave of absence, as coach Dick Sisler stepped in as acting manager.

The same month, Hutch graced *True* magazine with an "as told to" essay co-written by Al Hirshberg, "How I Live with Cancer." Stunningly detailed and frank, the 6,000-word article traced Hutch's discovery of the disease, his treatments, and his attitude toward it all. Laced with humility and gentle humor, the piece was comforting, as Hutch professed to worry more about the Reds' chances in 1964 than his own diagnosis: "If I was going to die, of course, worrying wouldn't save me. And if I was going to live, worrying was a waste of time. One thing was sure. I wasn't going to worry myself to death." The article was yet another courageous act in the face of certain demise. He even donated the $1,000 fee to a cancer research fund.

Hutch returned to Crosley Field on October 4, when, in a 10-0 drubbing by the collapsed Philadelphia Phillies, his Reds lost the 1964 pennant. In the clubhouse afterward, Sisler nodded in Hutch's direction and told reporters, "I'm only sorry we couldn't have won it for that gentleman there." Perhaps coldly but true to the winning drive he tried to instill, Hutch replied, "I'm only sorry they couldn't have won it for themselves."

Little more than a month later, on November 12 at a hospital near his Florida home, Hutch died. His body was flown to Seattle for a November 16 funeral at Rainier Beach Presbyterian Church across the street from his boyhood home and burial in nearby Renton.

But Hutch lives on. In February 1965, *Sport* magazine named him "Man of the Year." Sportswriters created the Hutch Award, whose first winner was Mickey Mantle. Honoring perseverance in the face of adversity, the Seattle-based award luncheon raises hundreds of thousands of dollars each year for the renowned Fred Hutchinson Cancer Research Center, founded in Hutch's name and opened by his brother, Bill, in 1975 with Joe DiMaggio and President Ford as guests. Bob Feller, who has twice graced Hutch Award festivities, uses Hutch-like bluntness to describe the beneficiary: "Nothing does more public good."

When Seattle's Safeco Field opened on July 15, 1999, a diamond-shaped banner that featured Hutch in his 1938 pitching form covered the infield. Hutch's 5-1/2-year-old

BY FRED HUTCHINSON
as told to Al Hirshberg

(Right) With the word "cancer" in screened headline type, the first page of Fred Hutchinson's 6,000-word, first-person article in the August 1964 *True* magazine signaled the ravages of the disease that soon would kill him.

(Below) This PCL game between the Seattle Angels and Hawaii Islanders raised funds to build the cancer research center bearing Hutch's name.

grandson Joey, in a bright red replica 1955 Rainiers hat and jersey, became the first person to run the bases. Also unveiled that day were stanchions at the end of every row of the posh stadium's seats — with Hutch in mid-windup depicted permanently in bas-relief on each one.

Five months later, on December 24, the eve of the new millennium, the *Seattle Post-Intelligencer* named Hutch the city's Athlete of the 20th Century, an eye-popping pick given that he was a pro player and manager in Seattle for just two and a half years. "No local athlete has been more revered than Hutch," reported Dan Raley. "Hutchinson was a leader, and there was never a question. He led people to championships. ... He led us to tears, sharing his own struggle with cancer in a very public and heroic manner."

Seattle Mariners center fielder Ken Griffey Jr., who had belted 398 homers for the team but had issued an unpopular — and, some said, crude — demand to be traded to a "winner," placed second to a man whom many regarded as one of the game's preeminent winners. ⚾

For more information on Fred Hutchinson and the cancer research center that was named for him, visit <http://www.fhcrc.org>.

A man named Sick made Seattle well

For 27 years, the Rainiers brought baseball home

By DAN RALEY

Home plate is still there. It sits in its actual spot in front of a busy South Seattle hardware store, accompanied by a plaque and small silhouette of a baseball player, barely noticeable to the person hurrying to pick up a gallon of paint or a bag of fertilizer.

As people wander aimlessly in and out of this place, most have no idea that the great Rogers Hornsby stood on the very spot, casually handing over his lineup card or bending the ear of some umpire. They may not know that a teen-age Fred Hutchinson spent a splendid summer peering intently at a catcher's mitt, mesmerizing his hometown if not all of pro baseball with each quality pitch. They might be oblivious that Leo Lassen's staccato voice magically carried from the general vicinity to every corner of the city, creating an unforgettable Seattle sound.

If ever there was a historical landmark for baseball in Seattle, this was it. Yet it's all gone now, unable to blunt urban sprawl, overrun by aisles of lumber, lawn mowers, and new sinks, wiped away by the inevitable arrival of major league baseball.

This obtrusive home-improvement center was once Sick's Stadium, from 1938 to 1964 home to the Seattle Rainiers, one of minor league baseball's most beloved and successful franchises, a place and a team that made people sit back and relish the game.

These Rainiers, funded and christened by a local brewery owner and some of the most hallowed members of the Pacific Coast League, were in operation for 27 seasons, a perfect fit for the Northwest. Playing against the backdrop of Mount Rainier looming over the right center-field fence like some oversized postcard, Seattle fans and players held a shared sense of joy as they gathered in a ballpark that resided on the aptly named Rainier Avenue South.

"I wish everybody who played ball could have played in Seattle," said Rainiers centerfielder Jim Rivera, the 1951 Pacific Coast League Most Valuable Player and later a member of the pennant-winning 1959 Chicago White Sox.

Five times the Rainiers led all of minor league baseball in attendance, pulling in a franchise-best 548,368 in 1947, and another 545,434 in 1949. They often outdrew several big league franchises before finally proposing that they become one, a request that was considered and denied. Five times they won the Pacific Coast League championship, giving Seattle, however far removed from the Eastern baseball mainstream, something to brag about.

At times when Hutchinson was pitching, such as the night he successfully went for his 19th victory on his 19th birthday in 1938, there was so much demand for seating, the outfield was roped off, allowing fans to huddle on the grass and reach for newly created ground-rule doubles that might be hit to them.

Emil Sick lorded over his franchise, despite knowing next to nothing about baseball. He'd jumped in for the adventure. He was a Tacoma-born, Stanford-educated man and had assumed control of his father's brewery holdings in the Northwest and western Canadian provinces, turning the business into the largest of its kind worldwide, annually producing a million barrels and $20 million in revenues.

While Sick was experiencing a financial boon selling his post-Prohibition alcohol, Seattle's pro baseball interests had gone as stale as flat beer. For nearly five decades, various teams had been in operation in the city, usually intriguing the masses and then losing them due to some calamity, such as a war or stock market crash or arson fire, with championships alternating with desperate cries for monetary support.

In 1937, the Seattle Indians were at the end of their tether as the city's PCL entry, nearing bankruptcy and eviction, playing in a converted football field, and drawing agonizingly little support from the local populace. Things were so bad that between games of the season-ending Sunday doubleheader at Civic Stadium, federal treasury agents, state patrol officers, and even someone representing the city simultaneously raided the ticket windows,

A late 1940s view of Sick's Stadium, after its apostrophe was moved one digit to the right. Originally, the stadium was named in sole recognition of owner Emil Sick. But he later gave the name a plural possessive to reflect family ownership of the team.

(Opposite page) The always resplendent Emil Sick, savior of Seattle baseball, enjoys a night at the ballpark.

Dan Raley has been a *Seattle Post-Intelligencer* sportswriter for the past 26 years, forced to choose this career path when his Charlie Sheen "Wild Thing" impersonation as a high school pitcher failed to inspire a pro career.

The beloved Rainiers manager Jack Lelivelt (right) takes a break with the Seattle Post-Intelligencer's legendary sports editor, Royal Brougham, at 1939 spring training, Anaheim.

This 1938 press pass marks the beginning of the greatest era of minor-league baseball in Seattle. Leo Lassen, sports reporter for the Seattle Post-Intelligencer, served as the play-by-play announcer starting in 1931 for the Seattle Indians and then the Rainiers. The card, issued at the beginning of the season before the opening of Sick's Stadium, includes an artist's rendering indicating "Sick's Rainier Park" as the name for the ballpark. But "Rainier" never appeared on the ballpark itself.

sweeping up what little cash was available, and trying to square outstanding bills run up by the club's management. Indians chief Bill Klepper had already announced the team was up for sale, and nobody wanted to be left with mere IOUs. Baseball was in bad shape in Seattle. Again. Paradoxically, a man named Sick made it well overnight.

Within two months of the money grab, Sick had purchased the Indians after being encouraged to save the summertime game in the Northwest by a good friend, fellow brewer and New York Yankees owner Col. Jacob Ruppert. There wasn't much money to be had in this venture, but it was great fun. Beer hadn't made Ruppert famous; but baseball did, particularly through his well-publicized contract dealings with one Babe Ruth.

Sick was eager to climb up onto this stage. He made an immediate impression by paying off the considerable franchise debt, and then by building an attractive, art deco-style stadium within six months with nearly $500,000 of his own money, and finally by promising to provide some new baseball heroes. His team would be called the Rainiers, named after his beer, which was named after that mountain, which was named after an English explorer.

This type of team typically revolved around a roster of players that had either failed to stick in the big leagues or were convinced they were on their way up and ready to land there soon. In contrast, Sick turned to the surrounding working-class neighborhoods and unearthed local talent that paid huge dividends. Among his finds were outfielder Edo Vanni and Hutchinson. They were local players who would generate nonstop newspaper headlines and help him sell that many more tickets. The owner encouraged Hutch to stay at home rather than sign directly with some big league club, and he wooed Vanni, also a shifty running back and accurate place-kicker, away from the University of Washington football team.

"Mr. Sick was the savior of baseball in Seattle," Vanni said in later years. "When he bought the ball club, baseball was at rock bottom. He built the ballpark, never asked

anybody for any money, paid for it himself. It was one of the nicest in minor league baseball. It had the best playing field. There wasn't a weed in that place. Everything was first class, the ballpark, ushers, parking guys, everything."

Hutchinson was so ready for pro baseball that he enjoyed just one sensational season at Sick's Stadium. The place usually was sold out whenever the guy with the droopy hound-dog face and volcanic temper was on the pitching mound. He was the South Seattle doctor's kid, a fearless competitor who did not have to be encouraged to knock someone down. He was a righthander so prepared for the moment that he won 25 of 32 pitching decisions, garnering him *The Sporting News* Minor League Player of the Year honors in 1938.

The Detroit Tigers subsequently acquired Hutch in a blockbuster winter-meeting trade after the Rainiers considered nearly a half-dozen other offers. The American League team forked over four players, including longtime starting center fielder Joyner "Jo-Jo" White, and $50,000 cash to complete the deal. The Pittsburgh Pirates had proposed exchanging double the amount of people for the Seattle pitcher, but the best one, first baseman Gus Suhr, said he wouldn't report, scrapping that proposal. Fans were sad to see Hutchinson leave, but the swap brought them enough talent to win three consecutive PCL championships before World War II and the dilution or abandonment of baseball at every level.

Vanni, 88, remains the only living member of the original Rainiers. He resides not far from where Civic Stadium once stood in the heart of the city, holding up his end as the curator of some of Seattle's oldest and most glorious baseball memories. He was the Rainiers' original

Posing at Sick's Stadium are the 1939 PCL-championship Seattle Rainiers, winners of the first of three straight Rainiers flags and of Seattle's first PCL pennant since the city's first PCL-leading team, the 1924 Seattle Indians.

right fielder, an early-day Ichiro, someone who would drive other teams crazy by slapping the ball anywhere for a hit and disrupting defenses as a baserunner. He was a little guy who would never back down from a fight if he felt it was necessary to the outcome of the game.

He saw it all unfold, this blossoming relationship between baseball and Seattle. He was a clubhouse boy for the old Seattle Indians, working the dressing area at now-defunct Dugdale Park in 1934 when Babe Ruth and a bunch of barnstorming big leaguers showed up for an off-season exhibition game on their way to Japan, rubbing up against the game's great ones. As a Rainier, he was Hutchinson's roommate and sounding board. They were two feisty local guys unable to wait for the next ball game, always plotting ways to get ahead.

"Hutch was tough," Vanni said. "They used to knock me down and he'd say, 'Wait till that son of a bitch's best hitter comes up and I'll knock him down.' Or he would get on my ass and say, 'How can you let a pitcher get on you like that? Why don't you drag bunt and run it up his ass?' That's how he was." After the 1940 season, *The Sporting News* reported the Pirates were willing to pay Seattle $100,000 for Vanni, with the ballplayer receiving a fourth of the cash.

The outbreak of World War II, however, stunted his career. After three years in the Navy, Vanni never captured his former glory or made it to the majors. Instead, Vanni finished his career as a playing manager in baseball's lower levels in the Northwest before returning first as a coach and then as the final field manager for the Rainiers.

Baseball took off in a big way in Seattle largely because the cast of talented, larger-than-life characters in uniform was constantly replenished. They weren't good enough to make a big splash in the big leagues, but the local fans worshipped them. Lassen, the broadcaster with a rat-a-tat delivery and considerable imagination, brought them all to life over the airwaves. Fans grew attached to the creatively christened Dick "The Needle" Gyselman, "Coffee Joe" Coscarart, "Broadway Bill" Schuster (also known as "Schuster the Rooster"), Alan "Inky" Strange, Paul "Pops" Gregory, Bill "High Pockets" Lawrence, "Farmer" Hal Turpin, and, best of all, "Kewpie" Dick Barrett.

Lawrence was a lanky 6-foot-4 player who could run like a gazelle, and was considered by some to be one of the best defensive center fielders to play the game at any level. If the ball were hit inside the outfield fences, he'd likely run it down. He would turn to Vanni in right and Jo-Jo White in left, tell them each to guard their respective foul lines, and assure them he'd catch everything else. If only Lawrence could have hit much, he wouldn't have been in Seattle long.

"I saw a lot of center fielders, and I worked for the Houston Astros and was in the Astrodome for 34 years, and the best outfielder I ever saw was Bill Lawrence," said Morris "Buddy" Hancken, who was part of the Detroit trade for Hutchinson as a catcher and later a big league bullpen coach. "I saw all the great ones. No one ever hit one over his head and kept it in the park."

Barrett played 28 seasons of pro ball, 11 of them in Seattle. With his round physique and bald head, he more

Notables on the 101-73 team: (Top row, from left) Mike Hunt, fourth; Dewey Soriano, fifth; Bill Lawrence, seventh; manager Jack Lelivelt, eighth; Dick Gyselman, 11th; and Paul Gregory, far right. (Bottom row, from left) George Archie, first; Jo-Jo White, third; Alan Strange, fourth, Edo Vanni, fifth; Hal Turpin, seventh; and Dick Barrett, ninth.

"Kewpie" Dick Barrett (above), emits an uncommonly serious stare as "Broadway Bill" Walker strolls by in 1939. (Right) Bill "High Pockets" Lawrence, one of the best defensive centerfielders ever, goes after a foul fly ball at Sick's Stadium. (Below) A 1947 card signifies membership in a fan club for Joyner White, the "JoJo Juniors."

closely resembled the local bartender or butcher or someone sitting in the stands watching him play. But the righthander was as competitive as anyone who had a washboard stomach, mixing two different curveballs with great effectiveness and posting seven 20-win seasons for the Indians and Rainiers. He was so good in 1942, compiling a 27-13 record, that he was named *The Sporting News* Minor League Player of the Year. He threw a seven-inning perfect game in 1948, near the end of his time in Seattle. His love for a post-game alcoholic beverage might have kept him from spending much time in the big leagues.

White, a Georgia man with a slow, garbled drawl and folksy charm, hardly sulked after moving from Detroit and the majors to the Rainiers. Shipped to a faraway city with Hancken, first baseman George Archie, and pitcher Ed Selway as payment for Hutchinson, White was the beneficiary of being better compensated, with a $10,000-per-season salary in Seattle, a good $2,000 more than his best year in the Motor City. He had a bigger following among his Rainiers fans, feted with his own fan club. People were drawn to his daredevil base-running style: he had a hook slide similar to his hero, fellow Georgian Ty Cobb, and would repeatedly kick-slide a ball out of an infielder's glove with a move he perfected on his own. He could routinely score from second base on a groundout and leg out inside-the-park home runs with the best of them. White later served as Rainiers manager, brought back by popular demand, before he was fired when it became apparent that the move didn't work well at all.

There were 19 different Rainiers managers. None brought more joy and sadness than the first, Jack Lelivelt. A former big league player, Sick hired him on Ruppert's recommendation, and was rewarded with a runner-up finish and then two PCL championships. He was the perfect man for the job of turning the franchise around in a hurry. The Lelivelt title run included the winningest Rainiers team, one that finished 112-66 and won the 1940 title by 9-1/2 games over the Los Angeles Angels, the club he had previously guided. Tragically, the popular manager was weeks away from opening spring training with his fourth Rainiers team in 1941 when he suffered a fatal heart attack while attending a Globetrotters basketball game in Seattle. He was only 55 years old.

"Lelivelt was one of the best managers in baseball," said Vanni, who sat with him at the basketball game. "I can remember his speeches (to us). He never ridiculed anyone. If a ballplayer weren't capable of playing his kind of baseball, he'd find a place for him. He'd kept good spirit on the ball club. It was very sad when he died. He just sort of slumped over, and that was it."

There wasn't much time to mourn. The Rainiers had to find a new leader with spring camp fast approaching. Always thinking of ways to make a big splash with his baseball team, Sick sent word to Babe Ruth, retired six years as a player, that there was a managerial vacancy in Seattle. Suffering from the flu at the time the telegram arrived, the Bambino said through his wife from New York

OFFICIAL BATTING ORDER

SEATTLE	Pos.	OPPOSITION	Pos.
1. Grabowski	SS		
2. Goldsberry	1B		
3. Rivera	CF		
4. Judson	LF		
5. Montalvo	C		
6. McGhee	RF		
7. Kismer	3B		
8. Hemner	2B		
9. Hall	P		

Rogers Hornsby

(Far left) The July 14, 1951, lineup card was filled out by one of the majors' greats — and then-Rainiers manager — Hall of Famer Rogers Hornsby, who (near left) hits fungoes during batting practice.

that he wasn't interested in the job. He might have been a little gun-shy after facing several rejections before and with owners convinced the free-spirited one couldn't be a good leader. But a few days later, Ruth reconsidered, sending a long letter to the Rainiers owner. Unfortunately for the Babe, it was too late. Sick had moved fast, hiring one of Ruth's former Yankees teammates, Bill Skiff.

Ten years later, Sick finally had a Hall of Famer running his team. Rogers Hornsby spent the 1951 summer in Seattle, alienating nearly everyone with whom he came into contact while leading the Rainiers to their fourth pennant. He built a team around "Jungle Jim" Rivera, a man who had spent a previous year in an American military stockade on a rape charge. As long as the guy could hit, it didn't matter to Hornsby what was on his record. Rivera, a hard-playing Pete Rose type, rewarded his manager's open-mindedness with the most productive offensive season of any Rainier. He led the league with a .352 batting average and 40 doubles, and also provided 16 triples, 20 home runs, 33 stolen bases, and 112 runs batted in. Rivera was an easy choice for PCL Player of the Year.

Hornsby, however, showed little patience for his players, never leaving the dugout to make a pitching change. He simply waved for one guy to replace the other. He had no interest in interacting with a struggling hurler.

"Rogers had a fine capacity to judge player talent and somehow got the utmost out of his players," Sick wrote in his memoir. "On the other hand, Rogers was not the most tactful man. He was very outspoken and often critical when talking to the press, and to an extent our public relations suffered."

The Rainiers won a fifth and final PCL championship in 1955, and this one was as special as any of the first four. Hutchinson, the one-time pitching sensation, had returned after walking away as the Detroit Tigers manager over a

> **Rogers (Hornsby) was not the most tactful man. He was very outspoken and often critical when talking to the press, and to an extent our public relations suffered.**
>
> **Emil Sick**

Seattle **RAINIERS 1951** OFFICIAL SCORECARD

15¢

SICKS' SEATTLE STADIUM

MANUEL JAMES RIVERA
Rainier outfielder. Nickname "Jim". Born in New York City, July 22, 1923. Height 5' 11". Weight 192. Bats left. Throws left. Came to the Rainiers from Pensacola, Southeastern League. Has had only two years in organized baseball. In 1949 he signed with Atlanta of the Southern Association but was sent to Gainesville where he finished the season. Last year with Pensacola he played in 124 games and had a batting average of .338. He also drove in 135 runs.

"Jungle Jim" Rivera added undeniable excitement to the Rainiers' PCL championship year in 1951.

(From left) Broadcaster Leo Lassen and Seattle Rainiers stalwarts Ray Orteig and Artie Wilson greet fans in 1953.

Sources:

Microfilm archives of the *Seattle Post-Intelligencer* and *Seattle Times*

A private Emil Sick memoir supplied by his family

Rainiers press guides and original interviews

Materials for in-progress book about the Rainiers in concert with Dave Eskenazi

contract squabble and guided his hometown team to greatness. He didn't have a .300 hitting regular or 20-game winner. He simply pushed all the right buttons. It was a one-year deal, though, and the St. Louis Cardinals signed him to return to the majors as their leader for 1956.

Yet he would come home once more. In 1959, Hutchinson assumed the Rainiers manager's job again, thinking he might get even more involved this time and stay longer. Sick was in frail health and considering selling his holdings. The big leagues had entered the Los Angeles and San Francisco markets and diluted a league considered one step below the big leagues and one above the rest of the minors. Sick had seen his profits dwindle. There was talk that Hutch was part of a group that would purchase the Seattle franchise and revitalize it.

Hutchinson, however, didn't last the season. In the middle of the 1959 summer, the Reds coaxed him back for his third stint as a big league manager. Two years later, he had his Cincinnati squad in the World Series.

Sick got out in 1960, turning his beloved baseball team over to the Boston Red Sox. More and more independent owners were going this route as the minors became more tightly affiliated with the major leagues. Sick was promised that the team would be well stocked with players and remain the Rainiers. Keith Jackson, known for his decades of ABC-TV football broadcasts, replaced an aging Lassen in the radio booth

Over the next four years, young prospects such as Jim Lonborg, Dick Radatz, Wilbur Wood, and Rico Petrocelli made summer stops in Seattle. Their careers were just getting launched, but they didn't know that they were also part of the end of a glorious era.

In 1964, the Rainiers played their last season, with Vanni, one of the original stars, serving as manager. But the final three outs of the franchise came off the field.

First, on November 10, seven weeks after the season had ended, 70-year-old Sick died of complications from surgery in a Seattle hospital. Forty-eight hours later, a 45-year-old Hutchinson, who had stepped down recently as the Reds manager, succumbed to lung cancer at his Florida winter home. Finally, 19 days later, the Los Angeles Angels bought out the Red Sox holdings, making it clear right away that they were changing the team name from Rainiers to Angels.

That same year, the Cleveland Indians had publicly toyed with the idea of moving to Seattle but stayed put. The big leagues would turn up briefly in Seattle in 1969, and for good eight years later. Sick's Stadium would meet its wrecking-ball demise in 1979, having given way to the Kingdome, which itself eventually yielded to Safeco Field.

Today though, home plate in Sick's field is still there, pointed in a southerly direction. It's next to the pre-made sheds, over by the stacks of fencing. ⚾

(Far left) Sick's Stadium was a sorrowful sight in 1979 when it was razed for retail development. (Left) Former Rainiers pitcher Pete Jonas poses in 1999 at the location of the former ballpark's home plate at then-Eagle Hardware, now Lowe's.

Yesler Way Park, Seattle: Yesler Way, between 12ᵗʰ and 14ᵗʰ avenues. Northwestern League: Siwashes 1907-08, Turks 1909, Giants 1910-13.

Back, back, back to the ballparks

Fields where dreams took root

By DAVID ESKENAZI

Here is an album of Northwest ballparks, told by images from their heyday. As you peruse them, imagine yourself in the stands or on the fields of these cathedrals of green. Better yet, imagine yourself in the ballpark of your youth, with all of the attendant sights, sounds, and smells.

In these nine cities — Seattle, Tacoma, Spokane, Aberdeen, Wenatchee, Yakima, Portland, Salem and Vancouver, B.C. — lie much of the region's professional baseball legacy, dating back more than 115 years.

While players created most fans' memories of these fields, it was the team owners who most often built and kept them running through good times and bad.

From D.E. Dugdale and Emil Sick in Seattle to Bob Brown in Vancouver, B.C., to the McCredies in Portland, the owners were the visionaries who knew that professional baseball was a key element in building community.

This photographic sampler showcases a century of Northwest ballparks, most of which exist now only in history, or in the fading, fond memories of a few. ⚾

From this majestic view at Yesler Way Park, the Seattle Turks gave city ball fans their first of two Northwestern League pennants. This intimate neighborhood ballpark was known as the "bandbox" for its small size.

Dugdale Park*: Rainier Avenue and McLellan Street. Northwestern League: Giants 1913-17, Ballard Pippins 1914. Pacific Coast International League: Giants 1918, 1920. International Northwestern League: Drydockers 1919. Pacific Coast League: Purple Sox 1919, Rainiers 1919-20, Indians 1920-32.*

Connie Mack, the dear old chap whose leadership of the Philadelphia Athletics is a legend in baseball, helped me lay out that park. He came through Seattle in 1912, touring the country with his world's champions.

I showed him the plans for the new park, and we went over them. He gave me a lot of suggestions, and I incorporated them in the plans before we started building.

Dan Dugdale, Seattle Daily Times, July 6, 1932

Civic Field*, Seattle: Harrison Street, between 3rd and 5th avenues. Pacific Coast League: Indians 1932-38. (Shown is a late 1930s boxing set-up.) At Civic, Joe DiMaggio of the 1933-35 San Francisco Seals hit .411, and eight games of his PCL-record 61-game hitting streak came there. But Ted Williams of the 1937 San Diego Padres hit just .120 at Civic.*

This early 1950s view of Sick's Stadium looks southeast along Rainier Avenue. Cut off at the top is Franklin High School, alma mater of famed Rainiers pitcher and manager Fred Hutchinson and Chicago Cubs perennial all-star third baseman Ron Santo, who in his youth had a summer job at the ballpark. In about 1950, the park's name shifted to the plural possessive "Sicks' Stadium" to reflect family ownership.

There'll be a fanfare of trumpets this afternoon such as Seattle's baseball history never has heard before ... marking the completion of the 'New Deal' in the National Pastime here.

Seattle Post-Intelligencer, special section, June 15, 1938, the date of the first game played at Sick's Stadium

Sick's Stadium, Seattle: Rainier Avenue and McLellan Street. Pacific Coast League: Rainiers 1938-64, Angels 1965-68. American League: Pilots 1969. Northwest League: Rainiers 1972-76.

In the Pacific Northwest, nothing compared to a summer's day spent at Sick's Stadium, as in this view from the rightfield bleachers in 1960.

Y ou know what I remember about Seattle? Every time I got up to bat when it's a clear day, I'd see Mount Rainier. I'd look right over the centerfield fence. Sick's Stadium was beautiful, a great place to play.

Hillis Layne, Seattle Rainiers infielder in 1947-50, who won a PCL batting title in 1947 at .367.

Safeco Field, *Seattle: First Avenue South and Edgar Martinez Drive South. American League: Mariners 1999-present.*

Natatorium Park, Spokane: Natatorium Amusement Park, Western Extension of Boone Avenue. Pacific Northwest League: Bunchgrassers 1901-02. Pacific National League: Inlanders 1903, Indians 1903-04. Northwestern League: Indians 1916-17. Pacific Coast International League: Indians 1918, 1920.

The ballpark, facing a tall bluff on the north side of the Spokane river, seated 1,000 in its original wood grandstand. The infield was dirt. A tall Ponderosa pine served as the left-field foul pole. After fire destroyed the grandstand on July 4, 1908, its replacement seated almost 2,500.

Jim Price, Northwest baseball historian, 'Indians 100 Years' special section, the Spokesman Review, June 21, 2003

Spokane Indians Baseball Stadium / Fairgrounds Ball Park / Seafirst Stadium / Avista Stadium, Spokane: 602 N. Havana St. Pacific Coast League: Indians 1958-71, 1973-82. Northwest League: Indians 1972, 1983-present.

In the center field of Tacoma's Athletic Park stood a Bull Durham billboard that was common in minor-league parks in the early 1900s. A player who homered by hitting the sign received a five-pound carton of Bull Durham smoking tobacco. Note the sign to the right, for the grocery distributor Amocat Goods. (Amocat is Tacoma spelled backwards.)

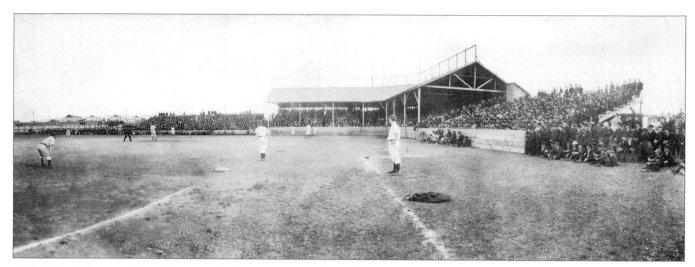

Athletic Park, Tacoma: 15*th* and Sprague. Northwestern League: Tigers 1907-17. Washington State League: Cubs 1910. Pacific Coast International League: Tigers 1918, 1920-21. International Northwestern League: Tigers 1919. Western International League: Tigers 1922.

Cheney Stadium was a model stadium for minor-league baseball when it opened in April 1960. Ben Cheney went out on a limb and guaranteed the cost and any overruns, and Concrete Tech brought its expertise to build the support structure. Amazingly, it was completed in 40-plus working days to be ready for the opener against the Portland Beavers.

Clay Huntington, chair of the committee that brought the Giants farm team to Tacoma

Cheney Stadium, Tacoma: 19*th* and Tyler. Pacific Coast League: Giants 1960-65, Cubs 1966-71, Twins 1972-77, Yankees 1978, Tugs 1979, Tigers 1980-94, Rainiers 1995-present. Many greats played here, including Gaylord Perry, Juan Marichal and Willie McCovey.

Electric Park, Aberdeen: Myrtle and Oak streets. Northwestern League: Grays Harbor Lumbermen 1906, Aberdeen Black Cats 1907, 1909, 1915, Grays Harbor Grays 1908. Washington State League: Aberdeen Black Cats 1910, 1912. Pacific Coast International League: Aberdeen Black Cats 1918.

Electric Park seated about 3,500 and overflow crowds for big games necessitated roping off the outfield. Admission cost between a dime and 50 cents, although, as South Aberdeen Swamp Hawk manager Aino 'Spike' Harkonen said with a wink, 'If some Finn was broke, we wouldn't argue about it.' Hundreds of fans would take in games from Kidder's Bluff overlooking leftfield.

Rick Anderson, sports editor, Daily World, Aberdeen, April 24, 1999

In the printed labels on these vintage postcard views, Electric Park was located in both Aberdeen and Hoquiam. In fact, Myrtle Street separated (and still separates) Aberdeen from Hoquiam, and the park was on the Aberdeen side, on the edge of Hoquiam.

Parker Field,
Yakima: Lennox Avenue and 12th. Western Int'l League: Pippins 1937-41, Stars 1946-47, Packers 1948, Bears 1949-54. Northwest League: Bears 1955-66, 1990-92. Photo circa 1951.

Parker Field was was about 330 down the lines, a legit home-run when you hit one. Left and right center were wide open. If you could run a little bit, you could get a triple.

Dario Lodigiani, manager, Yakima Bears, Western International League, 1952-53

Recreation Park in Wenatchee was a hitter's park.... The hitters would hit the ball out of there like popcorn. Still, I had some success there, going 18-9 in 1946 to help my team win the Western International League pennant.

Joe Vivalda, ace pitcher, 1946 Wenatchee Chiefs

(Above and left) ***Recreation Park***, *Wenatchee: Orondo at Cherry Street. Western International League: Chiefs 1937-41, 1946-54. Northwest League: Chiefs 1955-65.*

An evening game at Wenatchee's Recreation Park in 1963 shows off the stadium's just-installed lights.

Vaughn Street Park, *Portland: Vaughn Street, Northwest 25th Avenue and Northwest 24th Street. Pacific Northwest League: Webfooters 1901-02. Pacific Coast League: Browns 1903-04, Giants 1905, Beavers 1906-17, 1919-55. Northwestern League: Colts 1909, Pippins 1911, Colts 1912-14. Pacific Coast International League: Buckaroos 1918.*

Judge McCredie was much impressed with the new structure at the Polo Grounds in New York City, which is built in the form of an oval, and the Portland grandstand will be constructed along the same lines. It will be possible to seat 20,000 people without letting a single person on the playing field, and ground rules will be established which will allow for a home run whenever the ball is hit into the leftfield bleachers. Leftfield hitters will be the rage the coming season.

The Sporting News, Nov. 16, 1911

(Above and below) The venerable Vaughn Street Park had the longest tenure in PCL history, shortly after 1900 hosting the charter franchise Browns and Giants for three years and the Beavers for 50 more.

Multnomah Athletic Club and Stadium - Portland, Oregon

Multnomah Stadium / Civic Stadium / PGE Park, Portland: Salmon and Morrison streets, between SW 18th and SW 20th avenues. Pacific Coast League: Giants 1905, Beavers 1956-72, 1978-93, 2001-present. Northwest League: Mavericks 1973-77, Rockies 1995-2000.

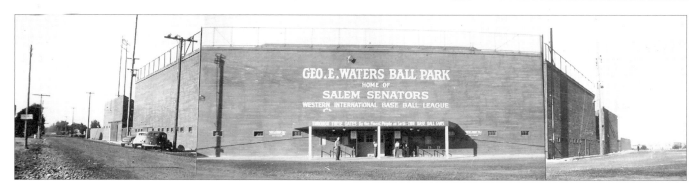

George Waters Park / Waters Field, Salem: 25th and Mission. Western International League: Senators 1940-42, 1946-54. Northwest League: Senators 1955-60, Dodgers 1961-65.

The Salem ballpark named for George Waters, shown in about 1950.

Waters Park was a pitcher's park. You really didn't have any short porches. It was about 345 down the lines and 400 to dead center. A guy earned his batting average at Waters Park. The first time I played there, Portland had sent me down to help Salem in the pennant race with Wenatchee in 1946. I got a line-drive base hit in my first at-bat. I knew better, but I led off first base a bit before pitcher Chuck Cronin was quite back on the mound. First baseman Dick Adams said, 'Hey, Spaeter,' showed me the ball, and tagged me out. They never let me forget that.

Al Spaeter, Salem Senators second baseman, 1946-1949

Robert P. Brown, PRESIDENT
James G. Potts, VICE-PRESIDENT

Harold D. Richardson, TREASURER
George Clink, SECRETARY

Athletic Park Company Limited

OFFICE AND PARK:
FIFTH AVE. AND HEMLOCK ST.

PHONE BAYVIEW 184

VANCOUVER, B. C.

Athletic Park, Vancouver, B.C.: 5th and 6th avenues, between Hemlock and Birch. Northwestern League: Beavers 1913-14, 1916-17, Champions 1915. Pacific Coast International League: Beavers 1918, 1920-21. International Northwestern League: Beavers 1919. Western International League: Beavers 1922. This letterhead was used in about 1915.

Our ball club opened the new park against Tacoma, and we drew more than 6,000 fans, a good start in a year that saw us draw 126,000 to those Northwest League games. That was a pretty fair record, by jingo, considering that Vancouver then was a town of barely 150,000 people.

Bob Brown, father of Vancouver baseball, as told to Eric Whitehead, Vancouver Province B.C Magazine, July 13, 1957

This plan for the siting of Athletic Park — printed on the back of letterhead for the Vancouver Athletic Club — indicates how the stadium was designed to fit in with the street patterns of Vancouver, B.C. The streets running vertically were (from left) Granville, Hemlock and Birch.

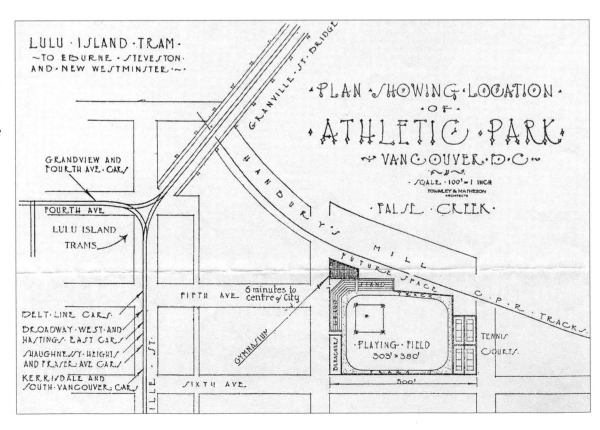

Capilano Stadium / Nat Bailey Stadium, *Vancouver, B.C.: Ontario Street at Queen Elizabeth Park. Western International League: Capilanos 1951-54. Pacific Coast League: Mounties 1956-62, 1965-69. Northwest League: Canadians 1978-present. The baby brother to Sick's Stadium, Capilano Stadium was modeled on its design. In fact, the old Sick's Stadium scoreboard is in operation today at Nat Bailey. This aerial photo was taken in 1951.*

A tree-lined hillside greeted fans at Capilano Stadium in 1960.

guess we were all looking forward, too, to the big day in June 1951, when we moved into the spanking new concrete and steel stadium on Little Mountain and an eventual place where we belonged, in the Coast League. Baseball folks downcoast got an indication themselves that year when we drew 171,000 fans to watch our Class B ball club. We'd have topped 200,000 if we had the whole season in the new stadium.

Bob Brown, as told to Eric Whitehead,
Vancouver Province B.C , July 13, 1957

The fife-and-drum corps turned out on Father's Day in 1915 when Tacoma's Tigers met the Indians in Spokane. "Iron Man" Joe McGinnity (back row, eighth from left) was among the pitchers, in a post-big-league career in the minors that stretched until age 54. Notable Spokane players included Earl Sheely (front row, sixth from left) and Ken Williams (front row, last player on right), who went on to the majors and slammed 196 homers, mostly for the St. Louis Browns.

Jim Price, a longtime copy editor and sports historian at the *Spokesman-Review* in Spokane, has been a Pacific Coast League play-by-play broadcaster and publicist, Northwest League and California League official scorer and public address announcer and a baseball beat writer. He spent 14 years as announcer and publicist for horse-racing tracks in six Western states and almost a decade as sports information director at Eastern Washington University. Marc Blau and Kevin Kalal contributed to this article.

You want stars, titles, nicknames? Tacoma's got 'em

From McGinnity to McCovey to McGwire, City of Destiny fields a baseball heritage second to none

BY JIM PRICE

When it comes to the professional baseball history of Tacoma, Washington, let's not quibble over details. Forgive those who believe there have been only two time periods, the Pacific Coast League era and the one before it. Forget pennants won, fans counted, ballpark amenities and profits and losses.

What is there to question in a city whose all-time pitching staff includes Hall of Fame members Clark Griffith, Joe McGinnity, Juan Marichal, and Gaylord Perry? Two other immortals, Walter Johnson and Willie McCovey, have worn a Tacoma uniform. So has New York Yankees star Alex Rodriguez, who's likely to make it. So too have the retired and now tarnished sluggers, Mark McGwire and Jose Canseco.

For the record, there have been two PCL eras. The first lasted barely two years, while the second stretch has been more strongly supported by the community. In 2006, Tacoma is playing its 47th consecutive season, the league's longest active streak.

Outside of the two PCL stints are 37 professional seasons that stretched from 1890 through 1951. Tacoma's teams in the Pacific Northwest League and its successors often were hobbled by inadequate financing and poor attendance. William H. Lucas managed the first team en route to becoming the region's most influential league executive in the Northwest.

Eight-five total baseball seasons have brought Tacoma several championships. The early fling with the Pacific Coast League produced the first in 1904, and the 1906 club won the Northwestern League pennant. Just before World War II, the city captured three Western International League playoff titles in four years, and since Tacoma rejoined the reborn PCL, it has taken two titles and shared two others.

After a March 14, 1890, organizational meeting in Captain Dodge's gun store at Tacoma, the City of Destiny joined Seattle, Portland, and Spokane to play the inaugural season of the Pacific Northwest League. Railroad man W.F. Carson served as president of the Tacoma franchise, and Mayor Henry Drum served on the board. Tacoma Baseball Park, built in 1885 at South 11th and L streets, became the city's first professional field. Midwest promoter John Barnes had needed fewer than six days to round up sponsorship in the region's largest cities. Barnes managed the franchise in Spokane, while Lucas, an old friend and rival, took charge at Tacoma.

The season began on Saturday, May 3, with Tacoma playing host to Seattle. Tacoma's captain, second baseman

J.J. McCabe, elected to have his team bat first. After his solo home run tied the score in the top of the ninth, the visitors scored in the bottom half to win, 7-6.

Spokane took command of the pennant race at the end of June, and finished in first by 6-1/2 games. Tacoma was second, led by former major league catcher Billy Earle, who hit .307. Teammate Frank March won 21 games and led the PNL with 197 strikeouts.

After the team declined to give Lucas a new contract, the league blacklisted him for sowing dissension, an odd charge against a man who became the game's regional czar. Without him, Tacoma won only 38 games in 1891. One of those came on May 16, when the home team beat Seattle 6-5 in a 22-inning game described at the time as the longest of all time.

In 1892, the merger between the National League and the American Association sent dozens of players back into the minor leagues. One of them was pitcher Clark Griffith. Together with outfielder Billy Goodenough — who lashed seven straight hits May 19 in Tacoma's 28-5 victory over Seattle — Griffith helped Tacoma finish second in both halves of a split season. However, the league folded before the schedule could be completed.

Tacoma participated in abortive revivals in 1896 and 1898. Early in the latter season, on May 26, Spokane's George Darby pitched a 15-0 perfect game at Tacoma.

Lucas and John McCloskey, an even better known minor league organizer, revitalized the Montana State League in 1900. While Lucas served as president, McCloskey managed Great Falls to the championship. Then they moved on, but thanks to them and Seattle's Dan Dugdale, the Pacific Northwest League was reborn on Feb. 22, 1901. Lucas was hired as the president, secretary and treasurer, while McCloskey managed Tacoma. The team became known as the Tigers, a nickname that stayed with the city's top ball clubs for half a century.

Portland dominated the first pennant race, finishing 16 games ahead of Tacoma, but Tigers third baseman Charley McIntyre, who had previously been the Montana champion, claimed the batting title, and Tigers lefthander Jimmy St. Vrain won 27 games. In 1902, when the PNL expanded to six teams, McCloskey moved to Butte, then a prosperous Montana mining center, and won the pennant, while Tacoma finished fifth.

From there, the league took an unhappy turn. In early December, Portland quit the PNL in favor of the California League, which also lined up a Seattle entry as part of launching the new Pacific Coast League. In retaliation, Lucas and his owners placed their own teams in Los Angeles and San Francisco, added a replacement in Portland, and morphed into the Pacific National League. With eight teams stretching from Southern California to Central Montana, the overstretched PNL didn't have a

chance.
By mid-August, Tacoma and Helena pulled out, and within days, the league's California teams quit, too.

On Feb. 2, 1904, the PCL, relishing its clear victory, received the blessing of the National Association and gained rights to Seattle, Portland, and Tacoma. Taking over the Sacramento franchise, the Tigers played in remodeled Tacoma Baseball Park, adding St. Vrain and outfielder Mike Lynch, another standout with the Pacific National club, to the newcomers. Tacoma won the first half of a split-season schedule, and shared the second-half title with Los Angeles before winning the playoff series, five games to four. Bobby Keefe won 34 games for the Tigers, two more than rookie Orvie Overall, while St. Vrain won 19. PCL immortal Truck Eagan claimed the second of his three straight home run titles. Small paying crowds spoiled the fun. Many people watched the games, but the majority climbed atop wood piles at a neighboring wood and coal yard and peered over the fence.

The 1905 club won the first half title again, but lost its playoff series to Los Angeles five games to one. After the season, the Tacoma club was relocated to Fresno for 1906. After two years in the new league, and one championship, it would be 54 years before they returned to the circuit.

Meanwhile, dapper Tacoma saloonkeeper George Shreeder acquired the Northwestern League's pennant-winning Everett franchise, moved it to Tacoma, and convinced Lynch to stay in town as player-manager for

Surrounding fashionable team owner George Shreeder, the 1908 Tacoma Tigers, second-place finishers in the Northwestern League, pose for a photo that gets a surreal treatment. Captain and outfielder Mike Lynch may have been Shreeder's best player, but veteran pitcher Ike Butler won 19 games.

1906. Led by Lynch (who took the batting title), and 20-game winner Ike Butler, the Tigers finished first by 8-1/2 games.

There was one sour note, although it wasn't notable at the time. On April 30, a hard-throwing Californian named Walter Johnson tried out with Tacoma. When Grays Harbor beat the teen-age righthander in an exhibition game, 4-3, Lynch sent him home, never to live that decision down.

Shreeder equipped the 1907 team with a new home, Athletic Park, at 15th and Sprague streets, and the Tigers won a league-high 90 games. But they played 13 more matches than Aberdeen, and lost eight of those, leaving the Black Cats with a higher winning percentage and the title. The season's highlight came on July 20, when Butler no-hit Seattle, gaining one of his 32 victories on the season. Butler won 19 more in 1908, but the Tigers had a hard time staying above .500 with a team that batted only .211. But one red-letter day came on Sunday, Sept. 27, when Tacoma beat visiting Spokane three times, topping the Indians 4-1 in a morning game, and then 7-0 and 7-3 in an afternoon twin bill.

After the season, Dan Dugdale lured Lynch to Seattle, paving the way for Russ Hall, who had spent two years at Butte after operating Seattle's short-lived original PCL franchise, to become Tacoma's manager. Seattle, last in 1908, finished first in 1909, while weak-hitting Tacoma wound up far behind. Butler's second no-hitter was about the only bright spot, as the 36-year-old righthander stopped Vancouver, 2-0, on April 24. A day later, Vancouver's Jack Hickey returned the favor, but the Tigers won that game, 1-0, on a three-hitter by young lefthander Jesse Baker.

Tacoma's 1910 and 1911 teams fared little better, despite the return of Lynch to manage the 1911 club. On April 18, Opening Day for the 1911 season, Victoria rookie Tom Lane no-hit Tacoma, 3-0, in a game in which he beaned Lynch and threw out his arm. He never pitched another professional game.

A poor last-place finish in 1912 ended Lynch's second tenure with the Tigers, paving the way for former major league star Joe McGinnity to become part-owner and manager. Still a useful pitcher at the age of 42, McGinnity was his own best player. Relying on slow curveballs, he won 22 games, helping the Tigers improve to 75 victories.

Unfortunately, by 1914 the Northwestern League was suffering, bogged down by lack of support from the major leagues and the public's growing interest in automobiles and motion pictures. In August, after war broke out in Europe, attendance in the league's Canadian cities fell off so badly that the season was shortened.

Tacoma's most memorable game that season came on May 9 at Tacoma, when McGinnity defeated Spokane's future Hall of Fame pitcher Stan Coveleski, 6-2, with the help of 10 putouts by left fielder Ten Million, the oddly named son of a Seattle judge. The game also saw Spokane's right fielder, George Kelly — himself headed to the Hall of Fame in the far-off future — turn a sinking liner into a

> **A poor last-place finish in 1912 ended Lynch's second tenure, paving the way for former major-league star Joe McGinnity to become part-owner and manager. Still a useful pitcher at age 42, McGinnity was his own best player.**

Mike Lynch started his playing career in Tacoma in 1901 and was part of the city's PCL championship team in 1904. The hard-drinking, redheaded outfielder managed four teams in the Northwestern League, sometimes offsetting his offensive, defensive and leadership skills with a conspicuous lack of self-control.

triple play. Another notable was Fred McMullin, in his third season as Tacoma's regular third baseman, and later to become one of eight Chicago White Sox banned for their parts in the 1919 World Series scandal.

Overshadowing each of the next four seasons were war-related issues that shrank crowds and, eventually, the pool of available players. In 1915, Victoria and Aberdeen disbanded on August 1, but Tacoma held on to win 86 games and finish second. Izzy Kaufman won 25 games, and McGinnity pitched a double-header shutout on closing day to reach the 20-win mark for the third straight year.

For 1916, after McGinnity transferred his holdings to Butte, Hall put together a new Tacoma franchise. The season only lasted until Labor Day, and Spokane easily won the pennant while Butte edged Tacoma for second place. Tigers righthander Harvey "Suds" Sutherland won a league-record 16 straight games.

Before the 1917 season, Tacoma manager Bill Leard traded jobs with Tealey Raymond, a Seattle mainstay since playing shortstop for Lynch on the 1909 NWL champion Seattle Turks, and a playing manager for Seattle since mid-1912. Sutherland pitched a 3-0 no-hit victory over Great Falls on May 8. On June 7, the Tigers enjoyed the biggest offensive show in their history, bashing 31 hits, seven by catcher Carl Stevens, to drub Butte 31-12.

Tacoma held a 2-1/2-game lead after sweeping a doubleheader on July 4. But with the U.S. now involved in the war, most minor leagues were crippled by sagging gate receipts, and the NWL called it quits on July 15. When Tacoma lost eight of its last nine games, Great Falls took the pennant. The Tigers wound up third, but outfielder Harry Harper won the batting title with a .382 average.

Between seasons, the Montana owners pulled out altogether. The remaining clubs added Aberdeen and Portland, which had lost its PCL franchise, and reorganized as the Pacific Coast International League. When play resumed in 1918, poor weather and the reduced level of play took their tolls early on; Tacoma dropped out on May 25, even though it occupied second place and Stevens (.369) was leading the hitters. The league quit on July 7.

Although the war ended that fall, pro ball remained a chancy business. The PCIL, including Tacoma, operated only on weekends in 1919, but it still folded in early June.

Tacoma was among six entries when the PCIL tried for a third time in 1920, and the league finally completed a season. The Tigers took the lead with a ten-game win streak in late July, but they then lost 12 of their last 18 to wind up fourth. They had already lost the Athletic Park stands, which burned down on May 23.

In 1921, Tacoma finished second to Yakima in both halves of a split season. Another reorganization preceded the 1922 season, as Tacoma and Vancouver joined Calgary and Edmonton in a far-flung, four-team circuit dubbed the Western International League. By mid-June, it suspended play, with Tacoma in last place.

Other than Pacific Coast League games at Seattle and Portland, the Northwest had no more professional baseball until a new Western International League was formed in 1937. Semipro ball had to fill the gap. Tacoma's hometown nine competed primarily in the Timber League, a high-quality circuit that represented the west, central, and southwestern parts of Washington.

In 1937 the WIL placed teams in Tacoma, Spokane, Yakima, and Vancouver. Lewiston, Idaho, about 90 miles south of Spokane, also agreed to participate, but it wasn't until the last moment that National Association organizer Peter B. Mitchell lined up a Wenatchee franchise to fill out a six-team field.

Tacoma banker Roger W. Peck was elected league president, and Mitchell became Tacoma's business manager. Games were played in front of a rebuilt grandstand at Athletic Park. The city's baseball fortunes immediately improved: although the Tigers never finished first, they won three playoff titles in short order. Pitcher Floyd "Lefty" Isekite and power-hitting outfielder Morry Abbott became local legends.

Willy League play started on April 27, 1937. On May 30, at Tacoma, lefthander Aldon Wilkie pitched a seven inning no-hitter to defeat Wenatchee 4-0. Wenatchee won the first half of the league's only split-season schedule, while the Tigers took the second half with a 42-25 record, finishing two games ahead of Vancouver. They then whipped Wenatchee four games to one in the playoff series. Isekite, a local product who had starred in the Timber League, won two of the four games. Infielder Harvey Storey was the team's best hitter, batting .347 with 51 doubles, 18 homers, 121 runs, 108 RBIs, and 20 stolen bases. Forty-year-old Hank Hulvey combined a 15-9 record with a league-leading 2.33 ERA.

Last in batting and fielding in 1938, Tacoma also finished last in the standings. Even so, outfielder Dave Goodman won the batting title with a .337 mark. Isekite won 16 games, took the first of his three straight WIL strikeout titles and posted a 2.01 ERA.

In 1939, a rebuilt offense vaulted Tacoma back up into second place. The Tigers clouted 108 home runs, a league

record 37 of them by Abbott, a Canadian-born former local semipro standout. Abbott also drove in 123 runs and scored 116. Isekite won 18 more games, posted a league-leading ERA, and on July 11 pitched a 3-0 no-hitter against first place Wenatchee.

In the Shaughnessy playoffs, Tacoma won three of four games from fourth-place Spokane (Abbott won the final game with a three-run, eighth inning homer), and then squared off with Wenatchee, which had beaten third-place Vancouver, four games to two. The Tigers opened the championship series with three straight victories at home. In Game Four, on Sept. 20 at Wenatchee, Isekite hooked up with future big leaguer Floyd "Bill" Bevens, who had thrown a no-hitter earlier that season. Rising to the occasions, Bevens hurled another as the Chiefs won 8-0. After Wenatchee won again in Game Five, Tacoma wrapped up the title with a 5-3 triumph in 10 innings, scoring twice on Jack Colbern's squeeze bunt.

The 1940 Tigers were preseason favorites, but wound up being hampered by injuries, finishing fourth behind an immensely talented Spokane club. In the playoffs, the Tigers, nearly back at full strength, defeated Yakima, two games to one, and then turned back Spokane, 3-2. Isekite, with an 18-9 record and a second place finish in ERA during the regular season, owned the Indians. He helped Tacoma gain a 7-5 victory when the championship series opened at Spokane's Ferris Field. After the Indians won the next two games, play shifted back to Tacoma. There, Isekite struck out 11 on the way to an 8-1 triumph to tie the series. Then the Tigers won the rubber game, 5-2.

In 1942, with world war again casting a shadow over the nation, Yakima and Wenatchee dropped out before play began, leaving only four teams. Tacoma finished second, 6-1/2 games behind Vancouver, and Abbott led the league in home runs and RBIs.

Because of manpower shortages, like many other minor leagues, the Western International League did not operate for the remainder of the war. When play resumed in 1946, it operated for the first time with eight teams. Tacoma did not field another good team until 1950, when the Tigers missed the pennant by one game.

The 1946 club played on new grounds, Tiger Park, built at 38th and Lawrence by the team's new owner, local sportsman Enoch Alexson. The Tigers finished fourth after a season marred by the Spokane team's tragic bus crash. Nineteen-year-old catcher Dick Kemper placed second in WIL batting with a .355 mark and 106 RBIs. His backup, Earl Kuper, hit .353. Lefthander Cy Greenlaw, Kuper's cousin, notched 18 victories, including a seven inning 3-0 no-hit triumph over Yakima on Memorial Day.

In 1947 Kuper won the batting crown with a record .389 mark, while Tacoma native Dick Greco, in his first full season, hit 21 home runs and drove in 102 runs. Despite the fireworks, the Tigers finished sixth. Tacoma finished fourth in 1948, when Greco batted .346 and drove in 126 runs. The club finished seventh in 1949, despite Greco's 33 home runs, 118 RBIs and 123 runs.

> **In 1939, a rebuilt offense vaulted Tacoma back up into second place. The Tigers clouted 108 home runs, a league record 37 of them by Morry Abbott, a Canadian-born former local semipro standout. Abbott also drove in 123 runs and scored 116.**

The 1949 Tacoma Tigers finished seventh in the Western International League but were buoyed by the 33 homers, 118 RBIs and 123 runs of rightfielder and Tacoma native Dick Greco.

In 1950, the Tigers, owned since 1948 by San Diego's PCL team, were a far better ball club, winning 90 games to finish one game behind Yakima. Greco enjoyed his best year, finishing second in the batting race at .360, and slamming 36 home runs (one short of Abbott's league record), and driving in another 154 runs. But after attendance skidded to 42,463 for the 1951 season, the Padres sold the debt ridden franchise to a group of Lewiston businessmen, who moved it to Idaho.

Pro ball did not return to Tacoma until 1960, two years after Brooklyn and New York had moved their National League teams to the West Coast. The Dodgers installed their top farm team in Spokane, while the Giants initially sent theirs to Phoenix. But not even the Pacific Coast League could draw big crowds to the Arizona city's ramshackle ballpark. General Manager Rosy Ryan brought the team to Tacoma, where he continued to run it.

Since being reborn with the San Francisco affiliation, Tacoma has been associated with the Cubs, Minnesota, the Yankees, Cleveland, Oakland, and Seattle.

Since being reborn with the San Francisco affiliation, Tacoma has been associated with the Cubs, Minnesota, the Yankees, Cleveland, Oakland, and Seattle. The Giants and the Cubs owned the team for six years apiece, while the working agreement with Oakland lasted 14 years. The relationship with the Mariners entered its 12th season in 2006. For more than two decades, Tacoma teams bore the nicknames of their parent club. The traditional Tigers nickname was restored in 1980, and stayed in use through 1994. Since then, they've been Rainiers, Seattle's longtime PCL nickname.

Acting on the promise of a Coast League franchise, lumber baron Ben Cheney donated $100,000 to help build an appropriate ballparl. and in 1960 Cheney Stadium was built in 105 days. Seats and light towers were acquired

from San Francisco's Seals Stadium. Well-known minor league manager Johnny "Red" Davis, who had followed the franchise from Arizona, directed Tacoma's first three PCL teams.

For that first squad, Willie McCovey played in a mere 17 games, Juan Marichal finished 11-5 before his recall to San Francisco, and Gaylord Perry pitched once near the end of the season. Helped by a second-place debut, Tacoma drew 270,024 fans, the most in the PCL.

In 1961, the Giants finished first in attendance again and did equally well in the standings, where their 97-57 record was the best in the city's modern history. Perry and Ron Herbel each won 16 games, and versatile Dick Phillips was the league MVP.

Perry led the PCL in ERA with 2.48 in 1962, a season in which Tacoma shared second place with Salt Lake City. After the league expanded to ten teams and split into divisions for 1963, the Giants took third in the North. They had their first losing Triple-A season in 1964, when the PCL grew again, this time to 12 teams.

Tacoma did not have another contender until former big league standout Whitey Lockman managed the Cubs-owned 1969 aggregation to the championship. At that point, the league was back down to eight teams. Tacoma easily won the Northern Division, and cut down Southern Division winner Eugene, three games to two, in the playoffs. Lockman was named manager of the year.

After a dismal 1970 season, Tacoma had the league's best record in 1971, before falling to Salt Lake City in the playoffs. Adrian Garrett won the home run title with 43, the league's top figure since 1957. Burt Hooton, on the verge of starting a fine big league career, set a PCL record by striking out 19 Eugene batters on Aug. 17.

Despite its on-field success, the Cubs decided to move their top farm club to Wichita. Stepping into the breach, Stan Naccarato, an enthusiastic former professional pitcher who ran a local shoe store, raised $100,000 with a 16-hour telethon that convinced 21 businessmen to support a community-owned team. The concept survived 19 years. Naccarato became president and general manager, stayed on the job for most of that time and won several awards.

Thus saved from oblivion, Tacoma's first working agreement was struck with Minnesota. After two losing seasons, Cal Ermer managed three straight teams to second place. Bob Gorinski's 28 homers and 110 RBIs led the league in 1976, when the Twins lost a one-game division playoff game to Hawaii. In 1977, Randy Bass hit four home runs for Tacoma's Twins in a June 9 game against Phoenix.

After a losing season in 1977, the Yankees moved in for a one-year affiliation. Larry McCall gave Tacoma its fourth ERA leader in five years, and future major league general manager Jim Beattie pitched a no-hitter as the Yankees won the Western Division by 4-1/2 games. Heavy rain broke up the playoffs, leaving division winners Tacoma and Albuquerque as co-champions.

Cleveland then became the club's parent organization.

After finishing second and third, Tacoma captured the Northern Division in 1981. That was as good as it got, though. Led by Triple Crown winner Mike Marshall, Albuquerque easily won both halves of the split season in the South, then enhanced its splendid 94-38 record with a 3-0 sweep in the finals.

Oakland began its long relationship with the Tigers in 1981. Tacoma's Ed Nottle, PCL Manager of the Year in 1981, again guided the Tigers to the division's best record in 1982. They won the first half, and finished right behind Spokane in the second, but dropped two of three to the Indians in the playoffs. Chris Codiroli became Tacoma's latest ERA leader with a 1.90 mark that was the league's lowest in 23 years.

Although Tacoma continued to put up impressive attendance figures, it was 1987 before the city fielded a winner. Keith Lieppman earned manager of the year honors for taking a team short on stars to the first-half title. However, second-half winner Calgary won the best-of-five series division playoffs. From 1985 to 1987, Jose Canseco, Mark McGwire and Walt Weiss, respectively, each spent part of the season in Tacoma. Each then joined Oakland and became an American League Rookie of the Year.

The Tigers had the league's worst record in 1988, but then the North Division's best in 1989, yet by failing to win either half of the split season, they didn't garner a spot in the playoffs. In 1990, they won the first half before bowing 3-2 to Edmonton, the second-half winner. They had the worst record again in 1992, despite Troy Neel's league-leading .351 average. They had the division's worst mark in 1993 and 1994 as Oakland's stay came to a disappointing end. Enforcing the perception that there is little correlation between minor league attendance and good teams, the 1994 Tigers drew 350,919 fans. That's still the city record.

Seattle has provided the talent and the club's nickname ever since. Although the 1995 squad included Alex Rodriguez for two months, Tacoma did not have another winning season until 1997, when the Rainiers fielded the first of four teams built on solid pitching.

Tacoma has greeted the 21st century in style. Dan Rohn was named manager of the year three times in five years, a period that has brought a share of one title, a second division crown and a near-miss for a third. Rohn has a team-record 375 victories.

Tacoma, which easily had the best pitching, put up the league's best record in 2001. The North Division winners and New Orleans, best in the South, were declared co-champions when the playoff finals were canceled because of the Sept. 11 terrorist attacks. The season did have more happily memorable moments, however. On July 7, John Halama, who spent most of the season with Seattle, pitched the first nine-inning perfect game in the PCL's 99-year history. He defeated Calgary 6-0 at Tacoma, four days after teammate Brett Tomko had no-hit Oklahoma 7-0. Denny Stark went 14-2 and captured the city's 13th Coast League ERA title.

The 2002 and 2003 Rainiers finished last, but Rohn earned his other manager of the year awards with overachievers. A weak-hitting, poor-fielding 2004 team took second place in the Northern Division with a good 79-63 record. In 2005, Tacoma edged Salt Lake City by one game for the division title before losing to Nashville in the playoffs. No pitcher had more than nine victories — not even Felix Hernandez, who was called up to the Mariners after 88 spectacular innings but was still named the PCL's Pitcher of the Year.

Whether Hernandez goes to the Hall of Fame is to be determined, but the 2004 and 2005 teams have balanced the books. After 46 years in the PCL, Tacoma's record is 3,330-3,317.

(Right) Future Hall of Famer (and spitballer) Gaylord Perry won 16 games for the first-place Tacoma Giants in 1961 and led the PCL with a 2.48 ERA in 1962. (Below) Willie McCovey shares a moment with the builder of the modern-day stadium bearing his name — ebullient Tacoma Giants owner Ben Cheney — at spring training in 1961 in Casa Grande, Arizona. McCovey played in 17 games for Tacoma tin 1960.

PHOTOS COURTESY
MARC BLAU COLLECTION

Sources

Reach Baseball Guide, 1890-1905 editions

The *Spokesman-Review,* Spokane

The *Spokane Daily Chronicle,* Spokane

The author's unpublished history of Spokane baseball

Dobbins, Dick, and Jon Twichell. *Nuggets on the Diamond.* San Francisco: Woodford Press, 1994

Wolff and Johnson. *The Encyclopedia of Minor League Baseball*

Gallacci, Blau & McArthur. *Playgrounds to the Pros.* Tacoma, Wash., Athletic Commission, 2005

Spalding, John E. *Sacramento Senators and Solons.* Manhattan, Kansas: Ag Press, 1995

Juan Marichal, the Tacoma Giant

Debuting with 11-5 record, high-kicking 'Laughing Boy' helped christen Cheney Stadium

By ANTHONY SALAZAR

Anthony Salazar is a
member of SABR's
Pacific Northwest
chapter and is the chair
of SABR36. He is also
the co-vice chair of the
Latino baseball
committee and edits its
quarterly publication, *La
Prensa del Béisbol
Latino.*

I t was 1960, the first year of Triple-A baseball in Tacoma (after a five-decade absence), and Juan Marichal proved the perfect man to help excite the region about the new team. The future "Dominican Dandy" enjoyed his four months in the Northwest, recently reflecting, "the people of Tacoma were very nice to me. I have very fond memories of my time there."

Juan Marichal was born on October 20, 1937 in Laguna Verde in the Dominican Republic, and like many of his compatriots, he began his life living in poverty. Marichal was just 3 when his father died, leaving behind a wife and five children, including four sons. It was Juan's brothers who were responsible for his introduction to baseball.

Marichal played shortstop as a boy but was converted into a pitcher when he played for company teams in 1956-57. He was drafted into the air force, and then to Rafael Trujillo's Winter League team in Escogido. It was there that he attracted the attention of the New York Giants, with whom he signed. Armed with a curveball, slider, screwball, and blazing fastball, he spent the next 18 years pitching in the United States.

In 1958 the Giants, relocated to San Francisco, sent the 20-year-old Marichal to their Class D Michigan City (Indiana) club in the Midwest League, where he tossed 245 innings in 35 games, finishing 21-8, with a league-leading 1.87 ERA and 246 strikeouts. The next season it was on to Springfield (Massachusetts) of the Eastern League, where he paced the league in wins (18, against 13 losses) and ERA (2.39), while pitching 271 innings in 37 games. Not surprisingly, Marichal was now deemed ready for Tacoma, the doorstep of the major leagues.

On April 16, 1960, the 22-year-old phenom started the second game of an Opening Day doubleheader against the Portland Beavers, in the christening of Tacoma's Ben Cheney Stadium. The pitcher, already dubbed "Laughing Boy" by the local media for his ever-present smile, shut out the Beavers 11-0.

In his next start, Marichal notched his second complete-game win, besting the neighboring Seattle Rainiers, 3-2. The Dominican already had become a fan favorite, and an "impressive" crowd of 4,101 home fans turned out to watch the pitcher hurl another complete victory, again over the Beavers. Marichal took his 3-0 record to Spokane, where he promptly disposed of the Indians, 3-1, his fourth complete game in as many outings.

On May 9, Marichal kept rolling when he shut out the Rainiers 1-0, ringing up nine strikeouts against only three hits, allowing no runners past second base. By now, he had fanned a league-leading 41 batters in 44 innings, while also pacing the circuit with a "gaudy" 1.23 ERA. The *Tacoma News-Tribune* noted that an overflow crowd of 8,255 fans clamored to watch Marichal work his magic. (Stadium capacity was only 7,000.) The paper remarked, "If Juan Marichal will only take out citizen papers, he can be elected to whatever Tacoma or Pierce County political office he chooses."

On Friday, May 13, Marichal suffered his first loss of the season, 11-5 at the hands of the Salt Lake Bees, lasting only six innings, allowing six hits and six runs, five of them earned. The young moundsman bounced back on May 18 in San Diego, holding the Padres to only five hits in a 1-0 victory, his third shutout of the season. The high-kicking hurler had allowed only two runners past second base.

His next outing in Salt Lake was a 5-2 victory. This time, the Laughing Boy gave up eight hits but struck out seven batters. The *Tacoma News-Tribune* observed that Marichal's beguiling countenance gave "no hint of the pure poison lurking in his pitching arm." A week later against the pesky Solons, Marichal suffered only his second loss, 3-1, when he allowed a two-run double in the 12th inning. He set down the first 14 batters, and did not allow a hit until one was out in the seventh. The Solons tied the game in the ninth, as Marichal battled the Sacramento batters through the 10th, 11th, and finally the 12th inning before the double ended the game. Despite the loss, Marichal had struck out 11 Sacramento batters.

Facing Vancouver for the first time in early June, Marichal, referred to as the "Dominican Dandy" for the first time in the local paper, showed the Mounties what all the fuss was about in a 5-2 victory. He recorded a season-high 14 strikeouts, allowing six hits and two runs, running his season record to 8-2.

Marichal's prowess on the mound did not escape the notice of the parent Giants. Carl Hubbell, former Giants star pitcher and their then-farm director, said, "When we first brought Marichal up ... we stuck him in Michigan City. He was just too good for the [Midwest] League. ... The next season, we jumped him to Springfield, and he found it a lot tougher. He got whacked around good early in the season. He learned he couldn't throw up just anything and the hitters would strike out. [In Tacoma] Marichal is a quick-thinking young fellow, and he started studying hitters and learning how to move the ball around — up and down, in and out. He started winning."

It wasn't until June 22 that Marichal suffered his third loss, 5-4 to Spokane, losing a 4-0 lead. The hurler lasted "only" 6-2/3 innings, giving up seven hits, five runs, four earned, while striking out only four Indians. In his next outing Marichal was bested again, 12-2 by Seattle. According to the *News-Tribune*, the Rainiers "treated Marichal like a batting practice hurler." In his fourth loss of the season, he gave up seven runs in 1-2/3 innings and did not strike out a batter. In his next outing, in Vancouver, he lost his third straight start, 8-7. Marichal was now 9-5 with 106 strikeouts and a 3.27 ERA in 133 innings. The *News-Tribune* speculated that Marichal had "lost his magic."

On July 4, Marichal picked up a much-need win, his tenth overall, as Tacoma bested Salt Lake City, 13-3. Five days later he notched his 11th victory in a 3-1 win over Sacramento, the only PCL team he hadn't beat.

Two days later, Marichal was recalled by the parent San Francisco Giants and jubilantly declared that he could "win right away" as a major leaguer. He departed immediately for San Francisco to meet his destiny as the premier Latino pitcher of his era.

Tacoma Giants manager John "Red" Davis was surprised by the move. Though he felt that Marichal had all the tools to become a star in the big leagues, he worried that the call-up was premature and thought that Sherman Jones, a pitcher performing better than Marichal, would be the one to make the leap to San Francisco. (Jones would make his debut at Candlestick Park later in the summer.)

In 18 starts for Tacoma, Marichal compiled an 11-5 record and 3.11 ERA over 138-2/3 innings. He struck out 121 batters, giving up 34 walks, 116 hits, and 48 earned runs. Despite Davis' reservations, Marichal succeeded in San Francisco right away, finishing the 1960 season with a 6-2 record and an ERA of 2.67 in 18 games. Over the course of 139 innings, he struck out 58 batters, while walking 28.

Other Latinos, among them Mateo Alou and Jose Pagan, were on that 1960 Tacoma Giants team. In the early to mid-1960s, Tacoma also employed Manny Mota, Jose Cardenal, Jesus Alou, and Tito Fuentes, each of whom was destined to make his mark in the big leagues.

Marichal, though, was the first famous Latin hero on the diamond in Tacoma, a fan favorite. To this day, his name uttered in Cheney Stadium is met with a nod of the head and a smile of remembrance. ⚾

Marichal is a quick-thinking young fellow, and he started studying hitters and learning how to move the ball around — up and down, in and out. He started winning.

Carl Hubbell then-farm director, San Francisco Giants

Sources

Cowan, Philip, *Tacoma's First Pitching Prospect*, Tacoma Rainiers Annual Program, 2000

Tacoma News-Tribune, April-July 1960

Stars leapt to bigs through Spokane

Glory to gloom to glory — that's the Inland baseball story

BY JIM PRICE

There is a widely-held perception that pro baseball reached Spokane, Washington, in the late 1950s, when Brooklyn headed west and moved its Los Angeles PCL team to Spokane. Readers from outside the Pacific Northwest need not be embarrassed. This perception is as well entrenched within the Inland Northwest as it may be anywhere else in the country.

The Dodgers era was indeed a grand period in the annals of Spokane baseball. It certainly set the standard for the city's quarter-century of Pacific Coast League play. But the former Bums from Brooklyn didn't bring pro ball to Spokane, and their stay wasn't the only golden age of baseball there. Professional baseball has been in Spokane since your great grandmother wore button shoes. Here's the scorecard: 116 years, 88 teams, 18 championships, and combined attendance that is bearing down on the 11 million mark.

The very first Spokane team, in 1890, won the initial Pacific Northwest League pennant. The nine-year period from 1908 to 1916, coincident with some of the city's greatest expansion, brought two championships and rosters that included two future Hall of Fame members, at least one near-miss, and two men destined for infamy.

The Western International League, founded in 1937, brought Spokane a fresh generation of splendid teams, highly admired minor league stars, and outstanding attendance figures. Although excessive ambition and the growing popularity of television finished off the WIL in the fall of 1954, the league was reborn within hours as the Northwest League. Unfortunately, Spokane barely lasted two years, and it had no pro team in 1957.

Gloom, however, turned to glory in an instant. In 1958, the Dodgers and the New York Giants moved to Los Angeles and San Francisco, respectively, forcing three Pacific Coast League teams to find new homes. For 14 years, the Dodgers pushed top prospects through Spokane, often in front of large crowds. Tom Lasorda headed the last three PCL teams of the Dodgers era, future Hall of Fame pitchers Hoyt Wilhelm and Don Sutton spent time with the Indians, and Duke Snider, on the verge of enshrinement as a player, managed Spokane for most of 1965.

After the Dodgers shifted their Triple A operations to

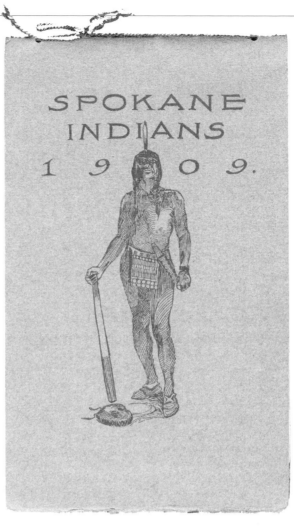

This 1909 Spokane yearbook may be the most handsome publication ever turned out by a Northwest minor-league baseball team.

(Opposite page) A brilliant all-around player when he manned right field for Spokane in 1959, Tommy Davis won two batting titles for the Los Angeles Dodgers and recovered from a serious injury to become the first top designated hitter.

Albuquerque, New Mexico, four other organizations provided ten more years of Triple A play in Spokane. When the franchise finally slunk off to Las Vegas in 1983, Spokane rejoined the Single A Northwest League. With out-of-town ownership and a parent team that badly misjudged the league's talent level, the first three entries finished last.

However, future Hall of Fame third baseman George Brett and his three brothers came to the rescue, taking control in 1986. With Bobby Brett as managing partner, the brothers restored Spokane's tradition of winning teams, record attendance, and excellent facilities. The Indians have won seven Northwest League titles in the ownership's first 20 years.

Right from the start, baseball was very, very good to Spokane. The original franchise was run by John S. Barnes, an experienced baseball organizer from the Midwest. Barnes was a 19th century huckster, an early-day Jack LaLanne with a touch of Tex Rickard, and his promotions always included jobs for himself. Seattle, Portland, and Tacoma, all 300 miles or so to the west of Spokane constituted the other Pacific Northwest League franchises. In Spokane, a grandstand that had been erected in an abortive 1889 housing tract was dismantled, and rebuilt near the corner of Boone Avenue and A Street, about two miles northwest of downtown.

Jim Price, a longtime copy editor and sports historian at the Spokesman-Review in Spokane, has been a Pacific Coast League play-by-play broadcaster and publicist, Northwest League and California League official scorer and public address announcer and a baseball beat writer. He also spent 14 years as track announcer and publicist for horse-racing tracks in six Western states and almost a decade as sports information director at Eastern Washington University.

The 1912 Spokane Indians have some pregame fun in the sun with Wally Cartwright (left) and Watt Powell standing up at the plate, where Bill Johnson's parasol shields "catcher" Phil Cooney. Dutch Altman looks on, while Fielder Jones Jr., son of the Northwestern League president, sneaks a peek.

The Spokesman-Review conducted a contest to give the Spokane team its first official nickname.

The winning entry was 'Inlanders.'

The inaugural season opened on a down note. When play began at Spokane on May 3, 1890, Portland scratched out an 8-7 victory in 11 innings. Spokane settled for earning its first triumph the next day, winning 14-8. The pennant race took a dramatic turn at mid-June: after Galveston built an insurmountable lead in the Texas League, the league collapsed, turning some of the country's best-known minor leaguers into free agents. Five wound up in Spokane. They were second baseman Frank "Piggy" Ward, pitcher Happy Jack Huston, shortstop Kid Peeples, roly-poly outfielder Mark Polhemus, and first baseman Tom McGuirk. The International League folded five weeks later, freeing up Abner Powell — later the most important figure in New Orleans baseball — to move into Spokane's outfield.

When the Texas Leaguers arrived, Spokane was 14-12, just behind Tacoma and Seattle. Portland was far behind. Shored up, Spokane won two-thirds of its remaining games, and finished with a 61-35 record, 6-1/2 games ahead of Tacoma. Ward, a demonstrative, base-stealing switch-hitter, beat out Polhemus for the batting title by hitting .367. Huston led the pitchers with a 28-8 record.

Spokane could have won again in 1891. By Sept. 16, it led Portland by 3-1/2 games with ten left. But Portland beat Spokane in the season's final two games to claim the title.

With financial disorder overshadowing the entire region, the PNL fell apart three-quarters of the way through the 1892 season. Revivals failed in 1896 and 1898, but while Spokane fielded a team in the unrecognized Kootenay-Washington League in 1897, it was 1901 before the PNL was reestablished with its original four cities. Spokane played on a new diamond at Natatorium Park, an amusement park near the Spokane River, just west of the previous field.

Although Spokane's 1901 and 1902 teams finished last, the latter season brought George Ferris to town. Spokane's starting second baseman was Heinie Reitz, who had been a regular for the great Baltimore Orioles of the 1890s. However, when team owner W.V. Garrett tired of Reitz's "disappearances," he replaced him with Ferris, a young college man who was playing for Baker City (Oregon) of the Inland Empire League. Ferris played five seasons, served as player-manager in 1906, and went on to preside over the area's top semipro league while spending 20 years as the city's corporation counsel. He devoted a half-century to Spokane baseball, and the new ballpark used by the Western International League would be named in his honor.

The so-called Pacific Coast League invasion preceded the 1903 season. When the California League established franchises in Portland and Seattle and adopted its more-grandiose name, PNL president William H. Lucas talked his owners into retaliating. With teams of their own in Los Angeles and San Francisco, as well as two in Montana, the far-flung, re-named Pacific National League lost half of its eight teams by August. Having won the short-lived war, the PCL went legit in 1904, while retaining the rights to the Northwest's largest West Coast cities.

Anticipating the high-profile season, *The Spokesman-Review* conducted a contest to give the Spokane team its first official nickname. The winning entry was "Inlanders," but two weeks into the season, without explanation the local papers switched to "Indians," and it stuck.

Spokane had plenty of offense, and rookie righthander Ernie Nichols was burning up the league. However, on July 20, an off day, Nichols dropped dead after attending a semipro game. The San Franciscan, who had already built up a 20-4 record, was only 22 years old. Thus handicapped, the Indians wound up second. Outfielders Jack Hendricks and Frank Huelsman were on their way to better things: Hendricks became a noted minor league manager, and eventually headed up two National League teams. Huelsman's .392 average earned him the second of what became five minor league batting titles. Little lefthander

Bill Dammann, a former Spokane schoolboy who had made it to the National League, returned to the area and posted a fine 26-16 record.

Lucas was left with four teams in smaller markets for the PNL's 1904 season. Spokane finished second again, although righthander Bill Hogg, on his way to the big leagues, won 29 games. Dammann won 23.

In early 1905, Lucas proclaimed the Pacific National League defunct, and launched the Northwestern League, which pointedly excluded Spokane. The PNL continued without backing from the National Association, but it failed in June. Lucas had the last laugh. When his Victoria, British Columbia, franchise went broke, he sent the team to Spokane, where, it began play at new grounds named Recreation Park. Hastily built on land owned by railroad, streetcar, and mining millionaire Jay P. Graves, Recreation Park sat northeast of the Spokane Interstate Fairgrounds, a couple of miles east of downtown.

By 1907, the turnstiles were spinning, and fans were being treated to good baseball. The Indians often returned from road trips to find that additions had been made to the ballpark's wooden stands. Spokane claimed its second pennant in 1910. New manager Harry Ostdiek, a former Cleveland Indians and Red Sox catcher, would last three-and-a-half seasons, a tenure that has not been topped. Lefthanded pitcher Jesse Baker won 28 games. Righthander Jack Killilay won 24, running his Spokane career total to 75, still the record.

With the exception of 1913, the Indians fielded winning teams from 1909 through 1916, and many important players passed through their clubhouse. The 1909 team included Vean Gregg, a rawboned lefthander from Clarkston, Washington. Although Gregg endured some injuries, he was sold to Cleveland. After an amazing 1910 season with Portland, the hard-throwing curveballer won 20 big league games in three straight seasons.

In 1911, Earl Sheely, an Illinois native raised in Spokane, left North Central High School to turn pro. He didn't make it with the Indians until 1915, but the genial first baseman went on to hit .300 in nine major league seasons. Before, during, and after his big league days, the future college coach, PCL manager, and general manager was a Pacific Coast League great.

In 1912, first baseman Hap Myers stole an astonishing 116 bases. That winter, Myers, 25-game winner Win Noyes, and Paul Strand, a pitching phenom from a tiny Tacoma-area town, were sold to the Boston Braves. Strand later gained recognition as an immortal minor league batter. That year's Spokane team also included a real Indian, Minnesota-born pitcher William Cadreau, who won 21 games.

Although the 1913 team was Spokane's least successful in a decade, its pitching staff included Stan Coveleski and Phil Douglas. Coveleski earned induction to the Hall of Fame, but Douglas was banned for life in 1922 after soliciting a bribe. Swede Risberg, an early-season team

Earl "Blossom" Sheely bats for Walla Walla team during Western Tri-State League action in 1913. A former Spokane high-school student and Indians first-baseman in 1915-16, Sheely hit .300 in nine major-league seasons.

OSTDIEK, SPOKANE, N.W.L.

(Left) Catcher Harry Ostdiek, who had short stays with Cleveland's and Boston's American League team, managed Spokane for three-and-a-half seasons, 1910 until mid-1913. That remains the longest tenure for an Indians manager. (Right) You had the long and short of it when standout pitcher Walter "Sad Slim" Smith posed with young catcher Tom Downey Jr., son of teammate Tom Downey, at the Spokane's 1920 spring-training camp in Eugene, Oregon.

member, was later found among the eight Chicago White Sox blacklisted after the 1919 World Series scandal.

George Kelly began his Hall of Fame career with Spokane in 1914. However, one month into the season, the Indians sent Kelly and homegrown pitcher Walter (Sad Slim) Smith to hapless Victoria, considering them surplus

Spokane's 1916 Northwestern League champions, including future big-league standouts Ken Williams and Dutch Ruether (back row, fourth and fifth from left) and Earl Sheely (front row, far right), were managed by the well-known Nick Williams (back row, sixth from left). Abe Kemp, San Francisco's boy-wonder sportswriter before joining The Spokesman-Review, stands far left in the back row.

Spokane's opening-day first baseman was future Yankees standout Bob Meusel, who was cut after collecting only three hits in his first 22 at-bats.

talent. Coveleski won 20 games. The regular first baseman, Walter Holke, was also to become a fine big leaguer. In 1915, the Indians led by 4-1/2 games with 18 left to play, but they lost their last eight, and Seattle, 60-20 after Independence Day, pulled ahead for the title.

Richard L. "Nick" Williams, a well-known West Coast minor league figure, managed Spokane's 1916 champions. The Indians won by 11 games while playing at Natatorium Park for the first time since 1905. Future St. Louis Browns great Ken Williams, Sheely, and lefthanded pitcher Dutch Ruether (who sometimes played in the field) were the top prospects.

In 1917, as the U.S. entered World War I and players headed for military service or West Coast shipyards, the Northwestern League crumbled; play ended on July 15. Spokane's opening-day first baseman was future Yankees standout Bob Meusel, but he was cut after collecting only three hits in his first 22 at-bats. In 1918, the NWL dumped its two Montana teams and reorganized as the Pacific Coast International League, but the change didn't prevent another early finish, and Spokane lasted only 25 games.

Efforts to resume play failed in 1919. When the PCIL did come back in 1920, with four Washington teams and two from British Columbia, Spokane placed fifth. "Sad Slim" Smith was the ace of that team, and became the city's finest pitcher. Smith played irregularly as a pro, but he is well remembered as a player, manager, and sponsor in the area's best semipro leagues.

The Pacific Coast International lasted just two more years without Spokane. Then the lower minor leagues disappeared from the region. It took better economic times to inspire formation of the Western International League in

1937. And it took George Ferris' persistence to provide Spokane with a handsome new wood ballpark at the fairgrounds that the city named Ferris Field.

When no local backers could be found, Yakima's owner, mining heir Shirley Parker, funded the Spokane franchise as well. The team would be known as "Hawks" until downtown restaurant owner Bill Ulrich bought out Parker in 1939. Oakland provided manager Bernie deViveiros and several players. Spokane posted the league's best record, but failed to make the playoffs after placing second and third in a split season. Spokane broke the Class B attendance record in 1938, attracting a paid gate of 201,412 with a team that finished below .500.

In 1939, a midseason player revolt led Ulrich to replace the fiery deViveiros with mild-mannered Eddie Leishman. More happily, by season's end Spokane had topped its own attendance record by attracting 232,157 paid fans. Despite a fourth-place finish, a nucleus of well-known players was in place, including outfielders Levi McCormack and Dwight Aden, infielder Henry Martinez, outfielder-first baseman Frank Falconi, and pitchers Duke Windsor, Pete Jonas, and Major Serventi.

In 1940, the magic ingredient was legendary minor leaguer Smead Jolley, who had been cut loose by Oakland. Jolley was one of the greatest hitters who never had a chance to be a DH. At age 38, he won the batting title for Spokane with a .373 average, and he drove in an astonishing 181 runs. The Indians finished 6-1/2 games ahead of Yakima, but Tacoma's Tigers beat them in the final round of the Shaughnessy playoffs. All eight regulars batted above .300, and McCormack, a Native American from the Idaho Panhandle, combined a .327 average with 108 RBIs and 130 runs. Windsor won 20 games. By fielding that sort of quality, Leishman soon became one of the game's most honored executives.

The magic ingredient in 1941 was Gabriel "Pete" Hughes. Younger and less expensive, Hughes bumped Jolley out of right field on his way to leading the league in home runs, runs, and walks. Shunted off to Vancouver, Jolley nevertheless won his sixth batting title, and retired with a career minor league average of .366. With the Indians (89-44) headed to an 18-game victory over the rest of the league, the playoffs were canceled.

Manpower shortages caused by World War II hurt the 1942 campaign, and led to cancellation of the next three. After play resumed, a bus accident killed nine members of Spokane's 1946 team. However, the accident brought the Indians and the Brooklyn Dodgers together, when Brooklyn staffed the 1947 club with some of its top prospects. Spokane wound up second in one of minor league baseball's most thrilling races. Vancouver edged the Indians by .001, and Bremerton finished just one game behind. Spokane's attendance soared again, reaching 287,185, another record. Fans got to see pitcher Bob Costello, from nearby Sprague, Washington, win 21 games. Third baseman Bobby Morgan, shortstop Clarence "Buddy" Hicks, and outfielder George Schmees all would go on to play in the major leagues. First baseman Herb Gorman hit .351.

The Indians were sold before the 1948 season, so the Dodgers didn't stay affiliated with them. Nonetheless, Spokane won the pennant, even though manager Buddy Ryan, seriously ill, left the team at midseason. With one of his protégés, former National League slugger Dolph Camilli, cracking the whip, the Indians won 45 of their last 57 games to win the title going away.

Infielder Leo Thomas, a Dodgers castoff, and zany outfielder Edo Vanni starred at the plate. Vanni stole 76 bases for one of his three league records. Catcher Bud Sheely, Earl's son, hit .317. But the year ended on a sour note when, on Oct. 29, fire badly damaged Ferris Field. Thanks to inadequate repairs, changes in ownership and uncertain financing, things were never quite the same.

Vanni helped the Indians take another title in 1951, and center fielder Eddie Murphy broke Vanni's record with 90 steals. John Conant and Dick Bishop, destined to finish second and third on the team's all-time win list, won 16 games apiece. Conant and Bishop headed a similar veteran staff in 1952, when the team placed second.

After winning the second half of a split season in 1953, the Indians, now affiliated with the Philadelphia Phillies, claimed their fourth WIL title in a playoff series with Salem. Slugging outfielder Stan Palys and lefthanded pitcher Jack Spring, a Spokane native, led the way.

The Western International League had expanded to 10 teams, boosting itself to Class A status. Unfortunately, team owners overlooked the cost of added travel to their new Canadian franchises in Calgary and Edmonton and failed to recognize the thin line between profitability and failure. Spokane and Calgary folded before the halfway point in 1954, and the league folded at the year's end. When it was reborn as the Northwest League, Spokane had no owner, and relied on stock sales to the public to pay the bills. The under-funded Indians had the worst combined record in both 1955 and 1956. Then, they went broke, and there was no team in 1957.

Once again, when the situation looked its worst, things took a turn for the better. The major leagues headed west. In anticipation, the city and Spokane County built an earth-berm Pacific Coast League ballpark at the new fairgrounds, a half-mile east of Ferris Field, in 111 days. It remains in use today as one of the country's top minor league fields. After two weeks on the road, Spokane played its first PCL game on April 29, 1958, defeating Seattle 6-5 before an overflow crowd of 8,404. For the season, attendance totaled 270,297. The next two years were nearly as good.

Significantly, the Dodgers years provided the city with an astonishing run of talent. Most of the skippers wound up managing big league teams. Many of the players also made it to "The Show," including Maury Wills, Tommy Davis, Frank Howard, Willie Davis, Ron Fairly, Roy White, Bill Buckner, Steve Garvey, Davey Lopes, Ron Cey, and Charlie Hough.

Such wealth provided other pleasures, as some fans and

With former National League slugger Dolph Camilli cracking the whip, the 1948 Indians won 45 of their last 57 games to win the title going away.

Spokane's 1940 team won the regular-season title but lost in the playoffs despite a standout outfield that included minor-league legend Smead Jolley (back row, fourth from right), Levi McCormack (back row, third from right) and Dwight Aden (front row, fourth from right).

In 1951, the Spokane Indians, emulating Hollywood's Pacific Coast League team, wore shorts in warm weather. That's longtime pitching ace John Conant (back row, second from the right) and standout center fielder Eddie Murphy (front row, third from the right.)

historians argue to this day whether the 1960 Indians or the 1970 version was the best PCL team of the last half-century. *Baseball America* favored the latter, but the 1960 team won its league by 11-1/2 games with loads of offense from Willie Davis and Fairly.

To many, the youthful 1970 team had no shortcomings. They won their division by 26 games. Shortstop Bobby Valentine was the league MVP, and the team also included Garvey at third base and Lopes and Bill Russell in the outfield. Buckner and Hutton shared first base. Hough, Mike Strahler, and 18-game winner Jerry Stephenson led the pitching staff. After the Indians won the first three games of their playoff series with Hawaii, Greg Washburn hit Valentine in the face with the first pitch of Game 4. The enraged Indians then crushed the Islanders 16-2 to complete the sweep.

All good things come to an end, but when the Dodgers left in 1972, they salved the wound by provisioning a Northwest League team for one year. Owner Bill Cutler subsequently moved Portland's PCL franchise eastward in 1973. Backed by the Texas Rangers, the newcomers brought Spokane back-to-back championships. Bill Madlock, who would win four National League batting titles, starred for the 1973 team. In 1974, designated hitter Tom Robson became the league's MVP after hitting 41 home runs, the all-time Spokane record. After three years, the affiliation with the Rangers was supplanted by a new relationship with the Milwaukee Brewers.

Baseball in the 1970s brought strange sights, like the

When Bobby Bragan became Spokane's manager in mid-1958, he convinced shortstop Maury Wills to become a switch-hitter. The change, which let Wills capitalize on his speed, brought him 586 major-league stolen bases.

unimaginable image of the immense and aging ex-slugger Frank Howard clad in the 1976 club's orange uniforms. Very hairy outfielder Gorman Thomas hit 31 homers in 1977. In late 1978, Cutler sold the Indians to a partnership headed by Gonzaga University coach Larry Koentopp; Cutler became the league president. The new owners signed a working agreement with Seattle, whose farmhands fared no better than Milwaukee's. The 1979 team was long in the tooth, and outfielder Dave Henderson turned out to be the

SURE I BOUGHT SPOKANE INDIANS BASEBALL STOCK

When ailing owner Roy Hotchkiss surrendered the Spokane franchise following the 1954 season, the Indians sold stock to their fans in hopes of survival. Nonetheless, they went out of business two years later.

Some writers and fans believe the 1960 Spokane Indians were the city's finest team with a fine offensive lineup featuring Willie Davis (front row, second from right), Ron Fairly (middle row, third from left) and slugger Frank Howard (not pictured).

only top prospect on the squad in 1980-81.

The 1982 team, backed by the California Angels, was much better, winning the second-half title before losing in the playoff finals to Albuquerque. Unfortunately, that wasn't all Spokane lost. The liberal promotion policies of Koentopp's regime had generated impressive crowd figures, but little or no profit. The regular season ended in acrimony, with Koentopp denying he had a deal to move the team to Las Vegas while the Las Vegas Chamber of Commerce was inconveniently announcing it.

That put Spokane back in the Northwest League. The partnership that owned Tucson's PCL entry established a new Spokane franchise stocked with players from the San Diego organization. By now, the Northwest League played 70-game seasons, didn't open play until mid-June, and its rosters were dominated by recent draftees. The mid-1980s squads featured Mitch Williams, Sandy Alomar Jr., and Joey Cora, but the teams were pretty poor.

Enter the Bretts. Bobby Brett, who had made good money in Southern California real estate, told the parent San Diego Padres that he wanted better players, and he got

them. The 1986 team had a winning season, and the 1987 Indians won the first of four straight championships. When the player-development contract expired after a last-place finish in 1994, Spokane dropped the Padres in favor of Kansas City, George Brett's team. Eight years with the Royals produced only one title, but that team, the 1999 squad, was a very good one, winning a ding-dong race with Boise and Everett, and it swept the playoffs to take the title.

Nonetheless, three years later, after consecutive last-place seasons, the Indians parted ways with the Royals in favor of the Texas Rangers. Since then, Spokane has gained two pennants in three years.

The first title team, in 2003, had no stars, but it did have the league's best pitching and no glaring weakness. The second title was won in 2005, and had former San Diego manager Greg Riddoch at the helm. Riddoch rallied the Indians to first place in the East Division title on the season's closing day. Then, despite their 37-39 record, his overachievers defeated Vancouver (46-30) in the playoffs.

It was glory time again. ⚾

Sources

Wolff and Johnson. *The Encyclopedia of Minor League Baseball*

Reach Baseball Guide, 1890-1905 editions

The Spokesman-Review, Spokane

The Spokane Daily Chronicle, Spokane

The author's unpublished history of Spokane baseball

Dick Dobbins and John Twichell. *Nuggets on the Diamond.* San Francisco: Woodford Press, 1994

Whether the 1970 Indians were better than the 1960 aggregation may be argued, but there is no doubt that this team had more impact at the major-league level. Bill Buckner (center, far left), Davey Lopes (front, sixth from left), Doyle Alexander (back, third from left), Charlie Hough (back, eighth from left) and Steve Garvey and Bill Russell (both not pictured) had fine playing careers. Manager Tom Lasorda (center, fifth from left) is in the Hall of Fame. Shortstop Bobby Valentine (bottom row, second from left, and in larger photo, right) was the PCL's MVP. A terrible leg injury cut short his playing days, but he has managed in the major leagues and in Japan for more than two decades.

Devastating crash reverberates 60 years later

Bus accident near Snoqualmie Pass killed nine 1946 Indians

(Opposite top) Casey Stengel's PCL Oakland Oaks and the Seattle Rainiers played in Spokane on July 8, 1946, raising $16,000 for the survivors and families of those who died in the June 24 bus crash (opposite bottom, from Wenatchee Daily World).

By JIM PRICE

Sixty years ago, the Spokane Indians of the Western International League made the worst kind of baseball history. The team's bus plunged into a ravine about 50 miles east of Seattle, on the western slope of Snoqualmie Pass in the Cascade Mountains, where it tumbled down the steep hillside, erupted in flames, and cut short the lives of nine players. It remains the most devastating accident in the history of American professional sports.

That terrible event has seldom been rivaled, either in the United States or elsewhere in the world. But it stands as a somber reminder that good times can become bad ones in just a few seconds.

The accident helped make one man, third baseman Jack Lohrke, an instant legend. It has marked another, pitcher Darwin (Gus) Hallbourg, as a survivor. *The* survivor. The last man left of those who rode the bus.

Recalled by the San Diego Padres of the Pacific Coast League, Lohrke left the team during its dinner stop. Hallbourg, 86, lives in Central California's San Joaquin Valley, where he gratefully admitted a while back, "I'm bright-eyed and bushy-tailed."

Details of the accident are well known. The *Spokesman-Review* in Spokane has dutifully marked its major anniversaries. Cable television network CNN-SI included a story on the ill-fated team in its coverage of the 2001 All-Star Game.

The 1946 season was the first after World War II. Ballplayers whose careers had been interrupted or delayed by the war flooded professional baseball's training camps. As the season unfolded, other players started receiving their discharges, and headed back to a ballpark.

The Western International League had suspended operations after a dismal 1942 season marked by a shrinking supply of players. The WIL's usual complement of six cities included Spokane, Tacoma, Wenatchee, and Yakima, Washington, as well as Salem, Oregon, and Vancouver, British Columbia. Anticipating a postwar glut of players, league owners added Bremerton, Wash., and Victoria, B.C., for 1946.

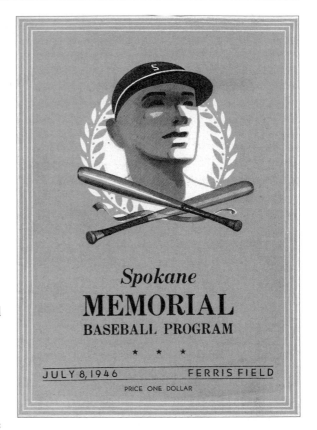

Spokane **MEMORIAL** BASEBALL PROGRAM ★ ★ ★ JULY 8, 1946   FERRIS FIELD PRICE ONE DOLLAR

EIGHT PERISH IN FLAMING BUS! Spokane Ball Team in Snoqualmie Death Plunge — *In Our OWN World* — THE WENATCHEE DAILY WORLD — Mel Cole Killed; Nine More Injured — Life-Giving Rain Turned On and Off at Monse

Jim Price, a longtime copy editor and sports historian at The Spokesman-Review in Spokane, has been a Pacific Coast League play-by-play broadcaster and publicist, Northwest League and California League official scorer and public address announcer and a baseball beat writer. He also spent 14 years as track announcer and publicist for horse-racing tracks in six Western states and almost a decade as sports information director at Eastern Washington University.

As Coast League players left military service and resumed their careers, teams demoted their stand-ins on an almost daily basis. Few Class B cities benefited more than Spokane, which regained some of its finest pre-war players, while also acquiring new ones, mostly from the Oakland Oaks. The Indians had a manager with top credentials, too, former National League shortstop Glenn Wright, who had led Wenatchee to a runaway WIL title in 1939.

Unfortunately, Wright had a serious drinking problem, perhaps related to the fact that his potentially Hall of Fame-caliber career had been derailed by a shoulder injury. When Wright went on a binge at the end of spring training, team owner Sam Collins replaced him with utility man Mel Cole.

The Indians started the season with a good team. They had four veteran starting pitchers and some hot infield prospects. Former New York Yankees farmhands Bob James and Bob Paterson joined popular Levi McCormack in the outfield. McCormack, a full-blooded Native American, had starred for the city's outstanding 1940 and 1941 teams.

The key pitchers were former Tacoma standout Milt Cadinha, his boyhood friend Joe Faria, ex-PCL righthander Dick Powers, and Hallbourg, a 15-game winner in the

California League in 1941. The infield prospects included Lohrke, shortstop George Risk, and Vic Picetti, who had come right out of high school the year before to play first base for Oakland.

Salem started the year like a house afire, winning its first 13 games, seven of them against Spokane. Nevertheless, it wasn't long before five teams were bunched near the top of the standings. After a 3-8 start, the Indians won 11 of their next 12 games. Their run was aided by a roster that improved almost weekly.

Oakland returned Bob Kinnaman, a former Washington State College star who had won 22 games for the Indians in 1941. Then, Collins acquired veteran infielder Ben Geraghty from the Brooklyn Dodgers, as well as Chris Hartje, who had been the bullpen catcher for the Yankees.

On Sunday, June 23, at Ferris Field in Spokane, Salem and Spokane split a day-night doubleheader. The Indians took the nightcap 10-9 by scoring three runs in the ninth inning. Second baseman Marty Martinez was hitting .353, Risk was batting .349, and Lohrke was right behind him at .345. Cadinha had an 8-1 record.

Monday, June 24, was an off-day, and devoted to travel. Shortly after 10 in the morning, driver Glen Berg headed the Washington Motor Coach bus toward Bremerton on a bleak, wet day. He had 16 players on board. Cadinha, Faria, and their wives left later by car, but joined their teammates for dinner at Webster's Food Shop, the best-known café in Ellensburg, which was about two-thirds of the way.

While the players ate, Berg drove to the bus company's local garage, complaining of brake and gear problems, and hoping to secure a replacement. Thanks to war-time parts shortages that had affected the entire country, there was nothing better on the lot.

As Lohrke, who already had avoided almost certain death in a postwar plane crash, hitched a ride back to Spokane, the bus headed west on U.S. Highway 10 into the rain and gathering darkness.

After the meal, at about 8 o'clock the coach labored over the Snoqualmie summit, traveling slower than 30 mph. Four miles down the grade, on a straight stretch that hugs the southern edge of the ravine, Berg said an eastbound

black car veered across the center line. Reluctant to use the brakes, he steered toward the shoulder. Both right wheels left the pavement. The front end regained the asphalt, but it whipped back toward the abyss, clipped off several concrete posts, tore through the restraining cables, and headed downhill. The bus struck a boulder, rolled onto its side, hit another very large rock, rolled twice more and burst into flames. Some players were thrown out of the bus as it plunged downward. A few scrambled out once it came to a rest.

Cole, Risk, Paterson, Kinnaman, Martinez, and James burned to death or died from head injuries. Picetti died en route to a Seattle hospital, pitcher George Lyden died the next day, and Hartje, burned terribly, lived until Wednesday.

Powers, with a fractured skull and broken back, was

This photograph of the 1946 Spokane Indians was taken on Sunday, June 23, little more than 24 hours before the team bus tumbled off the Snoqualmie Pass highway.

A full-blooded Nez Perce and Spokane Indian, bus-wreck survivor Levi McCormack was not above capitalizing on his heritage, whether he played for the old Seattle Indians of the PCL (shown at left with Alice Brougham, team "mascot" and daughter of Royal Brougham, at 1937 spring training) or the Spokane Indians of the Western International League.

(Above)
Spokane's 1946 season began on a note of turmoil when owner Sam Collins (right) named utility player Mel Cole to take over as the manager just before the Indians began their season.

Infielder Jack Lohrke, on option from San Diego of the Coast League, was spared when the Padres recalled him. Reached by telephone, Lohrke left the Indians during a dinner stop in Ellensburg, Wash., about two hours before the fatal accident.

A Spokane star before World War II, Bob Kinnaman was among the WIL's top pitchers again in 1946 when he died in the fiery accident that killed nine Spokane players.

Sources

Wolff and Johnson, *The Encyclopedia of Minor League Baseball*

Reach Baseball Guides, 1890-2005

The Spokesman-Review, Spokane

The Spokane Daily Chronicle, Spokane

Jim Price's unpublished history of Spokane baseball

Dick Dobbins and John Twichell, *Nuggets on the Diamond*, Woodford Press, San Francisco, 1994

hospitalized for six months. Geraghty had a broken kneecap and a long gash on his scalp, and reserve catcher Irv Konopka broke a shoulder. McCormack and pitcher Pete Barisoff had relatively minor injuries, while Hallbourg wriggled through a window and escaped with burns on his arms. Berg, the driver, was badly burned and hospitalized for months.

Wright had stayed in town, and became the manager with a ragtag roster made up of players borrowed from other teams and organizations, bad actors who were free agents, and some semipros. When they weren't pitching, Cadinha, Faria and Hallbourg played the outfield. Trainer John (Dutch) Anderson often played third base.

Even so, the re-stocked Indians did not return to action until the Fourth of July. They lost 52 of their final 74

games, and finished seventh, 29-1/2 games behind, as Wenatchee won the pennant.

In response to the tragedy, fans, teams, and leagues around the country donated close to $120,000, including $25,000 from Major League Baseball's All-Star Game. Widows or families of the players who died, and the men who were injured shared close to a quarter-million dollars from the fund and the bus company's insurance.

Of the six players who survived the accident, only Hallbourg and Powers lived past their 60th birthdays. Barisoff died in a 1949 house fire. Geraghty became a legendary minor league manager before he succumbed to a heart attack in 1963. Konopka died of cancer in 1970. McCormack had a fatal heart attack in 1974.

Berg, the driver, died less than two years ago. Apparently, he never talked about the accident, not even with his family. He drove local delivery trucks for half a century, establishing an enviable reputation for safety and as a mentor to young drivers.

Now, aside from Lohrke, only Hallbourg is left. In January, the Manteca, Calif., resident and his wife, Roberta, celebrated their 60th wedding anniversary. A cheery man who once was a fine amateur golfer, he had a 32-year career with the telephone company.

What are his thoughts about the accident?

"When I think about it, and I do on occasion," he said last winter, "I just think 'How lucky you were.' And that's for sure." ⚾

'Lucky Beavers' carve sole link to PCL's earliest days

Unassisted triple play, no-hitter spice Portland's long run

BY PAUL ANDRESEN AND KIP CARLSON

While most of the long-term PCL cities eventually landed a major league club, Portland remains the last link to the league's early years, and to its long run as an independent top-flight minor league. The Portland Beavers' recent history has been spotty on and off the field. The Golden Age of the Portland Beavers under Walter and W.W. McCredie (see page 22) ended in 1921. Since the McCredies' departure, Portland has won only three PCL titles and has twice watched the team owner pull up stakes for greener pastures. The Rose City's baseball story in recent decades is one of dashed hope.

After a string of disappointing years, the McCredies finally sold the Beavers after the 1921 season to Walter Klepper, former president of the Seattle team. The team rose to seventh place in 1922, but Klepper got in hot water with Organized Baseball after several players from Seattle ended up on the Portland team. Klepper was suspended by baseball commissioner Kenesaw Mountain Landis, but the feisty owner went to court and had the ruling overturned. In 1923 the Beavers posted their best mark of a dismal decade

with a third-place finish and a 107-89 record.

The 1924 season brought future Hall of Famer Mickey Cochrane. Not so coincidentally, the team was bought after that season by Philadelphia Athletics owners John and Tom Shibe and Roy Mack, son of A's manager Connie Mack, was made vice president and business manager. Cochrane was a fine player, but not enough to keep the Beavers from sliding back to seventh place. Not surprisingly, Cochrane was playing for the A's the next year.

Shorn of Cochrane, the Beavers turned to former major leaguers to entertain the home crowd. In 1925, the team brought in Duffy Lewis, a star outfielder for many years in the American League. The former Red Sox hero had won the PCL batting championship with Salt Lake City the previous year, but Lewis left the Beavers before 1925 was over. Elmer Smith, of 1920 World Series fame, joined the club for 1926-27, but despite leading the PCL in home runs in 1926 and 1927, the Beavers finished fourth and fifth. Another solid player on these teams was Doc Prothro, who had been a practicing dentist before beginning his major league career in 1920. Ten years later, Prothro would have the "honor" of managing three of the worst teams (1939-41) in Phillies history. The Prothro name would reappear in Oregon a generation later when Doc's son Tommy would serve as Oregon State's football coach from 1955 to 1964.

In 1928, eight Beavers hit over .300, but the team fell to seventh place at 79-112. Every Beaver pitcher, save one, had a losing record. In an equally poor 1929, Portland showed off the "reversible battery" of Ed Tomlin and Junk Walters, who on at least one occasion were the pitcher and catcher in the first game of a doubleheader, then exchanged positions for the second game.

The highlight of the 1930 Beaver season was second baseman William Rhiel's unassisted triple play, the last one recorded in the PCL through the 2005 season. Portland's pitching staff had veteran Carl Mays and longtime PCL stalwart Duster Mails, but even the .347 hitting of future

Kip Carlson and Paul Andresen are baseball researchers living in Corvallis, Oregon, and and both grew up watching PCL baseball. This article is largely adapted from their book *The Portland Beavers*, published by Arcadia in 2004.

James "Doc" Prothro, a practicing dentist, was a good-hitting third baseman for the Portland Beavers in 1926-27. He later managed the Philadelphia Phillies. His son, Tommy, coached football at Oregon State University and UCLA then moved on to Los Angeles and San Diego of the NFL.

———

In 1937, Portland dropped to fourth place, good enough to make the expanded playoffs, defeating San Francisco in the first round before losing to champion San Diego, which featured a skinny kid named Ted Williams in its outfield.

———

big league star Doc Cramer couldn't overcome a sky-high staff ERA. The Beavers closed out a decade of futility with a last-place finish in 1930.

In 1931, the Beavers changed hands once again, as Tom Turner bought the team from the Shibe brothers. Led by Ed Coleman's league-leading 275 hits and 183 RBI, the club improved to 100 victories and a third place finish. Better yet, the 1932 Beavers brought home Portland's first pennant since 1914. This club was the opposite of the great teams of the 1910s, as it had relatively weak pitching but exceptional hitting, relying on the strong bat of Pinky Higgins at third base, as well as outfielder Lou Finney's league-leading 268 hits.

The club slipped to second place in 1933, then tumbled back to the basement in 1934, going through three managers, including a stint by Turner himself. Attendance tumbled as well, setting an all-time franchise low of 50,731, fully one-quarter of whom showed up on Opening Day. Walter McCredie was brought back to manage but his poor health caused him to resign after a few weeks, and he died on the eve of a ceremony planned to honor him. The team changed hands again after the 1934 season, Turner selling out to E.J. Schefter. The team rose to fourth place, squeaking in one game over .500 in 1935. Perhaps more importantly, attendance rebounded to 228,000 for the year.

The most famous post-McCredie Beaver team came next. The team opened 1936 with ex-A's star Max Bishop as manager and second baseman. But Bishop wanted to play the promising Pete Coscarart at second, and Bishop

was fired when he wouldn't play himself enough. Bill Sweeney, the team's first baseman, stepped in and led the team to the regular season title on the season's last day. Portland then beat Seattle four games to none in the first playoff round and trounced Oakland four games to one in the championship series. Pitcher Ad Liska began his long career in Portland, winning the first 15 of his eventual 198 career victories for the Beavers.

In 1937, Portland dropped to fourth place but made the expanded playoffs, defeating San Francisco in the first round before losing to champion San Diego, which featured a skinny outfielder named Ted Williams. The 1938 outfit had strong pitchers in Whitey Hilcher, Bill Thomas and Ad Liska but showed little hitting and no power while the team dropped to sixth. Thomas and Liska each won 20 games and eight Beavers hit over .300 in 1939, but the team began a stretch of four straight years in the cellar.

The 1940 club produced the worst Beaver record (56-122) since 1921, and finished 56 games behind champion Seattle, and a full 25 games behind seventh-place San Francisco. Despite their dismal records, the club found a star in minor league veteran Ted Norbert. In 1942, Norbert ran away with the batting title with a .378 average, precisely 100 points higher than he hit for the Beavers in 1941. He also paced the league with 28 home runs.

In 1943 George Norgan, in partnership with former owner William Klepper (1922-24), purchased the team. The Beavers responded with their first winning record since 1937. With management dubbing them the "Lucky Beavers," Portland made the PCL playoffs, but lost to San Francisco in the first round. The pitching was much improved, led by Liska's 17-11 record.

By this point, World War II was savaging the ranks of major league baseball and the minors as well, but Portland managed to become "less bad" than the rest of the circuit and continued to move up, finishing second in 1944. The hitting was not spectacular, but solid from top to bottom, with seven players each contributing more than 40 RBIs.

Finally, in 1945, there was another Portland pennant, this time led by player-manager Marv Owen. Five regulars hit over .300, and each drove in at least 60 runs. Liska, Burt Pulford and Roy Helser each won exactly 20 games, and the Beavers took the pennant by 8-1/2 games. Again, the team was luckless in the playoffs, losing to San Francisco in the first round, but as a franchise, the Beavers had survived the war relatively well.

The end of World War II signaled a boom for baseball in general, including the Pacific Coast League. Following the pennant-winning season of 1945, George Norgan bought out William Klepper and became the sole owner of the Portland franchise. Unfortunately, the Beavers sank to seventh place in 1946, 41 games out of first, though Harvey Storey's .326 average (partially with Los Angeles) led the league, and Ad Liska tossed a no-hitter.

The next season, the Beavers set a team attendance record lasting more than a half-century, drawing 421,000

Future major-league standouts Bob Johnson and Pinky Higgins (back row, fourth, and tenth from left, respectively) were members of Portland's 1932 PCL champions. The Beavers were affiliated with the Philadelphia Athletics. Coach Nick Williams (middle row, sixth from left) had managed San Francisco to the 1931 PCL title.

fans to Vaughn Street, finishing third and returning to the playoffs. The 1947 season also marked the Portland debut of one of the most popular Beavers ever, second baseman Eddie Basinski. The man known as "The Fiddler" and "The Professor" would play for the club into the 1957 season and remain a local icon for decades after he left the game.

Portland spent the next several years drenched in mediocrity, placing between fourth and sixth each season from 1948 through 1953. The Beavers also integrated in 1949, as shortstop Frankie Austin and outfielder Luis Marquez joined the team.

In 1952, the PCL was granted "Open" status, placing it a step above the other Triple A leagues but a step below the major leagues. It was also the start of a four-season tenure as manager by Clay Hopper, who had helmed the Montreal Royals, helping guide Jackie Robinson as he broke the color line in Organized Baseball in 1946. After a last-place finish in 1954, Norgan sold the team into community ownership with shares available to the public for $10 each. Approximately 2,400 new owners saw Portland rise to fifth place, just nine games out of first, in 1955.

The first year of community ownership was also the last year for Vaughn Street. Prior to the season, the ball club's board of directors announced that the team would move to Multnomah Stadium for 1956. The final day at the old ballpark, September 11, saw the Beavers sweep a doubleheader from Oakland to wrap up a fifth-place finish.

The club's spacious new home had actually been around since 1926, and it led to a jump in attendance, from just under 200,000 to just over 300,000 for a third-place club in 1956. The next season saw the Beavers drop to last place in what was the final season of the "classic" Pacific Coast League, as the major league Dodgers and Giants subsequently moved to Los Angeles and San Francisco, displacing the PCL teams there. With the loss of the PCL's "Open" classification, Portland lost some of its baseball identity. Now in a circuit that included cities like Phoenix and Salt Lake City, the Beavers finished fourth in 1958.

From 1929 to 1963, Rollie Truitt broadcast Portland Beaver games. Truitt, who continued as public-address announcer through 1972, became team historian, publishing an annual booklet, "Rollie Truitt's Scrapbook." Despite a less than glib delivery, Truitt endeared himself to fans with his love of the game and knowledge of the team.

In the 1960s, the Beavers gradually but irretrievably lost their independence, as the "farm system" model took over the PCL. Signings, trades and releases that had long been left to the Beavers — they controlled the contracts of their players — were now made based on the needs of the major league team supplying the players. It didn't help that the Beavers spent 1962 and 1963 affiliated with the dreadful Kansas City Athletics, but Portland nevertheless managed to avoid the cellar both seasons. With Portland's parent affiliation changing regularly, there was little continuity of players from year to year.

In 1964 the Cleveland Indians sent a squad that included standout pitchers Luis Tiant, Sam McDowell and Tommy John. McDowell (8-0) and Tiant (15-1) earned promotions to the parent club, leaving Portland to finish just a game out

No, that's not Edward G. Robinson. It's E.J. Schefter, Portland Beavers president, peeking through the "1938" formed by (from left) Eddie Wilson, Steve Coscarart, Manager Bill Sweeney and Dudley Lee. Sweeney, who also managed PCL teams in Hollywood, Los Angeles and Seattle, led the Beavers to the PCL crown in 1936, his first year as Portland manager. Steve Coscarart was one of three Coscararts to play for Portland. Pete and Joe were the other two.

Outfielder and fan favorite Luis Marquez helped the Portland Beavers break the color line in 1949.

of first place in the Western Division. The next season, the Beavers won their first title of any type since the 1945 pennant winners by capturing the division title, but they fell to Oklahoma City in the PCL championship series.

Portland fans lost two other longtime ties with the ball club during the decade. Rollie Truitt, the team's radio voice since 1929, called his last game in 1963. (He continued to serve as public address announcer at the stadium through 1972.) Beloved groundskeeper Rocky Benevento hung up his rake in 1966 after 30 years on the job.

Minor league crowds dwindled across the nation, and Portland's attendance slipped under 200,000 for all but two years in the 1960s. Multnomah Stadium became less fan-friendly in 1969, when the city installed artificial turf, one of the first baseball parks to do so. That year, the Beavers were sold to a group of local businessman, who a year later sold it to Bill Cutler. After the 1972 season, Cutler moved the franchise to Spokane. For the next five years, Portland had to settle for the Mavericks, independent team in the Single A Northwest League.

The American League expansion by two teams in 1977 caused the PCL to follow suit a year later, and Portland was back in Triple A. This version of the Beavers lasted 16 years, highlighted by the zany promotions of Dave Hersh, the stints of Luis Tiant and Willie Horton in 1981, and a championship in 1983 (the first for the Beavers since 1936). Ex-Yankee and longtime minor league operator Joe Buzas bought the club in 1986, but after seven seasons of mediocre attendance, he moved the franchise to Salt Lake City. For the next six years, Portland was again entertained by a Northwest League team, a run that included a championship in 1997.

In 2000, Portland Family Entertainment (PFE) bought the Albuquerque Dukes and moved the franchise to Portland while also heavily renovating Civic (formerly Multnomah) Stadium. The ballpark, renamed PGE Park, drew great reviews for bringing back an old-time baseball atmosphere — an organ for music, a gargantuan hand-operated scoreboard in left-centerfield, dark green seats, fresh popcorn, a shoeshine stand — and nearly 440,000 fans came through the gates, breaking the single-season attendance record that had stood since 1947.

This operation was also expensive, and PGE investors soon ousted the group's management. Further financial difficulties turned to team over to a pension fund in 2003, and the PCL ran the club in 2004. The ownership situation became clearer in March 2005, when an agreement was reached for the Portland Baseball Investment Group (PBIG) to purchase the team. Among the investors were Abe Alizadeh, the majority owner, and Jack Cain, a Portland native and long-time baseball operator. The Beavers placed third in their division, drawing 360,772 fans.

Today, with the Pacific Coast League heading into its second century, Portland remains the sole link to the league's earliest days. Meanwhile, Oregon's largest city is looking for a promotion to the big leagues and again seeking to end a lengthy pennant drought. ⚾

Portland Beavers infielder Eddie Basinski, a 13-year veteran of the Pacific Coast League, found "smarter baseball" being played in the PCL than in the majors.

'Those were the most wonderful days I believe I ever had'

Players who lived the PCL story recall warmly their exhilaration in 'the third major league'

BY LARRY STONE

They are slowly disappearing, the men who made the Pacific Coast League such a rollicking, boisterous, and crackling fun place in its heyday in the 1930s, '40s and '50s. The march of time has a way of doing that. Long gone are many of the legends who were household names up and down the West Coast: Steve Bilko, Lou "the Mad Russian" Novikoff, Kewpie Dick Barrett, "Farmer Hal" Turpin, Marvin "Doo-

Dat" Gudat, Frenchy Uhalt. And yes, Joe DiMaggio and Ted Williams.

But the ones who survive, now in their 70s and 80s and even 90s, many infirm but still clear of mind, relish their memories of that circuit. They are militant in their assertion that the league — which spanned from San Diego in the south to Seattle in the north (with Vancouver, B.C., replacing Oakland after the 1956 season), finally dying out as an independent force when the Dodgers and Giants moved West in 1958 — was major league in every way but name.

Consider Larry Jansen, who won 30 games for the pennant-winning San Francisco Seals in 1946, then went to the New York Giants the following year and won 21 to start a productive major league career.

"They were awful close (in quality)," said Jansen, now 85 and living in Forest Grove, Oregon. "I went from here to there and did the same thing."

Consider Buddy Hancken, who caught one game in the majors for the Philadelphia A's in 1940, and caught for the Seattle Rainiers on their championship team of 1939.

"Lord have mercy, we had good players," he said of the PCL. "We made more money than they did in the big leagues, because we had another month of play. The weather was great, we were off every Monday. An awful lot

Larry Stone is the national baseball writer for the *Seattle Times*. A graduate of the University of California at Berkeley, he has covered major league baseball since 1986. Stone lives in Bellevue, Washington, with his wife of 21 years, Lisa; daughter Meredith, 9; and son, Jordan, 6. His daughter, Jessica, 19, just completed her sophomore year at Georgetown University.

Warming up along the third-base line in 1951 is Art Del Duca, who found manager Rogers Hornsby strict, "but if he liked you, he stayed with you."

The most I made in the majors was $6,000 in 1945, when I made the All-Star team. ...

I made more with Portland, $7,200. It was a little better than a plumber or electrician, but I had to work in the winter.

Those were great days — like Tom Brokaw says, the greatest generation.

Eddie Basinski

of guys said they'd rather stay there than go back and face the cold spring and fall in New York and Chicago."

Consider infielder Eddie Basinski, a starter with the Brooklyn Dodgers in 1945 who found himself out of a job the next year when Pee Wee Reese returned from the war. That allowed Basinski to forge a highly successful 13-year PCL career in Portland, Seattle, and Vancouver, interrupted only by a 56-game stint with the Pirates in 1947.

"I will say this. The difference between two leagues is that there was smarter baseball within the Coast League," observed Basinski. "Sure, the top pitchers were in the majors, and the Grade A home-run hitters. But all in all, our league was much smarter, and the product produced by the league was better. We double-stole, hit and ran, hit behind the runner, all those things. All the guys in the majors were going for the home runs. ... The Coast League was, in fact, the third major league. It was a great league. All the players loved it. We made more money than the big leagues, although that's not saying much."

"In my estimation," added Charlie Metro, who managed Vancouver in 1957-59 and would go on to have major league managerial stints with the Cubs and Royals, "every game, every series was a terrific, exhilarating thing."

It was "the grand minor league," as it was dubbed in a 1999 book by the late PCL historian Dick Dobbins. There were teams like the San Diego Padres, where Ted Williams got his start in 1936 at age 17 before he led them to their first PCL pennant the next year.

Teams like the Hollywood Stars — a PCL powerhouse in the early 1950s — and the Los Angeles Angels, whose bitter rivalry was nearly matched in intensity by that between the Bay Area titans, the San Francisco Seals of the DiMaggios and Lefty O'Doul and the Oakland Oaks of Casey Stengel and Billy Martin.

And teams like the Mission Bells, who were rechristened "Reds" after popular team manager Wade "Red" Killefer, and who shared San Francisco with the Seals for a time. Or the Sacramento Solons, who won the PCL pennant in 1942 while managed by St. Louis "Gas House Gang" hero Pepper Martin.

And here, especially, were the Northwest teams in the PCL: the Seattle Rainiers, whose reign of three pennants in 1939-41 under the ownership of beer baron Emil Sick established them as a powerhouse; the Portland Beavers, under the control of the Philadelphia A's in the 1930s, and who won it all in 1936; and the Vancouver Mounties, who were warmly received by Canadian fans when the Oakland Oaks moved north after the 1955 season. The Baltimore Orioles sent many of their young prospects to Vancouver, which is where a young third baseman named Brooks Robinson passed through in 1959 en route to Baltimore and, eventually, Cooperstown and the Hall of Fame.

Seven men who lived the PCL story tell it here. They traveled the circuit from San Diego to Vancouver, playing with and against the great teams that ruled the West Coast baseball world.

Eddie Basinski

He made "Ripley's Believe It or Not" as (according to the piece) the first person ever to go straight to the major leagues without playing high school or college baseball. With the majors decimated by World War II, he got signed at age 21 by Dodgers GM Branch Rickey in 1944 right out of the city leagues of Buffalo. One of his best friends growing up was a hot-shot pitcher named Warren Spahn, against whom he would often take batting practice. With the Pittsburgh Pirates in 1947, Basinski would face Spahn, then the ace of the Braves, and got two ringing doubles. After the second one, Spahn turned on the mound to face Basinski and said, "You SOB — Houghton Park in Buffalo. That's where you learned all those tricks." But Basinski, now 83 and still living in Portland, thrived most brightly in the PCL.

"There were no agents in those days. There was no reason, because there was no money. The most I made in the majors was $6,000 in 1945. I made more with Portland — $7,200. It was a little better than a plumber or electrician, but I had to work in the winter. Those were great days — like Tom Brokaw says, the greatest generation.

"I made my major league debut on May 20 against Cincinnati. Clyde Shoun was the pitcher. He had pitched a no-hitter the start before. I hit a triple my first time up in the pros. As I came around third, I'm going for home, because the city league parks in Buffalo had no fences. You

hit a long ball to left center, you got a home run. Leo Durocher had to tackle me as I went around third, and I crawled back to the bag. Durocher said, 'Where in the world did Rickey find you? Didn't you see the sign?' I said, 'What sign?' "

With many of the Dodgers off to war, Basinski played shortstop for the Dodgers in 1944-45, hitting .262 in 1945. But when Reese came back from the war for the next season, Durocher gave Pee Wee his old shortstop job, and Basinski maneuvered a move to St. Paul, where he could play every day. From there, he was traded to the Yankees and went to their farm team in Newark. Then, in August 1947, Basinski was shipped to Portland, where his deceptively unathletic looks didn't make a good first impression on Portland manager Jim Turner.

"I could have gone back to the Yankees. They wanted me after the 1947 season with Portland. I couldn't do anything wrong with Portland that year. Every time I came up with the winning or tying run on base, I came through. Turner says, 'Ed, you and Charlie Silvera are going to the Yankees.' The reason I was a little stunned by that, when I flew from Newark to Seattle to join the Portland team in 1947, Jim Turner came in that day and later told me, 'You have no idea how disappointed I was when I saw you.' He was judging me by my appearance. That pissed me off. A year and a half later, he's telling me I'm going to the Yankees. I didn't take advantage of rubbing that in.

"I turned them down. I knew there was a lot of politics up there. Earlier with Brooklyn, I was hitting .389 after two weeks, leading the National League in hitting. I made a terrible mistake. A reporter came to my hotel to interview me. He said, 'Mr. Basinski, what do you think of the National League?' I should have kept by mouth shut. But I said, 'Any man who can't hit .300 in this league ought to go get a lunch bucket.' What a horrible mistake. Did they come after me! I found out what great curveballs are, and found out what knockdown pitches are. They called me bush league and every name in the world.

"When I turned the Yankees down, it was probably a terrible mistake. They won a lot pennants after that. I would have been part of all those great teams and made all that money. A lot of players who are just average players are highlighted because they won pennants.

"I went on with Portland in 1948 to have another great year. I loved the team, loved the guys. We finished in the first division, but we had to struggle because the owner was a Canadian man who owned Lucky Lager beer, and he wouldn't put the money out to get top pitchers or hitters. He was happy just making the first division.

"Portland fans, as far as loyalty, people supporting the team, were second only to Brooklyn fans, who were the greatest. They idolized you and would kill for you (while) Portland fans were conservative, but very loyal and appreciative. They even appreciated opposing players — not like San Francisco or L.A., where they would hang you by the neck if you did something good. In Oakland, they'd be shooting BB guns at you from the right field stands. One

night, our right fielder ran off the field in the middle of an inning. They had to get the cops to confiscate the BB guns. The next day, our manager, Bill Sweeney, brought his own pistol to the dugout. Dressen was the manager in Oakland. Sweeney was shooting him in the ass. Dressen thought his own fans were shooting him. Sweeney was laughing so hard he was crying.

"I had a great ten years with Portland. One record I'm very proud of is playing all the innings in 202 games in 1950. We had a 200-game schedule and two tie games. No player in the history of baseball has ever done that. I was proud of that, because a lot of guys looked at me and said a gust of wind would blow me over. But I was tough.

"I settled in Portland, married there, had a couple of boys. I think that had a lot to do with turning down the Yankees. I'm sure it was a mistake as far as money, but I had the great love and devotion of Portland all those years."

In 1957, after a dispute with general manager Joe Ziegler, Basinski was sold to the Seattle Rainiers, where he played under manager Lefty O'Doul.

"(Dewey) Soriano in Seattle picked me up for $100. I couldn't believe it. Two years later, he sold me for $10,000 to Vancouver. My popularity got Ziegler afraid. He even accused me of stealing his job. I hated Ziegler for that. Two of my best years were for Seattle because of that. I offered steak dinners to anyone who would drive in a run or win a game. Oh, I was mad. I came back and killed Portland, hit .484 in two years against them, with half my homers against them.

"I should have finished my career in Portland. But I loved O'Doul. I basically retired after 1959 with Vancouver. I had a chance there to rub shoulders with Brooks Robinson. What a fantastic ballplayer. Even while I was playing, I was already working for Consolidated Freightways. I spent 31 years with them. I loved the country out there, loved Portland. Still do."

Art Del Duca

Now 79, Del Duca lives in New Hampshire and still works full-time. He played in Seattle in 1951-53, the first year under manager Rogers Hornsby, the Hall of Famer whom he had first met while playing Double A ball in the Yankees organization.

"If there was any other place I was going to live, it would be Seattle. I loved it there. I kind of clicked with Hornsby when I met him in Beaumont. We won the pennant down there, and then they shipped me to San Francisco. I got a bad cold when I got out there in spring from the change in climate. I couldn't get going. Hornsby had become manager of Seattle, and he traded for me. I ended up with another pennant winner in 1951.

"I went to spring training one year with the Yankees, that was it. But I still follow the Yankees. I drive a Mercedes, and on the plate frame it says "New York Yankees." The team we had in Seattle could have beaten some of the lower

If there was any other place I was going to live, it would be Seattle. I loved it there.

I ended up with another pennant winner in 1951.

Art Del Duca

(From left) Larry Jansen, player-coach for the Seattle Rainiers, chats with fellow hurlers Elmer Singleton and Bud Podbielan in the dugout of Sick's Stadium in 1955.

teams in the American League and National League. The PCL was a good league.

"I had to work in the off-season. My brother was in the construction business. The best I got was $300 a week, maybe. It wasn't bad money. You could save some, believe it or not. In those days, you were supposed to go nine innings. When you signed a contract, you said you were going to go nine innings. You tried your best.

"We had Jungle Jim Rivera in Seattle. He went to the big leagues the very next year. He was a great player, (but) very controversial. The night life, geez. I went out with him one night. Finally, I said, 'You do what you do. I'm going to bed.' He stayed out all night, played a doubleheader the next day, and was drag bunting like he had never been out. I behaved.

"Hornsby was kind of strict, but if he liked you, he stayed with you. I had won two games with Kansas City, then they optioned me to Beaumont, which I thought they shouldn't have done. When I got down there, I lost my first five games. Hornsby got me in a room and said, 'I'm going to stick with you.' I didn't lose a game the rest of the year. I won 11 in a row. A lot of guys didn't like him, thought he was as crude as could be. I never spoke to him much, but I knew he was there, and he knew I was there."

Larry Jansen

Jansen was the last 30-game winner in the PCL for the pennant-winning Seals in 1946, just two years after a PCL career that began with San Francisco in 1941 was interrupted by World War II.

> **The slider just chewed everyone up. ...**
>
> **The slider was a very, very new pitch. Everyone thought it was a fastball. They hit ground ball after ground ball.**
>
> **Larry Jansen**

"I was very fortunate. When the war started, during the winter I was working on our farm in Oregon. The next spring, I called the draft board and said, 'I'm supposed to leave for spring training tomorrow.' They said, 'What's your address? We'll send the induction forms right to you.' I said, 'I have two children. What happens if I stay on the farm?' They said they'd give me a deferment for a while. I said, 'I'm not going to spring training.' I skipped 1943 and 1944, and part of 1945.

"Before I left the PCL, my catcher taught me a slider. It was a pitch that had hardly ever been used. I learned it before the season ended in 1942. I worked on it playing in semipro leagues. When the war ended, San Francisco called and asked if I could pitch. I said I had to call the draft board. I told them the San Francisco Seals wanted me to play baseball. They asked me if I had taken any vacations while I worked on the farm. I said no. They said, 'We'll give you a five-week vacation.' I went down and went 4-1, helped get them into the playoffs. But I couldn't play in the playoffs because I hadn't gotten there in time. I went home, and they went on to win the playoffs and the pennant. They sent me a full share.

"The next year, I went 30-6. The slider just chewed everyone up. That's why I was such a good pitcher in the big leagues. The slider was a very, very new pitch. Everyone thought it was a fastball. They hit ground ball after ground ball.

"In 1947, I went to the New York Giants. Mel Ott was my manager. In spring training, Bob Feller hit a line drive back at me in Tucson, the first game I pitched, and I was out. When the season was starting, I hadn't pitched for awhile, and I relieved a little bit. I hadn't relieved in my life. Three or four days before cutting time, the pitching coach said, 'You've got to give Jansen a chance to start. He won 30 games last year.' They started me in Boston and I beat them 3-2, and four days later in St. Louis, he pitches me again, and I beat them. I made the team, and went on to win 21 games."

After going 120-86 in the major leagues for the Giants from 1947-54, Jansen returned to the PCL in 1955 with Seattle. He was a player-coach for Fred Hutchinson on the Rainiers' 1955 championship team, and for Lefty O'Doul in 1957, O'Doul's last season managing in the PCL. He also played for Portland in the late 1950s and early 1960s.

"Lefty O'Doul, my manager in Seattle, was a great, great guy. We were playing one day in San Francisco, at the old Seals Stadium. Only two or three balls had ever been hit over the center field fence. I was pitching for Seattle that day, and I hit one over the center field fence. O'Doul was coaching third, and as I round third, there's O'Doul laying flat on his back, yelling, 'Stop and pick me up.' I stopped and picked him up. The next day, I'm running in the outfield, and San Francisco's manager came up and told me, 'The guy you hit the home run off is gone to Fort Worth.'

"I had a pretty good stretch in Seattle. In 1956, I was 11-2. The Cincinnati Reds brought me up. They had a chance to win the pennant. They pitched me against the Braves because I used to pitch well against them. I beat them, and then the Braves came into Cincinnati, and I beat them again. But they made the mistake of pitching me against three more teams."

Rinaldo "Rugger" Ardizoia

Born in Oleggio, Italy, Ardizoia still lives at age 86 in the same San Francisco house he bought in 1940 on his 21st birthday for $5,000 — the same day he bought a new Pontiac for $1,000. Talk about a cup of coffee in the majors, Ardizoia had just a sip, pitching one game in the majors for the New York Yankees in 1947. Before that, he roamed the PCL to pitch for Mission, Hollywood, and Oakland. In 1938, he played for the Bellingham Chinooks of the Western International League, and took the mound for Seattle in 1949-50. Ardizoia works out at the gym three times a week and still works security for basketball and football games at two San Francisco high schools. "A lot of people don't believe my age," he said. "I keep in good shape. Going up and down stairs, I have to have a railing. Other than that, what the heck. At least I'm six feet over and not six feet under."

"We were between the majors and Triple A in the PCL. Doggone right we were as good as the major leagues. I'd like to see a better center fielder anywhere than Bill Lawrence.

"It was a real pleasure playing for Emil Sick. He was a hell of a nice owner. As a pitcher, I liked Sick's Stadium, because the ball didn't carry as well as in other parks.

Pitch counts were non-existent in the PCL, says Rinaldo "Rugger" Ardizoia, who pitched for Seattle in 1949 and 1950. "If you could get them out, you got them out. You couldn't get sore arms, because someone was looking over your shoulder."

"I started with Mission way back in 1937, but two teams were playing in Seals Stadium, and we weren't drawing. So Mission moved to Hollywood in 1938. Oh, boy, I was only 19, a free spirit. George Raft, Ronald Reagan, the Marx Brothers, the Bowery Boys, you name it, I met them all. One night before I pitched, our manager let me out into the stands and I sat with Desi Arnaz and Lucille Ball. They were in box seats.

"We had a big rivalry with the Angels. There was a self-centered sportswriter for the Los Angeles Herald named John B. Olds who was always getting on Frenchy Uhalt, who was hot-tempered, too. One time, between games of a doubleheader, Olds came in the clubhouse after we lost the first game. Him and Frenchy got into it. We got our traveling trunks and made a ring. Frenchy beat the hell out of him. Olds didn't say much after that.

"In 1941 and 1942, I went to spring training with the Yankees. They farmed me to Newark, but I was born in Italy and I wasn't an American citizen. Montreal and Toronto were in the International League, and they wouldn't let me in as an alien, so they sent me to Kansas City. In 1943, the U.S. Army drafted me. I was in the service three years, and I still wasn't a citizen. I came out, went before a judge, raised my hand and became a citizen.

"When I came out, I was 27, old for a rookie. They sent me to Oakland with Casey Stengel. I was 15-7 with a 2.83 ERA, and I thought this was it. I had a cup of coffee with the Yankees in 1947, but they sent me back to Hollywood.

"Playing for Casey in Oakland was a lot of fun. Every game we won, he gave us two cases of beer. When we won certain games, he gave us $3. That was for steak dinners in those days. He'd joke around, talk, keep you relaxed.

With a .367 average, Seattle Rainiers infielder Hillis Layne won the PCL batting title in 1947.

"We were real close. We traveled by train, always together in the same car, uppers and lowers. You waited for someone to go in a taxi with you when you went off to dinner. We flew one time only. We were in San Diego and had to play the next night in Seattle. The train would never make it, so Emil Sick flew us up there. It was the only time we ever flew.

"I had 108 complete games in my first six years. They didn't count pitches. If you could get them out, you got them out. You couldn't get sore arms, because someone was looking over your shoulder. One time with Bellingham I pitched 18 innings against Wenatchee. I pitched 15 innings for Hollywood against Los Angeles. It was not that unusual. Some guys pitched both games of a doubleheader.

"Once, Dickie Barrett was pitching for Seattle in Civic Stadium, before Sick's Stadium. He had won 18 games, and if he won 20 games, he would get a bonus. The owner told the manager if he pitched Barrett the second game of the doubleheader, he was firing him. The manager said, 'You'd better fire me now. He's pitching both games.' He didn't know about the bonus. Barrett won both games and won 20 games."

Hillis Layne

The 88-year-old Layne lives on Signal Mountain near Chattanooga, Tennessee. He has been mostly confined to a wheelchair for the last 16 years after falling out of a tree while cutting limbs. Now, he says, "I sit around and reminisce and think of the good old days." Though he played parts of three seasons with the

Washington Senators (1941, 1944 and 1945), the best seasons for Layne were in Seattle with the Rainiers in 1947-50, including winning a PCL batting title in 1947 with a .367 average.

"My best years were in Seattle, at Sick's Stadium. I really enjoyed the people out there. I hate to say this, but I enjoyed it more than the big leagues, what time I played. That PCL was probably the best league at the time of any of them. We had all those big league managers, Lefty O'Doul, Jimmy Dykes, Fred Hutchinson, Jo Jo White.

"I played for Jo Jo White in Seattle. Ol' Jo Jo was a good one. I remember mainly leading the league in 1947. I'd led the league all year with Chattanooga (in 1946) until the last day of the season, and a guy beat me out by five points, .374 to .369. Then I go to Seattle and hit .367. My best year was in 1948. We played a 200-game schedule. I got up to bat 664 times and got 227 hits. I hit .342. I remember Lou Novikoff, the 'Mad Russian' — we were kind of rivals. He'd come out of Chicago with the Cubs. I remember very distinctly, they said they'd give $100 to the one that hit the first home run. I wasn't a home run hitter, but I hit the ball pretty sharp and hit a home run. Lou said he could hardly breathe because Layne got the prize. One hundred dollars was a lot of money.

"Mr. Torchy Torrance (Seattle's general manager) was an officer in the Navy at the time, and he saw me play at Washington. He invited me and my wife to his house for dinner, and said, 'Hillis, I've told everyone that when I get out of the Navy, I'm going to buy you.' He bought me for $18,000.

"One thing I miss is Mount Rainier. I tell everyone: You know what I remember about Seattle? Every time I got up to bat when it's a clear day, I'd see Mount Rainier. I'd look right over the center field fence. Sick's Stadium was beautiful, a great place to play. Mr. Emil Sick treated us royally. It was kind of a big league outfit as far as playing conditions.

"In baseball now, the competition is keen in a way, but I do wish they'd be more competitive. I'm thinking about writing a letter to the commissioner. These guys now are grinning, going to first base and laughing. I had a roommate for four years named Tony York, a real good second baseman. One night, he planned to have me eat out in Seattle. I was playing for Portland then. He was making a double play, standing right over me. I tried to knock him out of the double play. He said, 'You're trying to kill your buddy, aren't you?' I got up and brushed myself off and grinned a little. That's how we played in those days.

"I was playing for the Chattanooga Lookouts, Double A, in my hometown, when they called three of us, three infielders, and told us we were going to Senators. One of the players was driving, and we heard the end of the broadcast. The announcer said, 'Pitching for Cleveland tomorrow against Washington is Bob Feller.'

The next afternoon, at 2 o'clock, I was facing Bob Feller. They had timed him at 110, 112 mph. I told my buddies after the game, if they throw like that up here, I'm in the wrong business. He struck out 17, beat us 2-0. I never did strike out much. I'm not bragging, but I was tough with two strikes. I hit the ball good twice, went 0-for-4, but me and Cecil Travis were the only two Bob didn't strike out. I thought that was a great thing."

Buddy Hancken

Hancken's major league cup of coffee was as brief as Ardizoia's — one game with Connie Mack's Philadelphia A's in 1940, a year after he played in Seattle on the Rainiers' first championship team. Now age 91, he lives in Orange, Texas, and enjoys spending time with his "lady friend."

"I had the greatest career anyone ever had–one game. Old man Mack signed me, because I had caught

knuckleballers at one time. He had a couple of knuckleballers. We trained in Anaheim in 1940, and damned if he didn't send the knuckleballers away. There I was left. I was out of luck. He sold me down to Buffalo.

"I thought Seattle was the greatest place in the world to play ball. We had great times, riding that train back and forth. The Seattle fans were great because we were winning. I don't

Buddy Hancken

know how they'd have been if we lost. We made some money for that club. We had 'Kewpie' Dick Barrett, one of the greatest showmen in all baseball. We had the best center fielder I saw in all my life, Bill Lawrence. As far as I'm concerned, he was better than DiMaggio. The second DiMaggio, Dom, was a great one, too. But I never saw a ball hit over Lawrence's head that stayed inside the park."

Charlie Metro

Metro played in the PCL for Oakland and Seattle, had a three-year major league career with the Tigers and A's in 1943-45 and managed the Vancouver Mounties in 1957-59 after the Hollywood franchise moved to Canada. He had partial-year stints managing the major league Chicago Cubs in 1962 and Kansas City Royals in 1970. Now 87, he lives in Colorado, where he settled after managing the Denver Bears. He remembers Vancouver fondly.

"Those were the most wonderful days I believe I ever had. Cedric Tallis gave me the job. They had had a rough year the year before, but we drew over a million people. I had a great time. I had played for Oakland and Seattle, then wound up in Vancouver. Boy, I had a great ride. The only thing was, I didn't get a raise each time.

"In Vancouver, they weren't allowed to sell tickets for Sunday. They broke that Sunday rule because we had a good club. We did a lot of politicking and got them to let us play on Sunday. But we couldn't play beyond 6 p.m. If the game was not over, we'd stop and pick it up. It was great. The fans were wonderful. I don't think I've ever seen fans

VANCOUVER *Mounties*
BASEBALL CLUB

CHARLIE METRO
MANAGER

Vancouver relented and played Sunday baseball but wouldn't allow games to run beyond 6 p.m., recalls Charlie Metro, manager of the Mounties in 1957-59.

like that anywhere. It was a beautiful setting, even though the place only seated seven or eight thousand. I wintered there. The kids loved it. I was offered a job to stay over, but I think the rule was, if you stayed four years, you lost your citizenship. My sons were getting ready to play Little League. I came back.

"I had Brooks Robinson, Ron Hansen, Chuck Estrada, George Bamberger, Jim Marshall. I had three guys that became big league managers: Bamberger, Marshall and Joe Frazier. People say I was a tough manager. I like to say 'demanding.' I didn't take any foolishness when it came to playing. In other words, you played hard. I told the players my job was to improve them and send them to the big leagues. And I did. We had a whole bunch of them go up.

"We finished second, third and second. One year we got beat out in the last week of season. It was a terrific league, the PCL. We had all those great managers, guys like Lefty O'Doul and Tommy Heath, and great ball clubs.

"One strange thing, in 1957, we never had a game rained out. It seemed like every time we went south, it rained like heck, but we never lost a game in Vancouver. The next year was reversed. It was a disaster. Opening Day was delayed a week. I tried to find a warm place to have people warm up. I found it under a bridge over toward the airport. I ran players around one of those concrete pillars that held up the bridge.

> We had all those great managers, guys like Lefty O'Doul and Tommy Heath, and great ball clubs.
>
> Charlie Metro

Seattle Rainiers sparkplug Edo Vanni admires a new car prior to a game in 1940 at Sick's Stadium.

Brooks Robinson was fabulous. I couldn't hit a ball by him. I'd hit them wicked, slice them, one hoppers, short hops. He gobbled up everything.

Charlie Metro

"Brooks Robinson was fabulous. I always hit infield to him, and I was pretty tricky with that fungo. He caught on to everything I did. I couldn't hit a ball by him. I'd hit them wicked, slice them, one hoppers, short hops. He gobbled up everything. My favorite story, our dugout in Vancouver had a screen hanging over some hooks. A guy took half the screen down but forgot the hooks. Brooks came over for a foul, slipped and threw his arm up. A hook caught his arm at the right elbow. I grabbed his arm, he had a 24-inch cut. If he had fallen, he would have been done. Every time I see him, I say, 'Let me see that arm.'

"One day, I put Jim Marshall, a lefthanded hitter, in there against a lefty. He said to me, 'I'm not supposed to be able to hit lefthanders.' I was about to exchange lineups. I said, 'Jim, you have three minutes to learn how.'

"I had been teammates with Paul Richards, who was the general manager and manager of Baltimore. He knew me very well, saw me playing on the Tigers. Our paths had crossed quite a bit. He just called me up and sent me the ballplayers. When we needed one, I'd call him and say, 'I need a pitcher,' and here they came. Unofficially, we were a farm club of theirs, but we got ballplayers from everywhere."

Edo Vanni

Now 88, Vanni is without question the dean of Seattle professional baseball. He attended Queen Anne High School in the city (where his classmates included "Dennis the Menace" creator Hank Ketcham, and Rudy Zallinger, who became artist-in-residence at Yale and won a Pulitzer Prize for his murals). He went to the University of Washington, played on the first Rainiers team in 1938, after beer magnate Emil Sick bought the old Seattle Indians. He also managed the last Rainiers club in 1964, just before they became the Seattle Angels. He was a speedy outfielder, a fiery manager, a wheeling-dealing general manager, and also served as director of group sales for the ill-fated Seattle Pilots in their one season of existence. Vanni's greatest days, however, were with the powerhouse Rainiers club that won three straight Pacific Coast League pennants in 1939-41. Still living in the same Queen Anne home he purchased during his career, Vanni is a treasure trove of memories about the old PCL.

"I went to the University of Washington on a football and baseball scholarship. I was a kicker. They were paying me $150 a month, my books, and a tutor. Then my dad had

a stroke, and I had to make a decision. Fred Hutchinson had just signed with the Seattle ball club, and they were after me. They wanted to meet. Torchy Torrance, a big alum at the university, was the secretary of the Rainiers. He called me and said, 'We'd like to talk to you,' so we set up a meeting.

"I told the football coach, Jim Phelan, what was going on. He said, 'Listen, if those SOBs want to take you, I want to sit in on the meeting.' There was him and Bobby Morris (a legendary football referee and future King County auditor). They were guidance to me. We had a meeting at Western Printing. They told me they would give me a $4,000 bonus, all this stuff. Bobby Morris said, 'Look, you're taking the kid away from college, where he has a dual scholarship. If he's willing to sacrifice his scholarship to play pro baseball, what are you guys going to compensate him with, if he gets hurt?' That's when they came up with these incentive bonuses: "If this kid hits .300, he gets a $250 bonus. If he scores 100 runs, he gets a $250 bonus. If he plays 180 games, he gets a $250 bonus. If you guys win the championship, he gets $250; if you make the playoffs, he gets $250."

"They went back and had a meeting, and came back out. They said that would be agreeable. Mr. Sick was in on the meeting, too. Phelan, the football coach, said, 'Mr. Sick, you're not a young man in the brewing industry here in Seattle. We want 4,000 shares of Rainier Beer stock at 25 cents a share included.' They looked at each other. I says to myself, 'They'll never get that.' They went into another meeting. They came out and said, 'You've got it.' That's where I made all my money. It wasn't in baseball I made it. That beer stock went up from 25 cents a share to $18 dollars a share.

"My first year with them, going into the last two games of the season, I was hitting just under .300, going for the bonus. The manager, Jack Lelivelt, came up to me and said, 'You don't have to play; we're giving you the bonus.' I said, 'No, I'm going to play.' We're playing San Diego. I said, 'I'm going to play this game, and I'm going to play the second game, too.' By God, we played the doubleheader, and I got 6 for 8. Ended up hitting .300. I said, 'I'm not going to sit down the last day.' Why would I sit down, lay down, and these guys think I'm chicken of them when they come to play next year?

"That Lelivelt was one of the best managers I ever played for. He knew how to handle ballplayers. We went to L.A. in the first series. I lost four games for the ball club in the seven-game series. Can you believe that? Everything. Missing first base, getting thrown out stealing third base, missing home plate. I'll never forget the last game of the doubleheader, I come in for a shoestring catch, and I kicked the ball out of my glove with my knee, and they win the ball game. I come in from the outfield, and only one guy was sitting in the dugout, and it was Jack Lelivelt. He said, 'Sit down.' He put his arm around me. He said, 'You had a tough week, didn't you?' I said, 'Yeah, everything I did was wrong, Jack.' So we're going up the ramp, to the clubhouse,

and there's Dick Barrett screaming like hell: 'If they don't get that kid out of the outfield, we're not going to win anything.' Lelivelt raised his hand and says, 'I knew the kid made all these mistakes this week, but he's the only one that got on base to make them.' It was the perfect thing to say. We went to San Diego and I won three out of seven games from the San Diego team. That was it. He could have ruined me right there. But he wasn't that kind of a manager. That's why Hutch was a success, and Hutch patterned his managing after him. I patterned after him, same thing. I had kids, I gave them a fair chance. I never bawled them out in front of anybody. Never. That's the way it should be done.

"Those pennant years, those were the most fun I've ever had. We traded Fred to Detroit and got four ballplayers in return — Jo Jo White, Buddy Hancken, Ed Selway, and George Archie. Four good ballplayers. Jo Jo White was a helluva competitor. He knew Ty Cobb, you know. I roomed with him. He says to me one day, 'You know, you are the weakest link on our ball club, so we've got to strengthen you up.' By God, he spent days with me at the ballpark, teaching me how to slide. By God, that paid off.

We were one-two in the batting order. We drove those pitchers nuts. The first four guys in our batting order in 1939 stole 112 bases. I was speedy. I hit a lot of singles and stole bases. That sparked everybody. Not that I was a great ballplayer, but that's the example we set for the other guys on the team, and they all followed in the pattern. We were strong. The first eight guys in the batting order, you couldn't get them out. We were tough.

"Then the town started rallying to the ball club. Oh, yeah. I'd go to the ballpark at 4 o'clock in the afternoon, and they'd be lined up for half a mile to get in. Then you'd walk around town, and everyone recognized you. It made you feel good. You'd say, 'Geez, I've got to go to the ballpark,' and then you'd go to the ballpark and have a hell of a time. It was fun playing baseball.

"The game has changed so much. Back when I played, all we had was a felt hat, and the pitcher — you were fair game. The pitcher would knock you on your ass, and they would throw at you. They would do anything they want. Then they came up with these helmets. Punch and Judy hitters like myself, we'd stand in there and just punch the ball. Those guys would buzz them under the chin; they'd have you jumping rope and everything. Then baseball wanted these home run hitters, so they started penalizing the pitchers for knocking the hitters down, so those guys could get home runs.

"Seattle is one of the best baseball towns in America. When Mr. Sick took over, and he put those winning teams in there, this was one of the best baseball towns. And it still is."

> We played the doubleheader, and I got 6 for 8. Ended up hitting .300.
>
> I said, 'I'm not going to sit down the last day.'
>
> Why would I sit down, lay down, and these guys think I'm chicken of them when they come to play next year?
>
> **Edo Vanni**

For a book so universally hailed as well-written, funny, and provocative, it is difficult to imagine that it was once so controversial or that its author would be shunned by people within the game for many years, and is still shunned. Yet it is so.

Staring down a photographer was the least of worries for Jim Bouton during his 1969 season with the Seattle Pilots, which he recounted with candor and humor in 'Ball Four.'

The revolution started here

The story behind the groundbreaking *Ball Four*

By MARK ARMOUR

Thirty-five years after its publication, one rarely encounters a negative opinion of *Ball Four*, Jim Bouton's 1970 journal recounting his previous season in the major leagues. A bestseller at the time of its publication, the book fundamentally changed sports literature and journalism — and the way we view our sports heroes. In 1995 the New York Public Library honored *Ball Four* as one of the greatest books published in the 20th century, alongside such classics as Anne Frank's *Diary of a Young Girl*, F. Scott Fitzgerald's *The Great Gatsby*, and Dr. Seuss's *The Cat in the Hat*.

Today's fans and writers, children or young adults when they first devoured the book, re-read it every few years. For a book so universally hailed as well-written, funny, and provocative, it is difficult to imagine that it was once so controversial or that its author would be shunned by people within the game for many years, and is still shunned. Yet it is so.

After decades of first-person sports books written mainly for high school boys, the first honest adult portrayal of the life a ballplayer predated *Ball Four* by ten years. *The Long Season* was pitcher Jim Brosnan's look at his 1959 season in the National League. Both it and his 1962 follow-up, *Pennant Race*, were well received outside the game and remain classics in sports literature. The great Jimmy Cannon called *The Long Season* "the greatest baseball book ever written." In the *New York Herald Tribune*, Red Smith hailed it as "a cocky book, caustic and candid and, in a way, courageous, for Brosnan calls him like he sees them, doesn't hesitate to name names, and employs ridicule like a stiletto."

In one of the more fascinating passages, Brosnan recalls a night that two of his Cardinal teammates spent in a bath house (essentially a brothel) while on the team's off-season trip to Japan. The book's publisher, Harper, required that Brosnan's original version be modified in deference to the two players, bachelors Joe Cunningham and Don Blasingame. As rewritten, the men partook in "a strenuous exercise or two." That instance aside, Brosnan said the rest of *The Long Season* appeared essentially as he wrote it.

Breaking from the typical ghosted autobiographies baseball had been serving up for years, and with scrappy determination mixed liberally with inspiration from God, family and country, Brosnan showed us real men — men who drank, chased women, argued over trivialities in the bullpen, and worried about their mortgages, families, and futures. Brosnan wanted to pitch well and especially to make more money, but there were many days that he would have just as soon called in sick and stayed home with his family. He also liked a martini or two after a hard-earned victory, or, for that matter, after a defeat. In other words, he had a lot in common with the rest of us, the people reading his book. Brosnan did not employ profanity, and, other than the single scene described above, did not reveal sexual encounters.

Inside the game, the book caused an uproar. Brosnan minced no words about several people he did not like, including his former manager Solly Hemus and Cardinal broadcaster Harry Caray ("an old blabbermouth"). Hemus was not amused, quipping, "You think Brosnan's writing is funny, wait until you see him pitch." Joe Garagiola called him a "kookie beatnik," complaining, "That stuff about him calling home to see if there were enough olives for martini hour. What kind of stuff is that to write about? How is that going to look to the kids?"

One young man who loved the book was Jim Bouton, a 21-year-old pitcher for the Yankees' Greensboro, North Carolina, farm club. "I really enjoyed it tremendously," he later recalled. "I remember when I was reading the book, the parts that excited me the most were whenever he would quote any of the players or coaches. ... It was fascinating to me what the ballplayers actually said to each other during games, in the bullpens, or after games. It really revealed them as personalities. What were these guys like? How did they think? What do they talk about? What's going on in their heads, you know?"

After Brosnan, inside looks at the real world of sports began to appear occasionally, though as most insiders could not write like Jim Brosnan, they required a collaborator. Former club owner Bill Veeck teamed with Ed Linn on *Veeck as in Wreck* (1962) and *The Hustler's Handbook* (1965), revealing his years of frustration over dealing with commissioners and his fellow owners. Bill Veeck was a man of many talents, but self-preservation was not one of them — his former colleagues blocked his attempts at buying another team until 1975. Jerry Kramer's *Instant Replay*, written with Dick Schaap in 1967, was a best-selling look at life with pro football's Green Bay Packers. More typically, Joe Namath and Schaap's *I Can't Wait Until Tomorrow ('Cause I Get Better Looking Every Day)* was about what you'd expect: salacious details of Joe's off-field adventures, with an occasional dose of football thrown in.

Sports reporting also evolved rapidly in the 1960s. Jimmy Cannon, the most admired sportswriter of his generation, for many years had written memorable prose celebrating the heroes of the era, men like Joe DiMaggio (who "stirred the dreams of countless boys") and Joe Louis ("a credit to his race — the human race"). But many of the men who arrived in the press boxes in the 1950s thought of

> It was fascinating to me what the ballplayers actually said to each other during games, in the bullpens, or after games. It really revealed them as personalities. What were these guys like?
>
> Jim Bouton on *The Long Season*

Mark Armour is a writer living in Corvallis, Oregon, with Jane, Maya and Drew. Mark's repeated reading of *Ball Four* as a boy hastened his own love for the game, and instilled in him a healthy dose of cynicism for the ways of the world.

themselves not merely as writers but as reporters, as men looking for a story. The new breed was down in the clubhouse asking the players and manager not just what they did, but "*Why?*" Why did you throw that pitch? Why did you try to steal the base? Why did you remove the pitcher?

Cannon was particularly contemptuous of this trend, referring to one especially aggressive group of reporters as "chipmunks." Cannon later complained to Jerome Holtzman, "The chipmunks love the big-word guys, the guys with the small batting averages but ... big vocabularies." Although Cannon used the term derisively, the "chipmunks" considered it a badge of honor, and other writers began to claim the nickname for themselves.

Cannon's targets included Leonard Shecter (*New York Post),* Stan Isaacs (*Newsday)* and Larry Merchant (*Philadelphia News*). As these writers saw it, their biggest crimes were a lack of deference to the New York Yankees, and an admiration for a new, outspoken generation of athletes, most especially Muhammad Ali, the controversial heavyweight boxing champion. These men (yes, they were all men) covered sports the way they would have covered politics or a fire, looking not just for news but for a provocative angle. Inevitably, the atmosphere in locker rooms grew tense.

Lenny Shecter was typical of the type, a skeptic about what he heard in locker rooms, an early supporter of Ali, and the author of a harsh *Esquire* piece on the widely revered Vince Lombardi. In 1968 Shecter wrote a powerful article for *Life* magazine, "Baseball: The Great American Myth." The story followed the Boston Red Sox, who had won a celebrated pennant the previous year but were going through a less newsworthy, injury-filled season, ultimately finishing fourth in a ten-team league. Shecter described players frustrated with their performance, worried about their futures, angry with manager Dick Williams, and bored with the drudgery of the road. There were no heroes or glamour in Shecter's story.

The following year, Shecter wrote *The Jocks,* a humorous and cynical broadside that laid waste to much of the sports establishment, including fellow newspapermen (pawns of the teams they covered), television (wielding too much power), the NCAA, all major professional sports, and many of the nation's biggest sports heroes, men like Joe DiMaggio, Mickey Mantle and Roger Maris. A fascinating and funny read, it was not all negative. He devoted an entire chapter to Casey Stengel, whom he had covered with the early Mets and loved dearly, and another chapter to people he calls "losers," athletes who were too bright and thoughtful to fit into the hypocritical sports world. One of these losers was Jim Bouton, a Yankee pitcher Shecter greatly admired.

When Bouton joined the Yankees in 1962, he was warned by his teammates about associating with reporters, especially Shecter, or "that fucking Shecter." Bouton rarely did what he was told, so he not only talked with the reporters, he became friends with many of them, including

> **He stands out because he is a decent young man in a game which does not recognize decency as valuable.**
>
> **Lenny Shecter on Jim Bouton in *Sport,* 1964**

Shecter. Bouton had early success with the Yankees, winning 39 games in the 1963 and 1964 seasons, and two of his three World Series starts (losing his other one, 1-0).

Shecter wrote a glowing piece on Bouton for *Sport* in 1964, revealing the pitcher's sense of humor, his broad set of interests, and his artwork, while dismissing Bouton's reputation as an oddball: "He stands out because he is a decent young man in a game which does not recognize decency as valuable." A few years later, when Shecter had left the *Post* and Bouton was struggling to hang on with the Yankees, Shecter published a story about Bouton and his wife adopting a Korean child. Bouton and Shecter were kindred spirits, bright men who loved the game, rankled at hypocrisy, and took pleasure in tweaking the stuffed shirts who ran the industry.

After the success of Kramer's *Instant Replay,* Shecter, now freelancing, wondered if the time was ripe for an honest baseball diary — a day-to-day inside look at the world of baseball. He approached Bouton during the fall of 1968, and was told, "Funny you should mention that. I've been keeping notes." Thus joined, their common purpose, as later recounted by Shecter, was "to illuminate the game as it never had been before." The illumination would include daily frustrations, meanness, and "extraordinary fun."

Shecter arranged a small advance from the World Publishing Group, though there was little reason to suppose that such a venture would be successful. For one thing, in 1968 Bouton had pitched, and not particularly well, for the Seattle Angels of the Triple A Pacific Coast League. In 1969, he was invited to spring training by the Seattle Pilots, a brand-new major league expansion team. There was no guarantee he would make the club or stick with the team long. When Jerry Kramer wrote *Instant Replay,* he was a star player on the best team in football. Bouton, if he made it, was a mediocre pitcher on a bad team. *If* he made it.

Bouton made the club, but just briefly — after two relief appearances he was sent to Triple A Vancouver. But he soon was back in Seattle and spent the rest of the season in the majors, enduring a trade to the Houston Astros in August. Between the majors and minors, he pitched in 81 games, almost all of them in relief, and finished the season in a National League pennant race. Given where he'd started in March, it had to be viewed as a wildly successful season.

More important for his place in history, Bouton spoke into a tape recorder almost every day all season. He then sent the tapes to Shecter, who had the transcripts typed up and ultimately turned them into a 1,500-page manuscript. The collaborators spent several months haggling over every word to reduce it to 520 manuscript pages, or about 400 in the book. Although the stories and opinions were 100 percent Bouton, the pitcher later credited Shecter for infusing the book with its humanity and sense of humor.

Another baseball diary beat *Ball Four* to the store shelves by several weeks in the spring of 1970. With the assistance of Steve Gelman and Dick

Schaap, Detroit Tigers catcher Bill Freehan penned *Behind The Mask* (World), a journal of his 1969 season. Freehan's book caused a stir for its candid look at some of the goings-on in the Detroit clubhouse, most notably Freehan's claim that the Tigers allowed star pitcher Denny McLain to flout team rules. As luck would have it, by the time excerpts from the book appeared in *Sports Illustrated* in March, McLain was being investigated by baseball for conspiring to operate a sports book, for which he would be suspended for half the 1970 season. Freehan was embarrassed by the contents of the book, apologized to his team, and more or less refused to talk about it ever again.

Early in the season Bouton asked Jim Owens, his Houston pitching coach and a man Bouton admired, whether there would be fallout if the team didn't like the book. Owens responded, "Depends on how you're doing at the time." Bouton was not doing well. He began the season in the rotation, was hit hard in a handful of starts, was relegated to the bullpen, and never got on track the entire season, finishing 4-6 with a 5.40 ERA.

Excerpts of *Ball Four* initially appeared in the June 2 and June 16 issues of *Look,* the first hitting the streets in mid-May. The selected passages in the initial issue included details of Bouton's contract negotiations with the Yankees, depictions of many players as ingenious Peeping Toms, salacious player dialogue that included sexual humor about each other's wives, the widespread use of amphetamines in the game, and playful kissing between inebriated Seattle Pilots on the team plane. Most of the passages were benignly funny and included Bouton's poignant insecurities about his place on the team, both on and off the field.

Although Bouton spent the majority of the book revealing day-to-day life with the Pilots and Astros, his comments on his years with the Yankees predictably generated the most controversy. Bouton described pitcher Whitey Ford's late-career chicanery, including illegally defacing the baseball. Mickey Mantle came off as a good-natured teammate who occasionally mistreated fans and who might have had a better career had he spent more time working out to recover from his injuries and less time drinking and carousing with his buddies. Though Mantle himself would one day adopt a nearly identical view of his own career, most of his ex-Yankee teammates were particularly unsettled by Bouton's comments about their beloved teammate.

Soon after the excerpts came out in *Look,* with the controversy still in full flower, the Astros came to New York to play a four-game series with the Mets (May 29-31). The New York press and fans were ready for Bouton, perhaps no one more so than Dick Young.

Young was the dean of New York sportswriters, a veteran of three decades with the *Daily News,* the beat writer for the Brooklyn Dodgers during their glory days, and a smart, tireless reporter. No fan of the modern athlete, Young was a vocal critic of Ali, unions, and any player expressing concerns for the world around him. A tireless high-handed moralist, he made a lot of enemies during his long career. In

My Life and Hard Times Throwing the Knuckleball in the Big Leagues

The most incisive, candid, revealing and, at the same time, the *funniest* book ever written about baseball and the people who make their living at it.
edited by Leonard Shecter

BALL FOUR by Jim Bouton

While sequels to Jim Bouton's 'Ball Four' have proliferated, original hardcover copies of the 1970 book have become hard to find.

his May 28 column, Young set his sights on *Ball Four:* "I feel sorry for Jim Bouton. He is a social leper. He didn't catch it, he developed it. His collaborator on the book, Leonard Shecter, is a social leper. People like this, embittered people, sit down in their time of deepest rejection and write. They write, oh, hell, everybody stinks, everybody but me, and it makes them feel better."

In Young's view, Bouton and Shecter used the book as revenge against the people who had rejected them. Bouton had written candidly of feeling out of place in the game: "I know about lonely summers. In my last years with the Yankees, I had a few of them. You stood around in a hotel lobby talking with guys at dinnertime, and they drift away, and some other guys come along, and they drift away, and soon they are gone. So you eat alone." Young saw the book as Bouton's chance to get even. Although he admires some of the book ("there are some beautiful passages"), he could not forgive what he saw as petty cruelty and disrespect for the game. To Young's displeasure, Bouton came across as being somewhat disinterested, even bored, with the game unless he was pitching in it.

Bouton finally took the mound on May 31 at Shea Stadium, and he was soundly thrashed, allowing three hits and three runs in one-third of an inning. He was booed from the time he began walking in from the bullpen until he retreated into the dugout after his appearance. He later wrote that it was his lowest moment ever on a baseball field.

The next day, Bouton met with commissioner Bowie Kuhn in Kuhn's Manhattan office. Also present were

> **I feel sorry for Jim Bouton. He is a social leper. He didn't catch it, he developed it. ...**
>
> **People like this, embittered people, sit down in their time of deepest rejection and write. They write, oh, hell, everybody stinks, everybody but me, and it makes them feel better.**
>
> **Dick Young, New York Daily News**

Marvin Miller, the head of the player's union, and Miller's aide Dick Moss. Kuhn told Bouton he was disappointed and shocked by the excerpts he had read, so much so that he felt compelled to remove the magazines from his house lest his sons read them. He was particularly uncomfortable with reports of drug use, sexually-themed verbal sparring among the players, and the playful kissing game on Seattle's team plane. Bouton responded that all of it was true, and that no harm would come from his revealing it.

Mainly, Kuhn brought Bouton in to force him to apologize, as Freehan had done earlier that spring, but Bouton did not give an inch. Failing that, Kuhn and Miller spent two and a half hours arguing over a suitable press release. What was finally agreed to was short and non-informative: "I advised Mr. Bouton of my displeasure with these writings and have warned him against future writings of this character. Under all the circumstances, I have concluded that no other action was necessary." After this brief statement was read, Bouton was asked if he regretted writing the book. "Absolutely not," responded the pitcher-author.

The aforementioned reaction predated the release of the book by several weeks. The *Look* selections included most of the salacious content of the book, and read in isolation they naturally prompted teammates and writers to wonder what other bombshells were coming. But the excerpts missed most of the heart of the book: Bouton's depiction of the day-to-day life of a baseball player.

*B*all Four's long-awaited release on June 21 brought mainly positive reviews from the nation's most respected book critics and columnists. As Robert Lipsyte wrote in the *New York Times*, reading the entire book provides the necessary context for the more revelatory passages, which appear as "a natural outgrowth of a game in which 25 young, insecure, undereducated men of narrow skills keep circling the country to play before fans who do not understand their problems or their work, and who use them as symbols for their own fantasies."

Within its four hundred pages, the locker room hijinks, the late nights, the players' occasional resentment of the fans, the petty rivalries, all seem perfectly natural to anyone who had spent time in the army or a high school locker room. The book struck a chord with so many people, perhaps, because while readers could not relate to throwing a 90-mph fastball or hitting a slider, they understood too well the frustrations of daily life, spending time in close quarters with people with whom they had nothing in common, and dealing with arbitrary and petty regulations enforced by unimaginative bosses.

Christopher Lehmann-Haupt, reviewing the book for the *Times*, wrote that it renewed his long dormant interest in the game. Rex Lardner Jr., in *The New York Times Book Review*, called it the "frankest book yet about the species *ballplayer satyriaticus*," concluding, "I hope he makes a million bucks." It was hailed in the *Washington Post* by David Markson as "a wry, understated, honest and memorable piece of Americana, by a good man they will

clobber because of it." John Gregory Dunne of the *Los Angeles Times* called it "an uncomfortably accurate look at life in the big leagues."

In the *New Yorker*, Roger Angell praised Bouton as a "day-to-day observer, hard thinker, angry victim, and unabashed lover" of the game, and lauded the book's portrayal of "his own survival as a human being caught up in an exhausting and ultimately unforgiving business." Given his role as a deeply respected chronicler of the game, it is telling that Angell was not in the least surprised or overly troubled by Bouton's more unsavory revelations. Instead, Angell regarded the volume as "a rare view of a highly complex public profession seen from the innermost inside, along with an even more rewarding inside view of an ironic and courageous mind. And, very likely, the funniest book of the year."

David Halberstam had won a Pulitzer Prize for his coverage of the Vietnam War for the *New York Times* but had yet to establish his eventual association with baseball. Writing for *Harper's Magazine*, he called *Ball Four* the "best sports book in years, a book deep in the American vein. ... It is a fine and funny book, with rare intelligence, wit, joy, and warmth; and a comparable insider's book about, say, the Congress of the United States, the Ford Motor Company, or the Joint Chiefs of Staff would be equally welcome." Halberstam believed he understood the resentment of the beat writers, the mythologizers and hero-makers — once "outflanked," they were compelled to attack the intentions of the writer. Thus, Bouton became a "social leper, and thus Sy Hersh, when he broke the My Lai story, became a 'peddler' to some of Washington's famous journalists."

His fellow players still did not like it. Joe Morgan, his teammate on the Astros, said, "I always thought he was a teammate, not an author. I told him some things I would never tell a sportswriter." By the time the book came out, the Seattle Pilots were extinct, having relocated to Milwaukee as the Brewers. Many of his ex-Pilot teammates, including Fred Talbot, Wayne Comer, and Don Mincher, deeply resented the book and Bouton. Jerry McNertney wasn't troubled by the book, and Gene Brabender, while not condoning it, did allow that it was "hilarious."

Jimmy Cannon, predictably, was not amused. Cannon blamed Shecter, though he never mentioned the collaborator by name in his scathing July 28 column. "The book is ugly with the small atrocities of the chipmunk's cruelty. In a way, Bouton is a chipmunk, a man who obviously cherishes himself as a social philosopher. The influence of the ghost is obvious. ... The literary critics take him seriously. It is as though he were assaulted with a sudden inspiration and rushed to a typewriter and put it all down in a flurry of creation. But he went to the spook, and one has to speculate where Bouton stops, and the ghost begins. Whose hatreds are these, whose theories? Which one's ethics governed the partnership?"

The diverse reaction to the book was part of the social

I advised Mr. Bouton of my displeasure with these writings and have warned him against future writings of this character. Under all the circumstances, I have concluded that no other action was necessary.

Bowie Kuhn, in a press release after meeting with Jim Bouton

For more information on 'Ball Four,' visit <http://www. ballfour.com>.

and political divide the country was going through. Bouton, a "Communist" to some of his critics, unabashedly supported the war protesters and held decidedly liberal views on civil rights, religion, the rights of women, the new players' union, poverty, and the other divisive issues of the time. What's more, he confidently stated his opinions in his book. Not surprisingly, the more liberal writers were more likely to praise it.

George Frazier, a *Boston Globe* columnist who later showed up on Richard Nixon's enemies list, called *Ball Four* "a revolutionary manifesto." In his strident and angry review, Frazier challenged the book's critics: "What is happening among baseball players, their doubting the divinity of demagogues ... is what is happening among housewives and their husbands who have had their fill of the shoddy wares and planned obsolescence foisted on them by American industry. Bouton is now being slandered by baseball's benevolent old men and their lackeys. Who the hell does Bowie Kuhn think he is?"

The most considered of *Ball Four*'s negative reviews was written for *Esquire* by Roger Kahn, a freelance writer still two years away from the publication of his masterpiece, *The Boys of Summer*. Kahn admired Shecter and Bouton, but was particularly critical of their depiction of life on the road, especially when Bouton named names. One member of the Pilots is quoted saying, "Boys, I had all the ingredients for a great piece of ass last night — plenty of time, and a hard-on. All I lacked was a broad." To Kahn, naming this player, and naming other players in other passages, represented a terrible "intrusion" on the privacy of the man and his family.

Bouton defended himself against this line of criticism, responding that he portrayed himself as a participant in the off-field stories, the drinking, the skirt chasing, and all the missed curfews. This is true, but Kahn correctly countered that Bouton did not show himself cheating on his wife, an act that carries an additional level of opprobrium. Bouton's wife Bobbie is shown as a loving supporter of her husband's career, laughing at all the rollicking good fun the players engaged in. (Kahn's view on issues of decorum evolved over the years. In his 1987 book *Joe and Marilyn*, for one example, he claims to reveal details of the famous couple's private body parts and discusses the quality of their lovemaking.)

Kahn's other serious concern with *Ball Four* was that Bouton and Shecter deceived the reader by suggesting that Bouton could still pitch. To Kahn, the book would have been better had Bouton written about his anxieties over the ending of his career, rather than continually blaming others for not being allowed to†pitch more. In fact, Bouton was leading the Pilots in games pitched (57) at the time he was traded, and his 73 games for the season were the fifth-highest total in the major leagues. So what, says Kahn, was he complaining about? What Bouton really wanted was a chance to start, or to pitch in tighter situations, and his statistics were actually significantly better than all of the Pilots' starting pitchers that season.

21st ANNUAL MID-WINTER SPORTS BANQUET, MONDAY, FEBRUARY 8, 1971, OLYMPIC HOTEL

ABE LEMONS

MASTER BUMMY

JIM BOUTON

Sponsored by the Puget Sound Sportswriters and Sportscasters Association

What Kahn missed, it seems, is that the book's narrative actually overflowed with self-doubt. The Jim Bouton of 1969 desperately wanted more of a chance because he loved the game and the competition, but he did not come across as someone with an outsized view of his abilities. One could understand a bad team's reluctance to invest a lot of innings in a 30-year-old knuckleballer coming off several bad seasons, but it was not realistic to expect that perspective from the pitcher himself. He wanted to pitch more, and he wanted his managers and coaches to let him pitch more. Why would he not? How else was he supposed to feel?

After being sent to the minor leagues in July 1970, pitching poorly and in the midst of the controversy over his book, Bouton soon retired from the game. Although he never used publicity surrounding *Ball Four* as an excuse, it is not hard to imagine the strain that the summer must have had on a mediocre pitcher trying to master a strange pitch. Bouton never lost his love for competition. After a few years pitching semi-pro ball while working in New York TV, he made two minor-league comebacks, the second of which culminated in a few starts for the Atlanta Braves in 1978. He was still pitching semi-pro ball at age 60.

Ball Four sold 200,000 hardcover copies and countless more in paperback. In 1971 Bouton and Shecter wrote a sequel, *I'm Glad You Didn't Take It Personally*, which Bouton slyly dedicated to Dick Young and Bowie Kuhn. Ball Four was reissued three times, every ten years, with epilogues updating Bouton's life and the lives of teammates and friends. His last installment, self-published in 2000 and subtitled *The Final Pitch*, touchingly described a reconciliation with Mickey Mantle prior to Mantle's death, and Bouton's 1998 Yankees Old-Timers Game appearance, ending the rift with the team for which he had starred. While promoting his beloved book, he routinely inscribes it with a phrase immortalized by his Pilots roommate Gary Bell in the original: "Smoke 'em inside." ⚾

No matter the controversy that Jim Bouton's 'Ball Four' encountered, the Seattle sportswriters welcomed the author as a guest speaker for their annual banquet in 1971.

Sources: Besides the books and reviews cited in the text, the author spoke with Jim Bouton and Stan Isaacs

Buses, beer and emboldened batboys

Jim Bouton recounts his days of revenge with that 70's team, the 'big bad' Portland Mavericks

BY JIM BOUTON

The Portland Mavericks were an independent franchise in the Northwest League from 1973 to 1977. They were very good — finishing first in their division four of their five seasons — but also gained notoriety and headlines for their behavior on and off the field.

Jim Bouton, during his on-again off-again comeback in the 1970s, pitched for the Mavericks in both 1975 and 1977, finishing a combined 9-2 in 14 starts.

In 2001, upon the Pacific Coast League's return to Portland, Bouton wrote a story for the April 29, 2001, edition of the (Portland) *Oregonian*, recalling his days with the Mavericks. The article is reprinted here with his permission.

Bouton's latest book is *Foul Ball: My Life and Hard Times Trying to Save an Old Ballpark, Plus Part II*, now in paperback from Lyons Press. He is waiting for a review from Bowie Kuhn.

I hear that Triple-A baseball is coming back to Portland. Evidently a team called the Beavers, wearing old-fashioned "classic" uniforms, and managed by a guy named Rick Sweet, will play at a place called PGE Park, recently refurbished with a "Family Deck" and a "vintage" soda fountain.

Not only that, but according to Beavers senior vice president and general manager Mike Higgins, "The players will be very visible in the community and they will give 150 percent every time they step on the field."

Isn't that swell? A bunch of boy scouts, following a leader named Sweet, will spend their afternoons carrying packages for little old ladies, before heading down to "ye olde ballyard" where they'll cavort on the field with some fan-friendly guy in a Beaver suit, while expending a level of effort that's scientifically impossible.

It all sounds so strange. Beavers? PGE Park? Soda fountains? What about the Mavericks? Civic Stadium. Beer coolers. And a general manager who doubled as a ticket taker and bus driver.

You want vintage? I'll give you vintage. Let's go back to the 1970s, prehistoric time, I realize, especially for some of you dot-commers, but a time to remember nonetheless.

The Portland Mavericks, boys and girls, were a baseball team that I'm proud to say I played for — twice. Once, for a few weeks in 1975, on vacation from my job as a sportscaster in New York, and again two years later when I quit TV altogether to begin my comeback to the major leagues. The sheer insanity of quitting a good job to play minor league baseball was what qualified me to be a Mav.

The "Big Bad Mavs" as we were known to friend and foe alike, were a collection of misfits, ne'er-do-wells, and degenerates who played ball and wreaked havoc in the Class A Northwest League from 1973 to 1977. Owned appropriately enough by actor Bing Russell of TV's "Bonanza," the team was made up of players who'd been released, or had never even been signed by a major league organization.

We made only $300 a month and had to double as the grounds crew. Our motivation was simple — revenge. We loved whomping fuzzy-cheeked college bonus babies owned by the Dodgers or Red Legs.

This was a league where men were men, and players rode buses, not airplanes. Our uniforms were vintage — vintage softball — solid red with black trim that would have made any devil proud. We were visible in the community too, if you happened to be out at four o'clock in the morning. And we strived to give 150 percent — but that was only after the game was over.

The Mavs were the most democratic team in America. A small newspaper ad for open tryouts attracted doctors, lawyers, plumbers, actors, gas station attendants, dope fiends and ex-cons from all over the country, who hitch-hiked, backpacked and slept in tents in the outfield just to try out for the Mavs. You didn't need a character reference to play. Which may explain why we led the league in umpires terrorized, hotel closets filled with empty beer cans and bar fights never started on purpose. "They're not bad boys, Father, just unruly."

The Mavs had more than their share of wackos, starting with the manager who, for the purposes of this story, we'll call Frank Peters. Frank, whose job it was to frisk the players before sending them into a game, spent time in jail for failing to distinguish between a felony and fan appreciation.

Our best player was Reggie "That's Not My Gun" Thomas, a fleet-footed outfielder who was famous for turning sure doubles into singles so he could steal second base and win free sandwiches awarded by the Souvlaki Stop Diner.

Then there was Phil "I Wish You Were Dead" Moreno. That's what Phil said to a Bellingham motel manager when his TV set wouldn't work. Six hours later the guy died of a heart attack. "Nice going, Phil," said one of the Mavs, "now we have to move to another motel."

The motels got further and further away from the ballparks as we wore out our welcomes at the closer locations. By the end of the season, the Mavs were staying 40 miles outside of whatever town we were playing in. Most of it was picky stuff, like our Cannonball Olympics in a motel pool in Boise. The diving board was only partially cracked and we cleaned up most of the watermelon.

Other characters included Steve "Cut" Colette, a third baseman who looked like a pirate; Jim "Swanee" Swanson, a left-handed catcher (you need a left-handed catcher in case anyone tries to steal first base); Joe "Dine and Dash" Garza, who was allergic to restaurant tabs; trainer Steve "Doc" Katz, who dispensed homeopathic remedies for sore arms and hangovers; and Rob "Baby Face" Nelson, who dreamed up Big League Chew in the bullpen in Civic Stadium. (By the way, will there be a plaque at PGE Park commemorating the only good idea to ever come out of a bullpen?)

The fastest thing to come out of a bullpen was our mascot, P. L. Maverick, a black Labrador retriever who specialized in running on the field to disrupt a game at key

moments. In the middle of a rally by the opposing team, for example, a ball would mysteriously come flying out of our bullpen with P. L. in hot pursuit. It usually took three umpires, four coaches and two cops at least 20 minutes to catch him — not counting cleanup — by which time the other team's momentum was broken.

The most famous Mav was Kurt Russell, who could have played in the big leagues if he hadn't gone into the acting business. Kurt was a good-fielding second baseman who could really pick 'em up, on and off the field. The whole team was a bunch of pick-up artists, in fact. And nobody was off limits — waitresses, bar maids, secretaries, opposing team girlfriends, umpire's wives. I never said we were smart.

But we were generous. Now the best education a young batboy can have is to spend time around his older heroes, picking up tips about baseball and life. Which may be how it happened that on the final road trip of the season, Miles Brandon and Todd Field, each 14 years old, were spotted at a diner in Eugene, at two o'clock in the morning, with "dates" they had picked up that night at the ballpark. Mamas don't let your babies grow up to be batboys.

Of course, we didn't have a marketing department back then. But we had something better — a beat-up old school bus, painted red and black to match our uniforms. Inside, the seats had been ripped out and replaced with mattresses on which the players lounged around playing cards and drinking beer.

Outside the bus, for some reason, was a loudspeaker operated by a portable microphone inside the bus. This gave each player the opportunity to make announcements to folks on the street.

"Hey lady," a voice would boom out at a stoplight in Salem, "that sure is an ugly baby you got there." Or, "You there in the blue shirt," the loudspeaker would blare at some overweight fellow, "mix in a salad." That night the stands would be filled with irate fans rooting passionately for our defeat.

Our manners weren't any better at the ballpark. Whenever the opposing pitcher got knocked out of the game (which was often), the Mavericks would line up on the top step of the dugout and serenade the departing player. It was always the same tune, a loud chorus of Roy Rogers' and Dale Evans' closing theme, sung with a smirk. "Happy traillls to youuuuu, until we meet againnnn. Happy

(Above, from left) actor and Maverick Kurt Russell, actor and laid-back team president Bing Russell and manager Frank Peters in 1973. Jim Bouton (left) helped lead the Mavs to a division title in 1975. Given the flavor of Bouton's memoir, the word "Go" in the button below may have had multiple meanings.

traillls to youuuu, keep smiling until thennnn."

One night the umpire came over to our dugout (umpires were always coming over to our dugout) and said we should knock it off because we had too much class for that. "Oh yeah," we hollered back. "Who says?"

The Mavs were an equal-opportunity disrespector. No one was spared, including this old right hander. One night I gave up what could be termed a fairly large home run to a guy named Don Reynolds, then with the Walla Walla Padres, and now assistant general manager with the Montreal Expos. Weeks later, my own teammates were saying, "you can still see it at night."

It should come as no surprise to learn that when the Mavs were fitted for championship rings, they measured our middle fingers.

But that was then and this is now. Which is not to say the Mavs wouldn't have enjoyed playing at the refurbished PGE Park. That new field-level bar and grill would have made a great dugout. "Just a beer and some fries, thanks, I'm up next inning."

Will there ever be a Mav Old Timers' Day, you ask? I doubt it. Too many players in the witness protection program. Wherever you guys are, I love you man.

Whenever the opposing pitcher got knocked out of the game (which was often), the Mavericks would line up on the top step of the dugout and serenade the departing player.

Jim Bouton

Excitement reigned at Sick's Stadium every time Tommy Harper got on base in 1969, as he chased the AL season record for steals. (Above) Second base, illustrated by Seattle artist Stu Moldrem, was presented to Harper on Aug. 22. (Right) One of the few unused tickets for Opening Day, which drew a capacity crowd of 15,014.

An exhilarating big league bust

Harper's stolen-base chase supplied thrills, but weak hitting, pitching, attendance, financing doomed Seattle's Pilots

BY **NICK ROUSSO**

O n a perfect spring day in 1969, major-league baseball breezed into Seattle. But one year later, it turned its back and stormed out, leaving the jewel of Puget Sound with fleeting memories of the first big-league franchise since 1901 to expire after one season.

These briefly present Pilots did not play good baseball, finishing with a 64-98 record, but in a region starved for big league action, they played exhilarating baseball. There were 16-13 slugfests and 1-0 pitchers duels, straight steals of home plate, brawls with both the venerable Yankees and the expansion Royals, and a brief pursuit of immortality by "Tailwind" Tommy Harper, the most exciting player in the American League.

Led by folksy manager Joe Schultz — who knew a lot about losing from his days as a player with the St. Louis Browns — and featuring a roster of shopworn veterans and fringe major leaguers, the Pilots swung from their heels, ran the bases with abandon, and got their uniforms dirty to the bitter end. When their season was over, the record book noted that the Pilots finished near the bottom of the 12-team American League in almost every offensive category. They did manage to finish fourth with 626 walks, as four players had at least 60. Most remarkably, they finished first with 167 stolen bases.

Schultz arrived in Seattle straight from the 1968 World Series, where he had served as third-base coach for the Cardinals and had the benefit of watching Lou Brock's base stealing exploits first-hand. Part of Schultz's grand offensive plan in Seattle was to put the speedy Harper at second base, install him at the top of the batting order, and let him run at will.

"The Great Experiment" was how Schultz termed the gambit, and it worked better than even he envisioned. Harper chased Ty Cobb's AL stolen base record for a while and finished with 73 bags, the most in the league since Cobb had stolen 96 in 1915. More important, Harper's exploits kept a quickly dwindling fan base enthralled as the

team plummeted to the bottom of the standings.

This was in part because clutch hitters the Pilots were not. They batted .234 as a team and hit only 125 home runs despite playing half of their games in Sick's Stadium, where the so-called power alleys were 345 feet from home plate. The Pilots grounded into 111 double plays and led the American League with 1,015 strikeouts — and their pitching was even worse than their hitting.

The Pilots' pitching staff finished third in the league with 963 strikeouts, but yielded 172 home runs, just 20 fewer than the 1962 Mets. Opponents scored in double digits 16 times and won 26 games by five runs or more. "I didn't ever think our pitching would get this bad," Schultz lamented in August as the Pilots planted themselves in the West Division's cellar. "It's tough to know from day to day which one can get a batter out."

The man responsible for those pitchers was general manager Marvin Milkes, a former California Angels executive with a voracious appetite for deal-making. "Players came and went like it was a bus station all summer," recalled Dick Rockne, then a 29-year-old baseball reporter for the Seattle Times. "The joke was that every night after the game there was a bus to Vancouver (the Pilots' Triple A affiliate) waiting outside. I think they

The ecstasy and the agony of the Seattle Pilots are reflected in the these 1969 portraits of owner Dewey Soriano (left) and general manager Marvin Milkes.

Nick Rousso is a Seattle native whose brush with baseball greatness occurred at age 9 when Bubba Morton moved in next door.

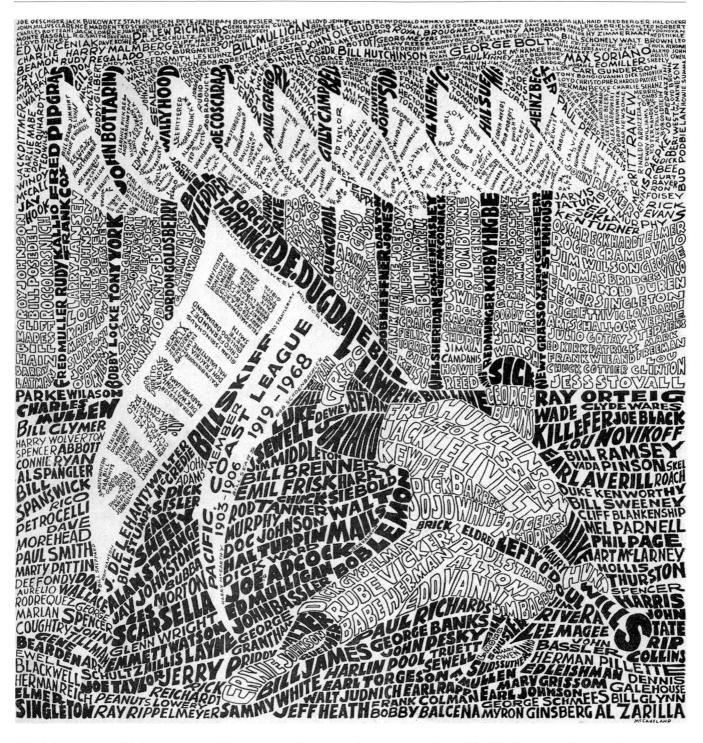

This Bob McCausland cartoon, which graced the cover of a 1968 Seattle Angels program, salutes the past while building excitement for the coming big-league Pilots.

might have set a record for number of players used. It was a big number."

The more moves Milkes made, the worse the Pilots performed. They had a 23-41 record after the All-Star break, and of the 25 players on the Opening Day roster, only 15 remained at the end of the season. All told, 53 players, including 25 pitchers, wore the distinctive Pilots uniform in at least one major league game.

No one knew it at the time, but Milkes cemented his Seattle legacy by trading Lou Piniella to Kansas City during spring training. An outspoken 25-year-old outfielder from Tampa, Fla., Piniella was having a terrific spring, but Milkes coveted Royals outfielder Steve Whitaker, a Tacoma native touted as the next Mickey Mantle during a brief stay with the Yankees. When the Royals offered Whitaker and pitcher John Gelnar for Piniella, Milkes happily closed the deal. Whitaker proceeded to hit .250 in 116 at-bats and was out of baseball a year later, while Gelnar went 3-10 with the Pilots, though with a respectable 3.31 ERA. Meanwhile, Piniella hit .282 for the Royals and was named the American League Rookie of the Year.

Milkes did make an inspired trade the day before the

The expansion Pilots brought many new faces to Seattle. (Left) Light-hitting shortstop Ray Oyler inspired a "Soc-It-To-Me" club organized by deejay Bob Hardwick, both of whom posed for this giveaway photo. (Center) Joe Schultz brought a laid-back approach to his hapless troupe. (Right) Gene Brabender, also shown on this book's cover, became the club's pitching ace with a 13-14 record.

Piniella deal when he sent Chico Salmon to Baltimore for pitcher Gene Brabender, a country-strong, 6-foot-7 right-hander from Black Earth, Wisconsin. Brabender won a team high 13 games, led the Pilots in innings pitched, complete games, and strikeouts, and became a fan favorite at Sick's Stadium as well as one of the most popular players in the clubhouse.

Most of the team's mainstays arrived through a major league dispersal draft that stocked expansion teams in Seattle, Kansas City, Montreal, and San Diego in November 1968. With their first pick, the Pilots selected first baseman Don Mincher from the Angels despite concerns about the long-term effects of a hit-by-pitch Mincher had suffered in 1968. "If I have to gamble, there's no one I'd rather gamble on than Mincher," Milkes said confidently. His bet paid off when Mincher, the club's cleanup hitter, hit a team-high 25 home runs.

Milkes then selected Harper with his second pick. Harper was a former top prospect in the Cincinnati system but had fallen on hard times. Traded to Cleveland after the 1967 season, he languished on the Indians' bench, hitting .217 in 1968 as a utility outfielder and pinch-hitter. He was used so infrequently that he stole only 11 bases. But Pilots scout Bobby Mattick had grown fond of Harper since signing the Oakland product to his first pro contract. He knew that Harper had led his Connie Mack team to a national championship at age 18, teamed with Willie Stargell on his high school baseball team, and had starred in football, basketball, and track. Harper was the kind of athletic leadoff hitter the Pilots coveted. It nevertheless came as a surprise to him when Schultz pulled Harper aside at spring training in Arizona and told him, "You've got the green light. Go make yourself some money."

The major league stolen base record belonged to former Seattle Rainiers shortstop Maury Wills, who had swiped 104 with the Dodgers in 1962. Harper took up the chase immediately and shadowed Wills' pace for about two months, with the Sick's Stadium denizens exhorting him

with chants of "Go, go, go!" But a batting slump in June and a thigh injury in July knocked him off stride. He entered the All-Star break with 44 stolen bases (not enough to win him a spot on the All-Star team) and finished with 73 — a remarkable total for a .235 hitter.

Officially, he tried to steal 91 times, getting thrown out on 18 attempts, but he also moved up several times when no stolen base was awarded because of catcher's indifference. "I'd never really picked up on the idea of stealing bases for numbers," Harper recalled a decade later on a visit to Seattle. "I'd just go with the flow of the game. But out here, I just stole every time I got on."

Harper's double-play partner was Ray Oyler, a weak-hitting shortstop renowned for his defense. Though Oyler had batted .125 with Detroit in 1968, playing sparingly as the season wore on, the Pilots were happy to have him. Said Schultz at spring training when asked whether Oyler's hitting would be a liability: "Ah, hell. Ray Oyler will bat .300 for us with his glove."

Embracing the underdog, Seattle disc jockey Bob Hardwick spearheaded a "Let's Help Ray Oyler Hit .300" drive, and thousands signed up for the Ray Oyler "Sock-It-To-Me" fan club. Lo and behold, Oyler hit .350 through the first two weeks of the season (though this encompassed just six games). He finished at .165. In addition to Mincher, Harper, and Oyler, the Opening Day lineup included Tommy Davis in left field, Jim Gosger in center, Mike Hegan in right, Rich Rollins at third base, and Jerry McNertney behind the plate.

It was a veteran group. Davis had won two National League batting titles with the Dodgers in the early 1960s, but came to Seattle with a bum ankle and other ailments. Rollins enjoyed several good seasons with the Twins, but had been relegated to a platoon role in 1968. McNertney was a career backup valued for his ability to handle a pitching staff. Gosger had kicked around, batting .180 with Oakland in 1968. Only Hegan looked like a potential star; the son of former Indians catcher Jim Hegan, Mike had a

If I have to gamble, there's no one I'd rather gamble on than Mincher.

Marvin Milkes, general manager

The 1969 Seattle Pilots: (back row, from left) Steve Whittaker, Steve Barber, Garry Roggenburk , Greg Goosen, Gene Brabender, Jim Pagiaroni, Don Mincher, John O'Donoghue , Jerry McNertney, (center, from left) Gordy Lund, Gus Gil, Jim Bouton, Ray Oyler, Marty Pattin, Fred Talbot, Diego Segui, Bob Locker, Dick Simpson, John Gelnar, Merritt Ranew, Tommy Davis, Steve Hovley, Ron Clark, (front, from left) equipment manager John McNamara, coaches Ron Plaza and Frank Crosetti, manager Joe Schultz, coaches Sal Maglie and Eddie O'Brien, John Donaldson, Tommy Harper, trainer Curt Rayer, (front center) Price, batboy.

The opening-day starter was righthander Marty Pattin, a 26-year-old former Seattle Angels standout who had reached the majors with California in 1968.

smooth swing and burgeoning power, but injuries proved to be his undoing during his time with the Pilots. He led the team in batting, slugging and on-base percentage (minimum 200 at-bats), but missed 67 games.

The Opening Day starter was right-hander Marty Pattin, a 26-year-old former Seattle Angels standout who had reached the majors with California in 1968. His first assignment was to face his former team in the Pilots' inaugural game, at the Big 'A' in Anaheim, on the evening of April 8, 1969.

Harper quickly got things started, ripping the game's third pitch down the left field line for a double. Hegan then blasted a two-run homer, and the Pilots were off and running, scoring four runs in their very first inning. Pattin made the lead hold up, yielding two hits over five innings before Schultz went to the bullpen. Diego Segui worked three innings, and then Jack Aker closed out the Angels in the ninth for a 4-3 Pilots victory.

Played in brilliant sunshine, the April 11 home opener, also was a rousing success. Gary Bell pitched a complete game and contributed a two-run double, and Mincher socked a two-run homer in a 7-0 victory over the White Sox. But while every available Sick's Stadium seat was taken, the crowd numbered just 15,014 because ballpark renovations had fallen woefully behind schedule. Concrete footings were all that existed beyond the right field fence, while in left field construction workers furiously hammered seats into place right up until Bell's first pitch.

Oyler hit a home run the next day as the Pilots ran their record to 3-1. But perhaps predictably, the team then began to struggle, losing 16 of its next 21 games. An exchange of punches turned into a full-fledged brawl during a game in Kansas City, and a loss to Oakland late in April dropped the Pilots into last place.

Then, suddenly and inexplicably, the Pilots began to play competitive baseball. During a 48-game stretch — more than a quarter of the season — the Pilots were winners, posting a 26-22 record and drawing enthusiastic crowds to Sick's Stadium.

Mike Marshall pitched a two-hitter to beat the Senators on May 9, and the next day the Pilots overcame an 11-3 deficit to win 16-13. Harper sparked a win over the Indians May 29 with three stolen bases (running his league-leading total to 25), and suddenly the Pilots had won 11 of 15 games. On July 1, the Pilots were 35-39 and in third place, 4-1/2 games ahead of their expansion siblings, the Royals.

Then the wheels came off. The Pilots were 9-20 in July, 6-22 in August, and 29-59 over the season's final three months. It was a numbing collapse. The Orioles outscored the Pilots 33-8 during a four-game sweep in mid-August, triggering a nosedive that produced 18 losses in 20 games, including eight agonizing one-run defeats. Opposing batters took aim at the short fences at Sick's Stadium, and the pitching staff imploded. The Pilots lost 15 consecutive home games before winning again in early September. Their home park had become a house of horrors.

"I remember the short porch in left field," Davis recalled two decades later, "and looking up at the people watching the game from their apartments. Sick's Stadium. Yeah, it probably was the most appropriately named stadium I ever played in."

With the Pilots in freefall, only 6,720 came out for Tommy Harper Night in late August. After being presented with second base in pre-game ceremonies, Harper ignited a rally in the ninth, but the Indians hit four home runs and sent the Pilots to their eighth consecutive loss. A few days later, Milkes voiced his displeasure with Schultz, suggesting that the popular manager would not return for the 1970 season. "Some maintain a manager who is loved, presumably by players and fans alike, should be retained," Milkes said. "Well, I'm not conducting a 'Love-In.' I'm running a major league baseball team." This was joined by a more ominous warning. Rumors from Texas suggested that the Pilots would relocate to Dallas for the 1970 season.

On the diamond, Harper's last hurrah came Sept. 12, when he stole three bases against the Angels to run his season total to 70, the most in the American League in 54 years.

The end for the Pilots came three weeks later, on a blustery October night at Sick's Stadium. The Athletics beat the Pilots 3-1 before an appreciative crowd of 5,473, McNertney going down swinging for the final out. A homemade sign fastened to the left field fence read: "So Long Pilots. See You Next Year — IN SEATTLE."

The season over, Schultz went home to St. Louis to await his fate. Milkes fired him a few days before Thanksgiving. "Joe was a realist in a grandfatherly kind of way," Rockne said. "He was a good guy for the job. He never got too excited about a victory, and he never got too excited about a loss. We'd go into his office after a game and he'd say, 'Aw shucks, as long as you get paid on the first and the 15th, who gives a (bleep).'"

Through it all, the franchise hemorrhaged red ink. The owners, an undercapitalized but earnest group led by Cleveland businessman William Daley and fronted by Seattle's Soriano brothers, Dewey and Max, had budgeted for attendance of one million to break even during the expansion season. Instead, the Pilots drew 677,944.

Dewey Soriano, a ship's pilot by trade but a baseball man at heart, had worked tirelessly to bring major league baseball to Seattle. Soriano attended Franklin High School, across the street from Sick's Stadium, pitched for the Rainiers and later became the club's general manager. In 1959, not yet 40 years old, he became president of the Pacific Coast League, staying in the job until 1968, when he took the helm of the Pilots. Yet Soriano had a fractured relationship with Seattle's business community that would come back to haunt him. More important, he and Max had to borrow to put up their stake in the Pilots.

"We were the only ones with borrowed capital," he recalled several years later. "You have to pay that interest, and we got hurt. We took a beating. People had us making an awful lot of money. We didn't make a dime on the sale of that club... We lost a lot of friends."

It's difficult to pinpoint the beginning of the end for the Pilots. When creditors began to call in their loans, or when the city threatened to evict the team from Sick's Stadium for non-payment of rent, or when civic leaders turned their backs on the club — all of those things conspired to topple the team's financial house of cards.

"Dewey was in a dream world. He had no money," Rockne said. "I swear to God, the whole franchise was being run on a Visa card."

Late on the evening of March 25, 1970, after a long winter of failed efforts to find a local buyer for the Pilots, the Soriano brothers were hanged in effigy from a ramp leading to the Monorail terminal in downtown Seattle. Affixed was a sign reading "Thanks Max and Dewey." Somehow Dewey, the kid who sold peanuts at Sick's Stadium, had become the man who helped kill baseball in Seattle.

The end came March 31, in federal bankruptcy court, where the Sorianos had petitioned to sell the franchise to Milwaukee car dealer Bud Selig for $10.8 million. The Sorianos argued that the club was broke and could not exist if forced to stay in Seattle, and bankruptcy referee Sidney Volinn finally agreed. As Volinn deliberated, a moving van loaded with Pilots equipment sat parked in Utah, awaiting orders to head northeast toward Milwaukee or northwest toward Seattle. The call came, the truck rumbled east and the Pilots were dead.

On some counts, the Pilots' legacy is easy to define. From their demise rose two major league franchises — the Brewers and then the Mariners — and the domed stadium intended to house the Pilots was eventually built and christened the Kingdome.

But otherwise, the memories have scattered like the players who wore the uniform — they left after the 1969

The 1969 Seattle Pilots drew mostly anemic crowds to Sick's Stadium, despite the hastily constructed outfield seating sections.

season and never returned. Oyler was the only one to make Seattle his home, returning in 1973 after being released by the Hawaii Islanders of the PCL. He sold cars, toiled on a Safeway loading dock, and finally got a job at Boeing. He died in 1981 of a heart attack, only 42 years old.

Schultz was branded a failure in his one season with the Pilots and, with the exception of a 28-game stint with the Tigers at the end of the 1973 season, never managed in the major leagues again. He left baseball and went to work for a railway supply company in St. Louis, taking his winters in Florida. He died in 1996.

Brabender returned to Black Earth after his baseball career and went to work as a carpenter. Mincher, never happy about playing for an expansion team, ended up running a Double A club in Alabama. Left-hander Steve Barber drove a school bus in Las Vegas. Greg Goossen, who hit 10 home runs in 52 second-half games, became a stand-in for actor Gene Hackman in Hollywood.

Most famously, Jim Bouton, reborn as a knuckleball pitcher with the Pilots, became a celebrated author when his tell-all diary, *Ball Four*, based largely on his four-month

Sources: the *Seattle Post-Intelligencer*, original interviews, *The Sporting News* and <www.baseball reference.com>

stint with the Pilots, made the bestseller list in 1970.

Some few former Pilots went on to greater achievements in baseball. Pattin won 104 games after leaving Seattle. Marshall developed into one of the game's best relief pitchers, winning the 1974 National League Cy Young Award with the Dodgers. Davis kicked around for seven more seasons, setting a major league record (since broken) when he hit home runs for nine different teams. And Harper, Seattle's favorite son for one rollicking summer, became the toast of Milwaukee in 1970, the fifth big league player to hit 30 home runs and steal 30 bases in the same season.

Milkes went with the Pilots to Milwaukee, where he continued to wheel and deal until Selig fired him following the 1970 season. It was his last chance as a major league general manager.

Dewey Soriano, his pride and passion for baseball severely wounded, went back to piloting ships. Opening Day in Seattle in 1970 came and went with no game. Sick's Stadium was shuttered, and everyone turned the page on a remarkably brief chapter in baseball history.

Working the free market

How the Seattle Mariners won 116 games in 2001

BY DAN LEVITT

Mariners Mark McLemore (left) and Mike Cameron wave a U.S. flag and lead teammates around Safeco Field following their 5-0 victory over the Anaheim Angels on Sept. 19, 2001, marking the clinching of the American League West title. Underlying the emotion was a patriotic fervor in the aftermath of the Sept. 11 terrorist attacks in New York City and Washington, D.C.

PHOTO BY BEN VANHOUTEN

The 2001 Seattle Mariners tied the major-league single-season record for wins (and set the American League record) with 116. This was particularly surprising because, after several disappointing years, the team achieved its big season despite losing three of the greatest players in the game — Randy Johnson, Ken Griffey Jr., and Alex Rodriguez. But by aggressively moving to trade the first two prior to their filing for free agency, and successfully working the free agent market themselves, the Mariners brilliantly reconstructed their roster to field a team that appeared to be a better sum of its parts. In doing so, they illustrated the extent to which free agency has dramatically altered both the problems and opportunities faced by major league front offices.

The record-setting 2001 Mariners had plenty of stars, and most of them were acquired as free agents. This team dramatically highlights how free agency has revised the tools available to a general manager in assembling a team. The table on the next page summarizes how the most significant 18 players (nine regular position players, two key reserves, the top four starters, and three best relievers) of the 2001 team were acquired.

Only Edgar Martinez and Bret Boone (who had been traded away and subsequently reacquired) were products of the Mariner farm system. Only seven of these players were on the roster during the 1999 season, two of whom arrived via a deadline deal in mid-1998. Nine of the other key contributors were the result of free-agent signings during the two subsequent off-seasons. Several other players were acquired as an indirect side effect of free agency: the forced trade of a star player threatening to play out his contract and sign elsewhere after the season.

Woody Woodward was the Seattle general manager in 1988-99 and at the time of his retirement was the longest-tenured GM in baseball. Woodward's reign was generally considered disappointing. To his credit, he assumed the direction of a historically hapless franchise, and in his 11 full seasons at the helm the club turned in their first five seasons above .500. But despite fielding teams built around several big-name stars, the Mariners never recorded more than 90 wins, only twice reached the playoffs, and advanced as far as the ALCS only once.

Woodward's final two years were particularly frustrating. The 1997 club had four of baseball's greatest players — Ken Griffey Jr., Alex Rodriguez, Edgar Martinez, and Randy Johnson, all enjoying strong seasons — yet the Mariners won just 90 games and lost in the first round of the playoffs. Woodward was unable to build on the foundation established by these four stars, and the Mariners slipped below .500 the next two seasons. In July 1998 Woodward was forced to trade a disgruntled Johnson, dealing him to the Astros for three minor leaguers: pitchers Freddie Garcia and John Halama, and infielder Carlos Guillen. Woodward deserves a lot of credit for this deal — Johnson's trade demand sapped the Mariners of any leverage, but all three players acquired in the deal would contribute to the Mariners' coming success.

After Woodward's retirement, the Mariner brain trust (president Chuck Armstrong, new chairman Howard Lincoln, and minority owner Chris Larson) chose veteran baseball man Pat Gillick as the team's new general manager. Sixty-two at the time, Gillick sported an impressive résumé. He had built and presided over a Blue Jays team that captured two straight World Series championships in the early 1990s before moving on to Baltimore where he reshuffled the team's talent into two consecutive playoff appearances — the team's first since 1983. Gillick was initially reluctant to resume the life of a general manager because, for one thing, his wife had recently opened an art gallery in Toronto. When she gave

The record-setting 2001 Mariners had plenty of stars, and most of them were acquired as free agents.

Dan Levitt is the co-author of *Paths to Glory: How Great Baseball Teams Got That Way*, winner of The Sporting News-SABR Baseball Research Award. Dan also has published numerous baseball articles and short biographies. He is currently writing a biography of Ed Barrow.

him an encouraging shove, Gillick accepted the job.

Gillick's early service in baseball included stints as an assistant farm director and as a regional scouting coordinator. Given this background, it is not surprising that he brought a traditional approach to player evaluation and stressed character, makeup, and chemistry. "When I'm scouting, I take character over physical ability every time." He later added, "I hate to say I put makeup ahead of ability, but the more I'm around the more I believe you have to do this. With the multi-year contracts we give out, makeup becomes more important. When you're in the midst of a five-year contract, one side is going to be upset." As to team chemistry, Gillick maintained, "Chemistry is unbelievably critical. If you come into the workplace, and there is inconsistency, there are disruptive employees or you don't know what to expect, then you won't be a motivated employee." Gillick extended this concept to the player's wives as well because "there can be a lot of one-upmanship with the ladies."

Shoring up the offense, Gillick used free-agency to bring home another Washington native, left-handed hitting first-baseman John Olerud.

With a new chairman and a new stadium (Safeco Field opened mid-1999), Seattle's management agreed to increase payroll as a means to improve the team. Acquiring free agents can be a risky strategy, because the mid-tier talents available on the market tend to be both overpriced and on the downside of their careers. Often teams assume that simply adding payroll should lead to success on the field, and have been surprised when it doesn't work out that way. In Pat Gillick, the Mariners had one of the few general managers who could make the strategy work, having done so to win the World Series twice over in Toronto.

In late October Gillick summed up his perspective on his new team. He observed, "The team needed a leadoff hitter, a lefthanded hitting outfielder and infielder (probably at first base), a lefthanded reliever, and a starting pitcher." For the starter, Gillick was looking for "a veteran-type guy who could fit in probably as a number two or a number three." The Mariners most significant outfield weakness was in left field, where Brian Hunter's 44 stolen bases couldn't mask a horrible season (he hit .231 with few walks and little power with the M's). The club was also undermanned at third base, with incumbent Russ Davis not being retained.

Unfortunately for Gillick, one of his first chores was to address the growing discontent of Griffey, one of the league's best players, who had become unhappy in Seattle. In November 1999 Griffey told Gillick and Lincoln that he planned to leave as a free agent after the 2000 season. Wanting to avoid a disruption caused by a disgruntled superstar, the Mariner brass opted to deal him. As a so-called "10-and-5 player" (a ten-year veteran, including five consecutive with his current team), Griffey had to approve any trade. By giving Gillick a list of only four teams to which he was willing to be dealt, Griffey further hampered Gillick's trade leverage.

The match turned out to be with the Reds, Griffey's hometown team and his father's longtime organization. Gillick showed that he was not a timid negotiator by initially asking for second baseman Pokey Reese, first

Key contributors in 2001

Pos	Name	How acquired
C	Dan Wilson	trade with Cincinnati 11/2/93
1B	John Olerud	free agent 12/15/99
2B	Bret Boone	free agent 12/22/00
3B	David Bell	trade with Cleveland 8/31/98
SS	Carlos Guillen	Randy Johnson trade 7/31/98
LF	Al Martin	trade with San Diego 7/31/00
CF	Mike Cameron	Ken Griffey trade 2/10/00
RF	Ichiro Suzuki	free agent 11/18/00
DH	Edgar Martinez	non-drafted free agent 12/19/82
UT	Mark McLemore	free agent 12/20/99
OF	Stan Javier	free agent 12/20/99
SP	Freddy Garcia	Randy Johnson trade 7/31/98
SP	Aaron Sele	free agent 1/10/00
SP	Jamie Moyer	trade with Boston 7/31/96
SP	Paul Abbott	free agent 1/10/97
RP	Jeff Nelson	free agent 12/4/00
RP	Arthur Rhodes	free agent 12/21/99
RP	Kazuhiro Sasaki	free agent 12/18/99

baseman Sean Casey, starter Denny Neagle, reliever Scott Williamson, and a top prospect. In the end Gillick landed none of the four major leaguers he coveted and was forced to settle for Mike Cameron, Brett Tomko, Antonio Perez, and Jake Meyer. Cameron would prove the only valuable addition from the trade.

The 1999 Mariners had trotted out one of the league's worst pitching staffs, and the bullpen had been anchored by the erratic Jose Mesa. To solve the latter problem, Gillick displayed some global creativity by signing Japanese closer Kaz Sasaki in December. A few days later, he shored up the pen even further by securing one of baseball's best lefthanded relievers, Arthur Rhodes. To land his starter, Gillick was the beneficiary of some good fortune. Aaron Sele, a solid mid-rotation pitcher, had agreed to a four-year, $30 million deal with the Orioles. After he took his physical, Baltimore scaled back its offer to only three years. The annoyed Sele instead signed with Seattle, in his home state, even though the deal was only two years and $15 million. With Sele added to Jamie Moyer and promising rookie Garcia (acquired in the Johnson deal), the Mariners hoped to field a stronger rotation in 2000.

Turning to the offense, Gillick used free agency to bring home another Washington native, lefthanded-hitting first baseman John Olerud. Gillick had drafted the player for the Blue Jays in 1989, even though Olerud was recovering from a brain aneurysm. Gillick had believed in him enough, in fact, to put him on the Blue Jays' big league roster that September, without having spent a day in the minor leagues. Gillick also signed infielder/outfielder Mark McLemore, a veteran with much-needed on-base skills. McLemore proved to be an extremely valuable player, filling in at a number of positions and regularly getting on base over the next few years. Finally, the club signed utility outfielder Stan Javier to bolster the bench.

Although the team's payroll increased only moderately, from $54.1 million to $58.9 million, it represented a significant outlay in new players, because 1999's two largest salaries — Griffey and pitcher Jeff Fassero — both came off of the roster.

The only in-season tinkering to the core group was with the left field position. McLemore started the season there, but soon moved to second base, with David Bell sliding over to third. After the New York Mets released Rickey Henderson, Gillick snapped him up in May to play left. At the trade deadline, the club dealt reserve outfielder John Mabry and a pitcher (Tom Davey) to San Diego for journeyman left fielder Al Martin. Henderson and Martin shared the spot over the last two months of the season.

All six off-season free-agent acquisitions — Sasaki, Rhodes, Sele, Olerud, Javier, and McLemore — delivered what the Mariners hoped for. Seattle rebounded to 91 wins and a trip to the playoffs, where they lost the ALCS to the Yankees. The team improved in all facets of the game: the offense moved up from sixth to fourth in the league in runs, despite playing a full season in pitcher-friendly Safeco Field; more significantly, the team jumped from 12th in runs allowed to second; and the defense had become one of the league's best.

The 2000-01 off-season proved as hectic and busy as the previous one had been. The over-arching story was the free agency of superstar shortstop Alex Rodriguez. Unlike the situations with Randy Johnson and Ken Griffey, when the Mariners had decided not to risk losing the player, the team had some hope that they could retain their shortstop. With or without Rodriguez, Gillick recognized that he needed to improve the club's offense for the coming season.

First, Gillick turned back to Japan for a solution outside of usual free agent pool, aggressively seeking and landing outfielder Ichiro Suzuki. First, he sent $13.125 million to the Orix club of the Japanese Pacific League for the right to negotiate with the player, then signed him on November 30 to a three-year deal for $14.088 million. The huge entourage of Japanese reporters following Ichiro during the season to come would add to the fishbowl atmosphere as the club entered what would be its record-setting season.

In December, Gillick further bolstered his bullpen by signing skilled setup man Jeff Nelson. He also inked veteran second baseman Bret Boone, filling one of the larger holes with a player who had begun his career with the Mariners in 1992. McLemore would move back to left field, splitting the job with the return of Al Martin.

In late January came the word the Mariners had been dreading — Alex Rodriguez signed a record ten-year, $252 million contract with the Texas Rangers. Coming as it did late in the off-season, the Mariners could only replace their superstar with young infielder Carlos Guillen, who had failed to win the third base position in 2000. Despite the loss of their best player, the various off-season moves increased the team's payroll to $74.7 million.

Heading into the 2001 season the Mariners were seen as

a good, but not great, ball club. Both *Sports Illustrated* and the *Sporting News* projected a second-place finish in the AL West. While the pitching was solid, the offense was still considered suspect. Boone, Suzuki and a full season from Martin were not expected to offset the loss of Rodriguez and the anticipated falloff in production from the injury-plagued Jay Buhner.

Disregarding any doubts, the team started on fire and stayed that way, reaching a high water mark of 47-12 after the games of June 8. At the All-Star break the team was at 63-24, with a commanding lead in the division. Even with the Mariners' hot start, Gillick was not completely satisfied with the makeup of his team. He argued at midseason, "If you want to go to the end, you basically have to have a number one starter. A number one starter is somebody when you get in a playoff situation, you need to have." And while Gillick liked Freddy Garcia (who would go on to lead the league in ERA that year), he was not fully sold on him as a staff ace. Even as the offense outperformed expectations, Gillick also hoped to upgrade his lineup. At various times he contemplated trading for San Diego third baseman Phil Nevin, Yankees' left fielder Chuck Knoblauch, Toronto left fielder Shannon Stewart, and Detroit outfielder Juan Encarnacion. But after considerable exploration of these opportunities, the Mariners made no midseason moves.

During the regular season, it certainly didn't matter. In the end, the team turned in a phenomenal 2001. In addition to their 116-46 record, the Mariners led the league in runs scored, fewest runs allowed, and attendance. In the playoffs, the Mariners first squeaked by the 91-win Cleveland Indians, three games to two, before falling once again to the Yankees in the ALCS.

So what happened next? How could a team win 116 games and revert to two consecutive 93-win seasons and no playoff appearances? In fairness, the two subsequent seasons rank as the second most wins in Mariner history. Nevertheless, a falloff of 23 games is significant and can be traced to several factors.

For one thing, the talent on the 2001 team was not as outstanding as its record implied, as several players had unaccountably outstanding seasons. Baseball researcher Phil Birnbaum has developed an objective method for measuring a team's "luck." After examining several factors, including how successful a team is in converting runs into wins, and how players performed compared to previous and subsequent seasons, Birnbaum concluded that the 2001 M's were the "luckiest" team since 1965 (at least). None of this is meant to detract in any way from the achievements of the team — the term "luckiest" is inappropriate, as the M's won the games and deserve the record. But in evaluating the potential for 2002, recognizing unaccountably strong seasons from players is essential. The 32-year-old Bret Boone was a lifetime .255 hitter, with a .312 on-base percentage and .413 slugging percentage, but in 2001 he recorded averages of .331/.372/.578, with 141 RBI. Looking forward, one should reasonably have expected a sharp drop-off, which is what transpired.

After examining several factors, including how successful a team is in converting runs into wins and how players perform compared to previous and subsequent seasons, Birnbaum concluded that the 2001 Seattle Mariners were the 'luckiest' team since at least 1965.

Further, Gillick lost his magic touch in filling holes. He followed up his two great off-seasons by acquiring journeymen to shore up his three weakest offensive positions: Ruben Sierra for left field, Jeff Cirillo to play third base, and Ben Davis to catch. To bolster the pitching staff Gillick brought in James Baldwin, another bottom-of-the-rotation starter. All four of these players proved unproductive in 2002.

Finally, the Mariners' drop-off highlights one of the pitfalls of building a team exclusively through free agency. Most free agents are nearing or past 30 by the time they become available on the open market, since they must have accrued six years of service time. Many of the nine players signed by the Mariners during those two great off-seasons were out of baseball or marginal contributors within a few years, and replacing them has proven difficult and expensive.

Nevertheless, the transformation of a mediocre 79-win team to the 116 wins in just two years was quite an accomplishment by the front office. Prior to free agency, such a dramatic leap forward would have required an unusually strong group of rookies, a lopsided trade or two, or purchases from a franchise looking to cash in its stars. Free agency changed this paradigm. As the 2001 Mariners demonstrated, teams can now materially alter their talent level on short notice. ⚾

Sources:

Seattle Post-Intelligencer, 1999-2001

Sports Illustrated, Aug. 27, 2001

Fast Company, June 14, 2002

Claxton, continued from page 45

Sources

Bailey, Arnold. "Obscure pitcher was first to break card color barrier," *Providence (R.I.) Journal*, Oct. 20, 2002

Dolgan, Bob. "Claxton was really first," (Cleveland)" *Plain Dealer*, Sept. 15, 1997

Hawthorn, Tom. "Before Jackie there was Jimmy," (Victoria, B.C.) *Times Colonist*, April 20, 1997

Olbermann, Keith. "Remembering a pioneer," *Sports Illustrated*, June 1, 1998, p. 90

Riley, James A. *The Biographical Encyclopedia of the Negro Baseball Leagues*. New York: Carroll and Graf, 1994

Walton, Dan. "Sports-log," Tacoma *News Tribune*, May 17, 1964

Weiss, William J. "The First Negro in 20th Century O.B.," *Baseball Research Journal*, 1979

Baltimore Afro-American, *Los Angeles Times*, *The Sporting News*, *Washington Post*

Interview with Marc Blau, Shanaman Sports Museum of Tacoma-Pierce County, Wash.

of his baseball career. *The Sporting News* reported that he was an Indian from "the wilds of Minnesein (sic)," while the *Washington Post* called "Big Chief Claxton" an "Osage Indian portsider."

As an itinerant moundsman, Claxton claimed to have pitched in all but two of the contiguous 48 states (missing Maine and, somehow, Texas). He began playing in Washington as a 13-year-old catcher for the town team in Roslyn, 50 miles east of Seattle, before becoming a pitcher with Chester, next door to Spokane, where he was said to have struck out 18 batters in his first start.

Claxton said he pitched for teams at Shasta, California; Good Thunder, Minnesota; Eurcka, South Dakota; as well as for town and industrial teams in Los Angeles (Jim Alexander's Giants), Seattle (Queen City Stars), Portland (Sellwood), Edmonds, Washington, and Tacoma, where he would long make his home. In 1924, he and brother-in-law Ernie Tanner belonged to a longshoreman's team admitted to the city's industrial league, their presence on the roster breaking its color line. Tanner had been instrumental in fighting for blacks' inclusion in the union in the first place.

In 1932, Claxton won a spot on a stellar pitching staff anchored by Luis (Lefty) Tiant, father of the future major league star hurler. Others in the rotation included Barney Brown, a screwball throwing left-hander sometimes billed as Brownez; Cuban all-rounder Lazaro Salazar, a reliable pitcher and a solid hitter; and, seven-foot-tall submariner Cuneo Galvez. The team played as the Cuban House of David in Florida during April, before heading north as the Cuban Stars to compete in the East-West League.

Claxton's league debut came in the season's second game, as he came in to relieve a game against the Detroit Wolves and slugging Mule Suttles. Down 5-0, Claxton failed to stop the bleeding, managing to record only a single out while being charged with three runs.

Claxton got the start in the second game of a May doubleheader against the Baltimore Black Sox, striking out seven in six innings. He also gave up seven hits, two walks, and six runs in being charged with the loss in a 7-6 defeat.

The Cuban Stars had seen enough, and Claxton was soon pitching for the rival Washington Pilots. He lost his first start, a scoreless first inning followed by a four-run second and a second loss. Two days later, the Pilots called on Claxton as a pinch-hitter in a game against his old team, and he came through with a single.

The East-West League would not survive the Depression, folding in midsummer 1932. Claxton's record was 1-2, his lone victory coming in relief. He had given up 25 hits and eight walks in just 21 innings pitched. He was age 39.

Claxton would have other barnstorming adventures in his career with the Nebraska Indians and others, even enjoying a 20-1 record with the Chicago Union Giants in a 43-game touring series against a House of David team.

He was still playing competitive baseball at age 52 for the South Tacoma Pines of the Valley League in his hometown, calling it a career after throwing a few token innings in an old-timer's game at age 63 in 1956.

In 1969, Claxton was inducted into the Tacoma-Pierce County Sports Hall of Fame. He died in Tacoma on March 3, 1970, survived by his wife, Juanita (who died in 1983), and a son who died in 1998. Ernie Tanner, who had married Claxton's sister, Emma, had been inducted as a three-sport star (baseball, football, and track) in 1964. Tanner had been a teammate on the Tacoma longshoreman's team. The Tanners had two children, one of them being Jack Edward Tanner, who sat as a judge at U.S. District Court in Tacoma until his death there at age 87 on Jan. 10, 2006.

Claxton's stint with the Oaks was so brief as to have seemed a dream, and forgivably, his memory expanded the length of his breakthrough. The proof of his short tenure on the Pacific Coast League club can be found on baseball card No. 25 of a 143-card set produced by the Collins-McCarthy Candy Company. These cards are better known by their brand name as Zee-nuts. One of the rare cards, rated by condition as a 3 out of 10, sold at auction by Sotheby's for $7,200 in June 2005.

It turns out that Claxton's week with the Oaks coincided with a visit by the candy company's photographer, making Claxton the first African-American baseball player to be depicted on a baseball card. ⚾

Round the horn: Santo to Pesky to Sandberg to Olerud

Northwest SABR presents the region's all-time team

COMPILED BY **ERIC SALLEE**

Here's the all-time, homegrown Pacific Northwest team, as selected by the members of the Northwest chapter of SABR. For our purposes, the Pacific Northwest encompasses the states of Washington, Oregon, Idaho, and Alaska, as well as the province of British Columbia.

Homegrown is defined as a person who first became proficient playing baseball while living in the Pacific Northwest, a person who became publicly known for his baseball skills while living and playing in the Pacific Northwest, and a person who was initially discovered by professional baseball while living and playing in the Pacific Northwest.

Ron Santo, catching for the all-city high school team in Sick's Stadium in 1957, first-team third baseman.

The Pacific Northwest encompasses the states of Washington, Oregon, Idaho and Alaska, and the province of British Columbia.

First team

First base: John Olerud, Bellevue, WA (Interlake HS, Washington St U)

Second base: Ryne Sandberg, Spokane, WA (North Central HS)

Shortstop: Johnny Pesky, Portland, OR (Lincoln HS)

Third base: Ron Santo, Seattle, WA (Franklin HS)

Outfield: Howard Earl Averill, Snohomish, WA (Snohomish HS)

Outfield: Larry Walker, Maple Ridge, BC (Maple Ridge Sr. Sec. School)

Outfield: Dale Murphy, Portland, OR (Wilson HS)

Catcher: Sammy White, Seattle, WA (Lincoln HS, U of Washington)

Multi-position regular: Harmon Killebrew, Payette, ID (Payette HS)

Righthanded starting pitcher: Mel Stottlemyre, Mabton, WA (Mabton HS)

Lefthanded starting pitcher: Mickey Lolich, Portland, OR (Lincoln HS)

Relief pitcher: Randy Myers, Vancouver, WA (Evergreen HS, Clark CC)

Manager: Fred Hutchinson, Seattle, WA (Franklin HS)

Second team

First base: Jack Fournier, Aberdeen, WA

Second base: Joe Gordon, Portland, OR (Jefferson HS, U of Oregon)

Shortstop: Kevin Stocker, Spokane, WA (Central Valley HS, U of Washington)

Third base: Ron Cey, Tacoma, WA (Mt. Tahoma HS, Washington St U)

Outfield: Bob Johnson, Tacoma, WA

Outfield: Ken Williams, Grants Pass, OR

Outfield: Jeff Heath, Seattle, WA (Garfield HS)

Catcher: Scott Hatteberg, Yakima, WA (Eisenhower HS, Washington St U)

Multi-position regular: Scott Brosius, Milwaukie, OR (Rex Putnam HS, Linfield College)

Righthanded starting pitcher: Larry Jackson, Boise, ID (Boise St U)

Lefthanded starting pitcher: Vean Gregg, Clarkston, WA

Relief pitcher: Mitch Williams, West Linn, OR (West Linn HS)

Manager: Del Baker, Sherwood, OR

Eric Sallee is a NWSABR chapter member and Seattle CPA who resides in Bellevue, Washington, with his wife, Sue, and two daughters.

(From left) Tacoma native Bob Johnson shown in 1932, second-team outfielder; Earl Torgeson, shown with the Seattle Rainiers in 1942, honorable mention outfielder; and Joe Gordon, shown in 1935 with Hop Gold brewery semipro team in Portland, second-team second baseman.

For more info on the Pacific Northwest chapter of SABR, visit: <http://nwsabr. sabr.org/>

Honorable mention
Position players

Wally Backman, Beaverton, OR (Aloha HS)

Jason Bay, Trail, BC (J. Lloyd Crowe Secondary School, N. Idaho CC, Gonzaga U)

Carson Bigbee, Waterloo, OR (U of Oregon)

Greg Brock, McMinnville, OR (McMinnville HS)

Ira Flagstead, Olympia, WA

Todd Hollandsworth, Bellevue, WA (Newport HS)

Brian Lee Hunter, Vancouver, WA (Fort Vancouver HS)

John Jaha, Portland, OR (David Douglas HS)

Roy Johnson, Tacoma, WA

Tom Lampkin, Seattle, WA (Blanchet HS, Edmonds CC, U of Portland)

Steve Lyons, Eugene, OR (Marist HS, Beaverton HS, Oregon St U)

Bill North, Seattle, WA (Garfield HS, Central Washington U)

Lyle Overbay, Centralia, WA (Centralia HS)

Harold Reynolds, Corvallis, OR (Corvallis HS)

Richie Sexson, Brush Prairie, WA (Prairie HS)

Earl Sheely, Spokane, WA (North Central HS)

Grady Sizemore, Everett, WA (Cascade HS)

Earl Torgeson, Snohomish, WA (Snohomish HS)

Pitchers

Larry Andersen, Bellevue, WA (Interlake HS, Bellevue CC)

Floyd Bannister, Seattle, WA (Kennedy HS)

Bud Black, Longview, WA (Mark Morris HS, Lower Columbia CC)

Ed Brandt, Spokane, WA (Lewis & Clark HS)

Leon Cadore, Sandpoint, ID (Gonzaga U)

Larry Christenson, Marysville, WA (Marysville HS)

Gene Conley, Richland, WA (Richland HS, Washington St U)

Fred Hutchinson, Seattle, WA (Franklin HS)

Larry Jansen, Forest Grove, OR

Syl Johnson, Portland, OR

Bruce Kison, Pasco, WA (Pasco HS)

Bill Krueger, McMinnville, OR (McMinnville HS, U of Portland)

Tom Niedenfuer, Redmond, WA (Redmond HS, Washington St U)

Steve Olin, Beaverton, OR (Beaverton HS, Portland St U)

Glendon Rusch, Shoreline, WA (Shorecrest HS)

Jason Schmidt, Kelso, WA (Kelso HS)

Aaron Sele, Poulsbo, WA (North Kitsap HS, Washington St U)

Dan Spillner, Federal Way, WA (Federal Way HS)

Gerry Staley, Brush Prairie, WA (Battle Ground HS)

Todd Stottlemyre, Yakima, WA (Davis HS)

Wayne Twitchell, Portland, OR (Wilson HS)

Dave Veres, Gresham, OR (Gresham HS, Mt. Hood CC)

Rube Walberg, Seattle, WA

Ray Washburn, Burbank, WA (Columbia-Burbank HS, Columbia Basin CC, Whitworth College)

Jack Wilson, Portland, OR (U of Portland)

Rick Wise, Portland, OR (Madison HS)